P9-DNN-799

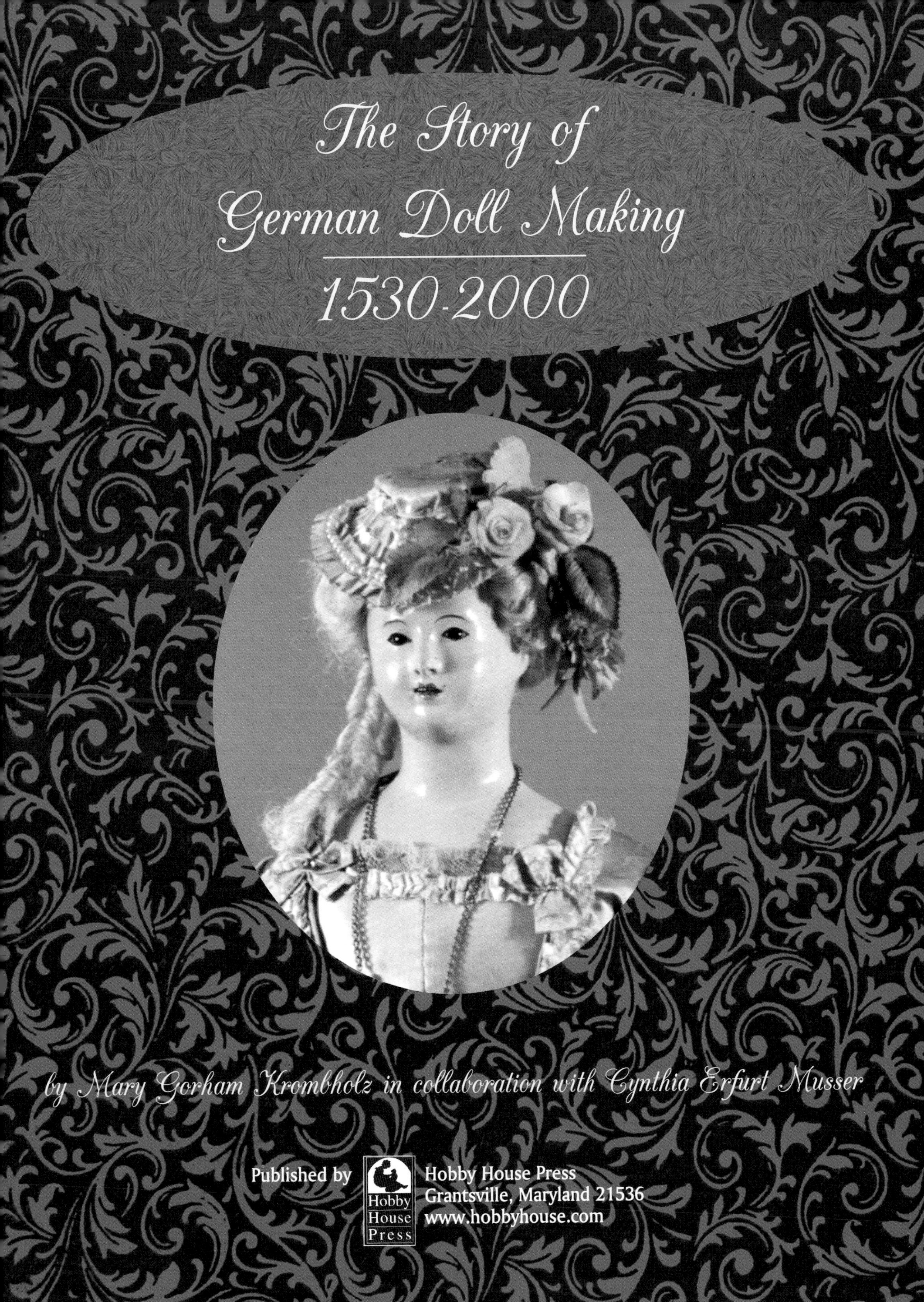
The Story of
German Doll Making
1530-2000
by Mary Gorham Krombholz in collaboration with Cynthia Erfurt Musser
Published by
Hobby House Press
Hobby House Press
Grantsville, Maryland 21536
www.hobbyhouse.com

Dedication

This book is dedicated to the memory of my friend, Carol Spalding Nagel. Carol brought such joy to my life because of our mutual love of dolls as well as a love of Germany.

The photographs of dolls and ephemera in the book are by Cynthia E. Musser.
All dolls, unless otherwise noted, are from the Krombholz and Erfurt/Musser Collections.

Additional copies of this book may be purchased at $39.95 (plus postage and handling) from
Hobby House Press, Inc.
1 Corporate Drive, Grantsville, MD 21536
1-800-554-1447
www.hobbyhouse.com
or from your favorite bookstore or dealer.

Printed in the United States of America

ISBN: 0-87588-602-7

This book would not have been possible without the help and support of my family. My husband, Herb, has been my main supporter and cheerleader through 43 years of marriage. He has encouraged my research of German dolls in Thuringia, although it meant leaving him for long periods of time.

I sincerely appreciate each and every contribution from my children, Lynn and Lee, and their spouses, Tim and Heather. My son Lee taught me to use a computer, so that I could write the book. My grandchildren, Kirtley and Isabelle, were the main inspiration for my book. As I watched them play with their dolls, following a visit to Sonneberg, I was finally able to understand the reality of a child's life in Thuringia during the doll making years.

I will always be grateful to my friend, Betty Matyas, for translating the "real" stories of doll making in the Sonneberg area as told by the children and grandchildren of the original doll makers. And, I'd especially like to thank Astrid Ledbetter for every word of her accurate translations from the German books and magazines in my library.

Special thanks to my German Doll Company friends. Without a doubt, I could not have written this book without your help. I would not have been able to find all the old porcelain factories without your knowledge of Germany.

I'd also like to thank Christiane Grafnitz for sharing her research on early German dolls and for acting as my tour guide throughout Thuringia.

I'd like to thank Mary and Josh Lytle for their fabulous Puppentours. The Lytles allowed me to "spread my wings" and research dolls in Germany without a single worry.

My best friend, Carol Nagel, took the pictures of the Thuringian buildings in the book. I wish she were alive to see her photographs in the book she encouraged me to write.

And last, but definitely not least, I'd like to thank Cynthia for her wonderful photographs of dolls and paper memorabilia. Her pictures have brought life to all my doll research and words.

Cynthia and I would like to thank our friends for allowing us to include their dolls in our book. The following friends shared their dolls: Mary Beard, Susan Bickert, Tim Dyar, Christiane Gräfnitz, Ana and Peter Kalinke, Karen Lintala, Marguerite Hoffman, Roland Schlegel, and Jane Walker.

Mary Krombholz

I thank my husband, Phil, who has understood my passion for researching and photographing dolls and toys especially in Thuringia where my family roots are. Phil has always supported me wholeheartedly through each of my projects. He has always been my best adviser.

I thank my children, Jonathan and Natalie, for always encouraging me to pursue my interests in studying and researching dolls even when it spilled over into our family time.

I will always appreciate my mother's part in all of this as we have collected, studied and photographed dolls and other toys together for most of my life. My mother has always been my great inspiration.

I especially thank Estelle Johnston for sharing some of her knowledge with me and teaching me to have a keen eye in studying and photographing dolls.

Finally, I would like to thank all of my friends in the United Federation of Doll Clubs for their friendship, encouragement and generosity in sharing dolls and information. This is the best support group a collector could want.

Cynthia Musser

Table of Contents

Chapter One

Chapter Two

Chapter Three

Chapter Four

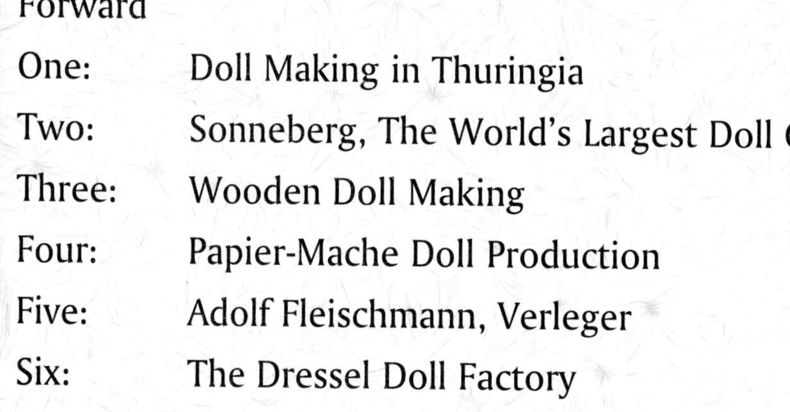

Chapter Five

Chapter Six

Chapter Seven

Chapter Eight

Chapter Nine

Chapter Ten

Chapter Eleven

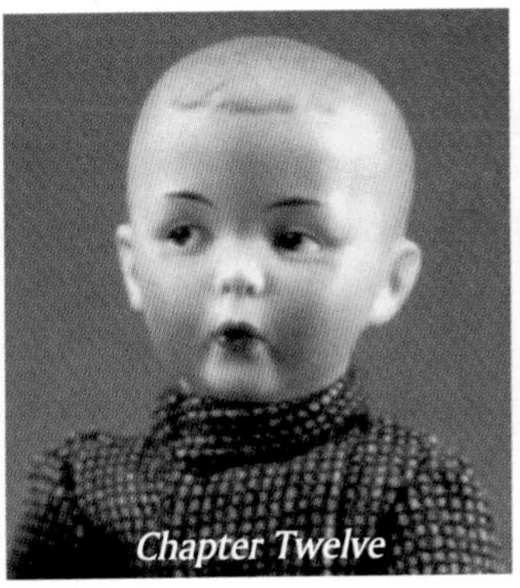
Chapter Twelve

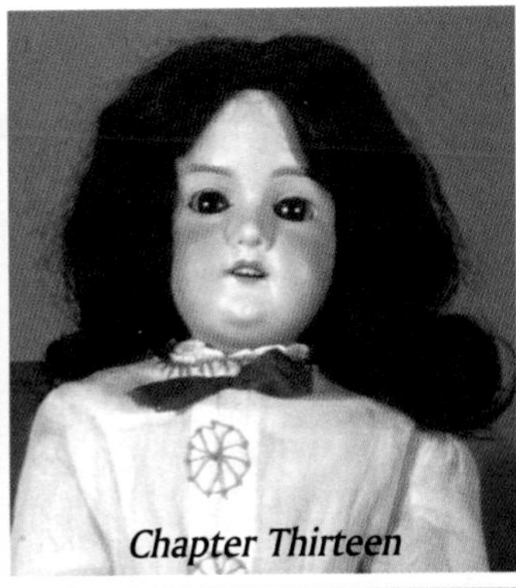
Chapter Thirteen

Chapter Fourteen

Chapter Fifteen

Chapter Sixteen

Chapter Seventeen

Chapter Eighteen

Chapter Nineteen

Chapter Twenty

Forward

For more than a hundred years, one German town was responsible for the manufacture of the majority of the dolls and toys found under American Christmas trees. Sonneberg doll makers made thousands of dolls a year during the 1600's and 1700's. By the 1800's, doll exports totaled from 300,000 to over 500,000 a year. From the 1880's until World War I, Sonneberg doll makers made millions of dolls a year. Yet, Sonneberg is seldom given credit for producing the majority of the world's dolls and toys. This small town, with a population of about 35,000 residents, looks much the same today as it did a hundred years ago when almost every resident, both young and old, was part of the doll scene. Over 200 former doll factories line the streets of Sonneberg today as reminders of the past. The Sonneberg Doll and Toy Museum paints an accurate picture of the years of doll making. By studying the Sonneberg dolls and toys in the museum, as well as the town's original entry in the 1910 Brussel's World's Fair, one is still able to revisit the doll making years. We will never know the names of all of the Sonneberg doll makers, but by collecting and preserving dolls, we are creating a permanent legacy in honor of the "No.1 Town of Dolls and Toys, in the Green Heart of Germany."

The photographs of dolls in the book are by Cynthia E. Musser. All dolls, unless otherwise noted, are from the Krombholz and ephemera Erfurt/Musser Collections.

Chapter One

Doll Making in Thuringia

A 1910 original postcard contains the message: "Direct from Sonneberg to Pittsburgh" and "Aus der Spielwarenstadt" (toy shop town); "Sonneberg i/Thueringen." A young girl is pictured kneeling on a shelf full of dolls and toys with the town of Sonneberg shown in the background. For years, American wholesale buyers, like the Pittsburgh Dry Goods Company, provided a stable market for the well made, inexpensive Sonneberg dolls and toys.

For more than four hundred years, the German doll and toy industry dominated the world market. The area of Germany known as the Thuringian Forest produced more dolls and toys than any other area in the world. Thuringia became the center of doll making for a number of reasons.

The Thuringian area doll makers made more dolls than the rest of the world combined. One of the most

The message on the reverse side of the Sonneberg postcard is: "The Pittsburgh Dry Goods Co. wishes to announce that their Doll Samples are ready and invite your inspection of same bought personally from the Manufacturers."

important reasons for this was the natural resources found there. The mature, dense forests provided ample wood for making dolls and doll parts. Wood was also used for heating houses and later to stoke the kilns for porcelain production. The abundant mountain streams in the area provided water for daily use as well as waterpower for the many factories. The large deposits of kaolin (fine, white clay used in the manufacture of porcelain) guaranteed the future of almost a hundred Thuringian porcelain factories. Quartz and feldspar, the other necessary ingredients in porcelain production, were also readily available. The Thuringian "slate mountains" provided slate, which could be sold all over the world. Slate was used to make slate boards, slate pencils and gravestones. Slate was also used to roof and side houses and factories. Thuringian merchants learned to market slate and other natural resources since the 1500's. The dolls and toys sold in later years were a natural progression.

Other factors contributed to the Thuringian area's success as well. Without a doubt, German workers succeeded in producing millions of dolls yearly in part because of their inborn skills and work ethics that were passed down from generation to generation. In addition, the German government aided the doll and toy industry by granting exemptions from taxes and duties for a number of years. Trade schools like the Sonneberg Industrial School were established to teach design, painting, sculpting, and mechanics. In 1838, 135 Sonnebergers founded the "Sonneberg Association of Trade." In 1843, the Association of Trade was cancelled; however, in 1883, the Sonneberg Chamber of Commerce agreed to establish "a school to intensify the local doll and toy industry." It was called the School of Industry.

In order to study this doll making area in the "green heart of Germany," I have divided the area into two identical circles. Each circle is similar to a wheel with spokes going 20 miles outward in every direction. Sonneberg is in the center of the Southern Circle while Waltershausen is in the center of the Northern Circle. With the help of the Ciesliks' *German Doll Encyclopedia*, I have compared the company listings in the commercial registers for the years 1800 to 1939.

Fir and spruce trees were abundant in the forests surrounding Sonneberg, shown in a 1910 original postcard.

The Sonneberg Industrial School, pictured in an original postcard, was established in 1883 to teach design, painting, sculpting and mechanics. The Sonneberg Doll and Toy Museum has been located in the 1910 building since the late 1930's.

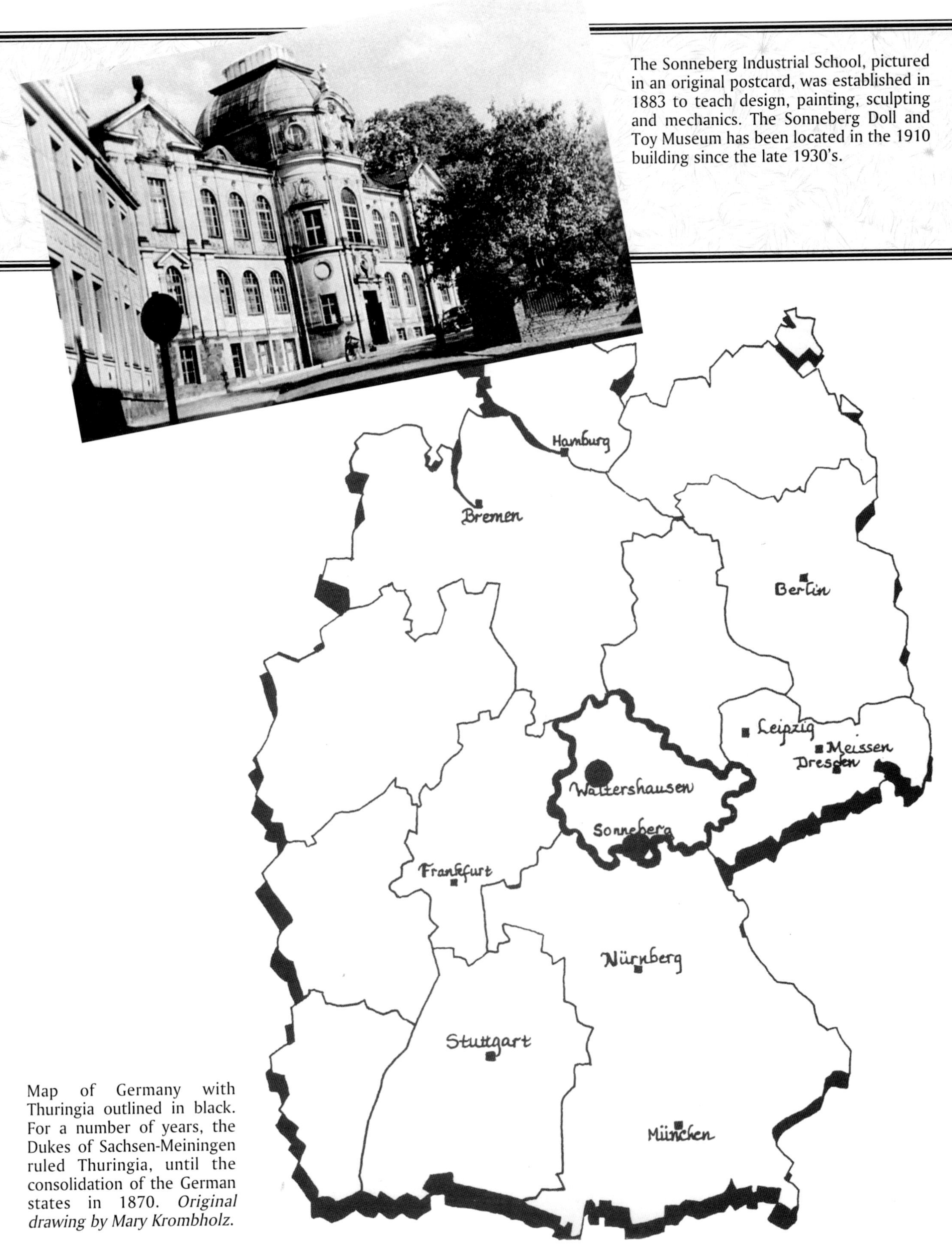

Map of Germany with Thuringia outlined in black. For a number of years, the Dukes of Sachsen-Meiningen ruled Thuringia, until the consolidation of the German states in 1870. *Original drawing by Mary Krombholz.*

The Northern Doll Making Circle with Waltershausen in the center. The majority of towns with former porcelain or doll factories, within 20 miles of Waltershausen, are shown on the map. *Original drawing by Mary Krombholz.*

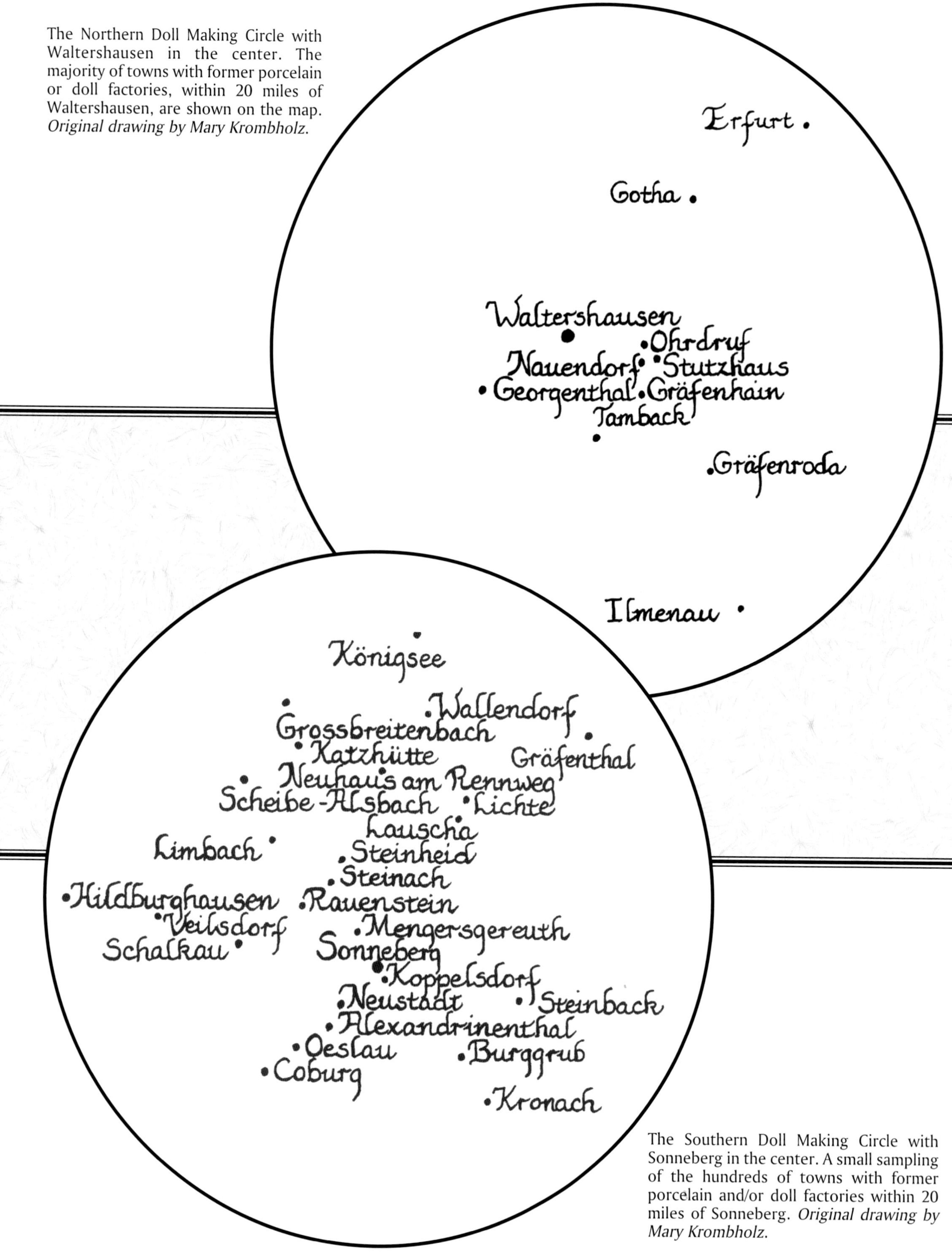

The Southern Doll Making Circle with Sonneberg in the center. A small sampling of the hundreds of towns with former porcelain and/or doll factories within 20 miles of Sonneberg. *Original drawing by Mary Krombholz.*

Over 500 doll firms were located in the Southern Circle no more than 20 miles from Sonneberg. It is important to note that of the Southern Circle's 500 doll firms, 278 were located in Sonneberg. A visit to Sonneberg today confirms the town's doll making role. Sonneberg is located in a picturesque valley surrounded by wooded hillsides. Although the town covers only six square miles, hundreds of two and three-story buildings (homes and factories) that mirror the Sonneberg success story are still standing today.

Unlike Sonneberg, Waltershausen is a typical small German town centered on a town square. There are about two-dozen doll factories and doll makers' homes to remind one of the many years of doll making. In the entire Northern Circle, there were only 87 doll factories listed in the commercial registers from 1800 to 1939. It is impossible to cover every doll and porcelain factory located in Thuringia, so I have chosen a few from each circle to tell the story of German doll making.

The creation of German dolls can be compared to the weaving of an intricate tapestry. Thousands of home and factory workers were involved in making the dolls we now collect. Every Thuringian doll and porcelain factory contributed "threads" to the doll-making tapestry. Some threads were more important than others were—doll heads and bodies were more important than cardboard boxes in the overall analysis. Yet, each contribution was part of the total picture. Many of the skills relating to doll making are no longer in use. The Thuringian doll factories brought together the work of the head makers, the body makers, the dressmakers, the shoemakers, the voice makers, the eye makers, the tress makers, the braid makers, the wig makers and the box makers, to name just a few. Innumerable, unidentified workers added millions of related parts to create dolls during the last four hundred years. The real story of German doll making is the story of each worker, young and old.

A 1990's photograph of Sonneberg home workers' houses below the "Castle on the Hill."

Scene No.1

Scene No. 2

Scene No. 3

Scene No. 4

Four original 1885 advertising cards picture German doll makers at work. Scene No.1: A typical Thuringian wooden doll factory with a line shaft shown on the left side of the picture. This mechanical device was an early form of mass production because a number of lathes could be turned from one source of power. Scene No. 2: Male workers dipping doll heads in liquefied wax in order to create wax-over papier-mâché doll heads. Scene No. 3: Women workers styling doll wigs and attaching the wigs to doll shoulder heads. Scene No. 4: A group of factory workers painting and dressing dolls. The reverse sides of the cards contain the Liebig Company's advertisements for "Fleisch-Extract."

Chapter Two

Sonneberg: The World's Largest Doll Center

On January 1, 1999, Sonneberg began celebrating its 650th Anniversary. Although there were small settlements in the southern Thuringian Forest in the early Middle Ages, the name "Sonneberg" did not appear in city records until 1207 when Knight Eberhard of Sonneberg recorded the name in the Cloister at Langheim in Lichtenfels. In about 1200, the Von Sonnebergs, descendants of the ruling duke, built the Sonneberg castle/fortress on "Sun Mountain". The German word "Sonne" means "sun" and "Berg" means "mountain." Shortly thereafter, families began building their homes in the valley below the Sonneberg castle.

The Sonneberg line died out in about 1310, and the rulers of Schaumberg inherited their possessions. The

An 1890's original postcard provides a view of Sonneberg including the site of the original "Castle on the Hill" and the heavily wooded mountains surrounding the town.

Schaumberg rulers had to give up their rights to the Sonneberg castle/fortress to Count von Henneberg in 1317 when he became the ruler of the Sonneberg area.

The Count died in 1347 and his Countess, Jutta von Henneberg, became regent of Sonneberg. January 5, 1349 is one of the most important dates in Sonneberg history. On that date, the Countess granted "City Rights" to Sonneberg, which gave residents the right to rule themselves through their own self-elected town council. They were also awarded the privilege of marketing their own goods. Additionally, they received the right to inherit previously owned estates.

By the mid-1500's, Sonneberg was a well-established stop on the trading routes from Nuremberg to Leipzig. Nuremberg merchants stopped in Sonneberg to rest their horses, to repair their wagons, and to hire guards to protect their goods from thieves while traveling through the densely wooded and dangerous mountain paths north of Sonneberg.

The first industry in Sonneberg was harvesting slate and grindstone followed by iron ore mining. The Thuringian "slate mountains" date back to the "Kambrium" formation. This valuable natural resource was an early source of income for the Sonneberg merchants. Sonnebergers traded slate and grinding stones (whetstones) for other goods carried by the Nuremberg merchants.

Farming was difficult due to the poor, rocky soil. Therefore, mining became the primary industry in the small town. During the long winters, the industrious Germans began carving articles from wood to trade to the Nurembergers who came through town in the spring. The first wooden goods were household articles such as spoons, plates, and bowls. Before long, Sonneberg wood carvers added dolls and toys to their sales line. The well-made inexpensive Sonneberg items were sold as "Nuremberg Wares" for many years.

Right: The "Scotsman's House" is the earliest building still standing in Sonneberg. Parts of the house date from the 1300's, and includes a cave containing a medieval baptismal font cut into the floor which is filled with water from the spring below. The cave is attached to the house, and it features a cross that is carved into the cave wall. The first Sonneberg Business School was located in this building.

A restored slate advertising picture on a building located in "Untere Marktstrasse." The picture signage advertises: "Ernst Schubart's Nachfolger (Successor)." The slate horses, pulling a covered wagon, remind one of the early days in Sonneberg when horses and wagons transported dolls and toys.

Wooden toys, like an 1850's Noah's Ark, were a popular Sonneberg export item. Sonneberg wood carvers and turners exported similar wooden toys to a worldwide market.

The Thirty-Years War, fought from 1618 to 1648, ended the Sonneberg/Nuremberg trading alliance. Three-fourths of the Sonneberg residents died during this devastating war. The town of Nuremberg was also heavily damaged, and like the Sonnebergers, a large number of Nurembergers lost their lives during the war.

For the first time, Sonneberg merchants were forced to trade on their own. In the beginning, the merchants traveled to nearby villages to sell their goods, but before long, they began to travel to the Leipzig Fairs. Between 1670 and 1700, the enterprising Sonneberg merchants had established export branches in other countries causing more wood carvers and turners to move to Sonneberg.

By 1735, the doll and toy makers in Sonneberg were making playthings in at least 35 different designs. According to company documents, Johann Philipp Dressel sold a variety of dolls and toys in 1757. Some of the earliest Sonneberg dolls and toys included turned wooden dolls, dancing and pull dolls, rattles, musical instruments like flutes and horns, and horses with riders.

Several important discoveries relating to doll making contributed to the town's success in the early years. In the late 1500's, a wood carver named Killian Dressel brought the art of bismuth painting to Sonneberg from his former home in Nuremberg. Bismuth is a metallic element used chiefly as a pigment in paints. The earliest wooden dolls and toys were generally sold unpainted, but from the late 1500's on, they were painted with vibrant, durable colors made from bismuth.

The use of bismuth to improve paints is just one of the reasons Sonneberg continued to grow and prosper as a doll and toy center during the next two centuries. The use of "Brotteig" (bread dough) was equally important. A low grade flour, often called "black flour", and gum water were mixed to make an inexpensive, malleable substance that could be applied to wooden dolls to create realistic details. Because bread dough was easily molded, an unskilled worker called a "Bossierer," or bread dough worker, could rapidly become modelers. Furthermore, unlike wood carving, the workers did not need to serve an apprenticeship to learn the trade.

By the late 1700's, bread dough workers and doll makers had formed their own guilds in Sonneberg. Trade guild regulations forbid one craftsman from doing the work of another. Dolls and toys had to be moved from workshop to workshop. The turned wooden dolls made in Neuenbau were embossed with dough (Brotteig) by the Sonneberg embossers. A Bossierer was only allowed to make dolls and toys, not to paint them. This was the responsibility of the bismuth painters. The bread dough workers and bismuth painters had many arguments over these rigid guild rules. To stop the quarreling and to encourage production, the Sonneberg ruling duke, Duke Georg the First, signed the "Great Sonneberg Privilege of Trade." This document changed Sonneberg forever and was the primary reason that Sonneberg became the world's largest doll and toy center.

This important document, which went into effect on February 24, 1789, gave 26 Sonneberg merchants and four from the neighboring villages of Judenbach, Neuenbau and Steinach the exclusive right of trade. Only these 30 men had the right to sell dolls and toys. These "privileged" men were given the title of "Verleger," which loosely translates to the English word "publisher." The "Privilege of Trade" contained one very unusual requirement. The members of the Verleger group were not allowed to own a doll factory for the next 73 years, until the "Privilege" was rescinded on June 16, 1862. In 1862, all Germans were given "the freedom to exercise a trade."

The work structure in Sonneberg changed drastically during the years the "Privilege" was in effect. The "privileged" merchants became extremely wealthy and powerful because they completely controlled all doll and toy production. Every doll and toy factory owner in the Sonneberg area was forbidden to sell dolls or toys except through a Verleger. Although a Verleger was not allowed to own an export company or a manufactory, he continued to make every important decision relating to

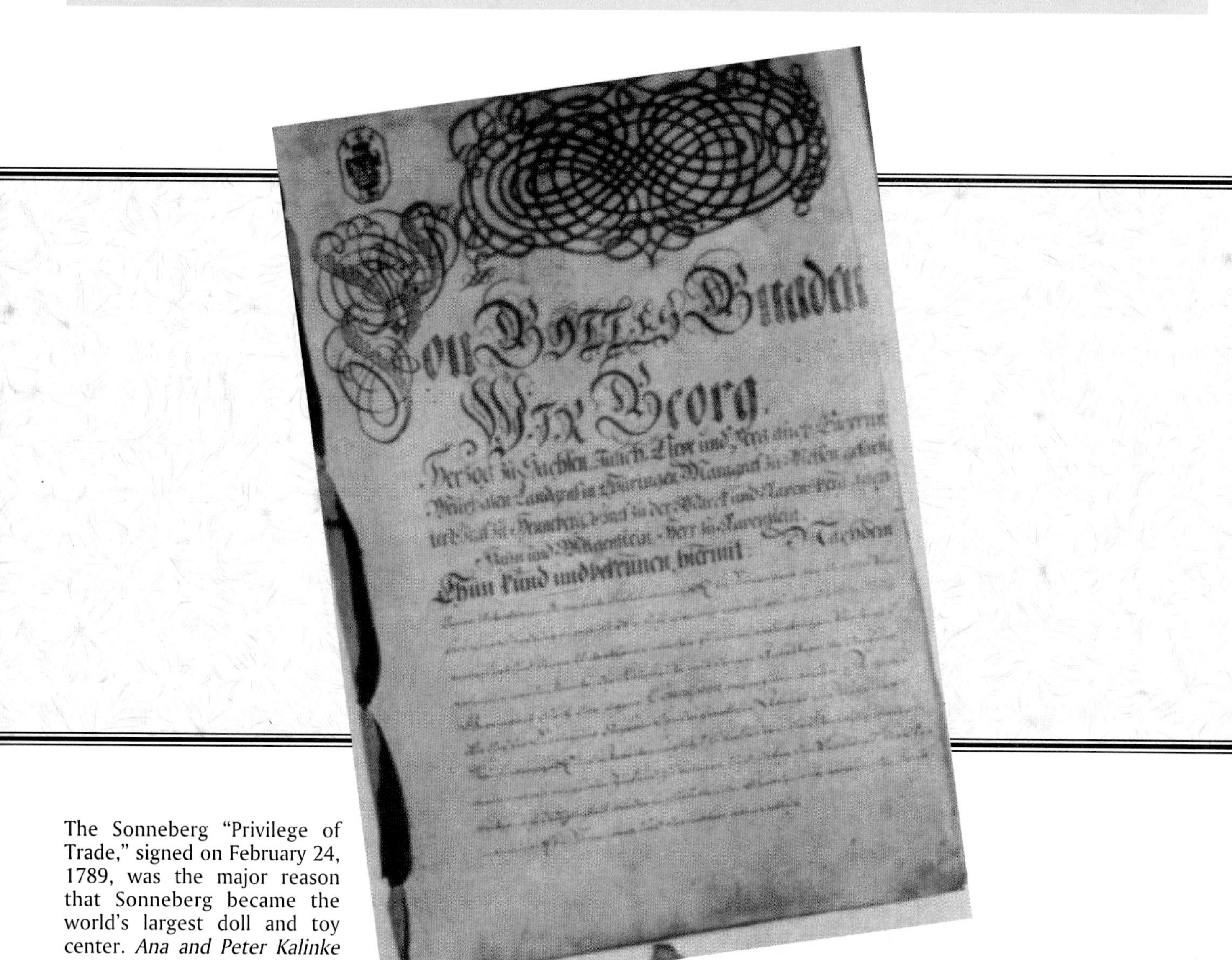
Von Gottes Gnaden
Wir Georg

Thun kund und bekennen hiermit

The Sonneberg "Privilege of Trade," signed on February 24, 1789, was the major reason that Sonneberg became the world's largest doll and toy center. *Ana and Peter Kalinke Collection.*

Untere Marktstrasse shown in a 1910 original postcard. The square was the main gathering place in Sonneberg during the years of doll making. Delivery day was typically Saturday, and from early morning on, workers delivered dolls and doll parts to the hundreds of doll factories in town. After they were paid for their work, home and factory workers bought groceries and other necessities at the stores and outdoor booths located around "Market Square."

An original 1910 Sonneberg postcard shows two small child's wagons full of dolls parked on the curb. The muddy streets filled with horses and wagons were a typical sight during the early doll-making years.

his own doll company. Each Verleger hired his own designers and sculptors to create new doll designs. He also placed and financed orders and arranged for delivery of his finished goods. The main difference during the era of the "Privilege" was the change in emphasis. For the first time in Sonneberg history, these 30 powerful Sonneberg area merchants were focused on creating more business rather than on the actual daily production of dolls and toys.

No other German town had such a large group of influential merchants whose main focus was on selling rather than producing dolls and toys. The merchants met once a week with the Lord Mayor and the brewery owners to develop "a feeling of unity." During the decades following 1789, many sons and daughters of these important Sonneberg merchants married creating an even stronger base for the doll and toy industry. As doll and toy sales increased, more workers moved into Sonneberg. The population increased dramatically. By 1826, over 10,000 people lived in Sonneberg, and during the next few decades, many more German families built houses within walking distance of Sonneberg in order to deliver their doll and toy related products every week. By the late 1880's, over 43,000 people lived in the immediate Sonneberg area. The dozens of villages surrounding Sonneberg were filled with home workers. Because of this "secondary" or "back-up" work force, any size Sonneberg doll order could be filled on time. The

Dressel doll factory often had between 20,000 and 30,000 dolls and toys in their sample rooms.

During the 73 years the "Privilege" was in effect, papier-mâché production, which started in the early 1800's, strengthened Sonneberg's hold on the world market. Unlike woodcarving and bread dough modeling, each item pressed into a mold came out looking exactly like the next item. Untrained workers could rapidly become a papier-mâché presser or "Drücker."

Early town records from 1823 indicate that "Sonneberg wares and products are known and sought everywhere." The number of workers and their special trades at that time was as follows: 37 wood carvers and turners, 20 bismuth painters, 21 papier-mâché molders, 10 children's violin and drum makers, 30 wood joiners, 2 guilders, 4 horn makers, 29 gravestone and pencil makers, 3 slate siding makers, 18 nailsmiths (and 40 journeymen), 2 tinsmiths, 2 coopers (barrel makers), 30 merchants and 12 shopkeepers. Other businesses included a lamp black business, a pine resin shop, a brick and a lime furnace, a brandy distillery, 2 marble mills, and 5 flour-making mills.

In 1896, the German government made a survey of the German residents directly involved in doll and toy making. According to that survey, 40,829 German residents were directly involved in the doll and toy industry. Of that number, 35,000 were Sonnebergers who were somehow contributing to making dolls and toys. Therefore, we can conclude that, aside from Sonneberg, only 5,829 workers were making dolls and toys in the remaining areas of Germany in 1896. We can also conclude that the majority of Sonneberg residents were directly involved in doll and toy making by the late 1800's.

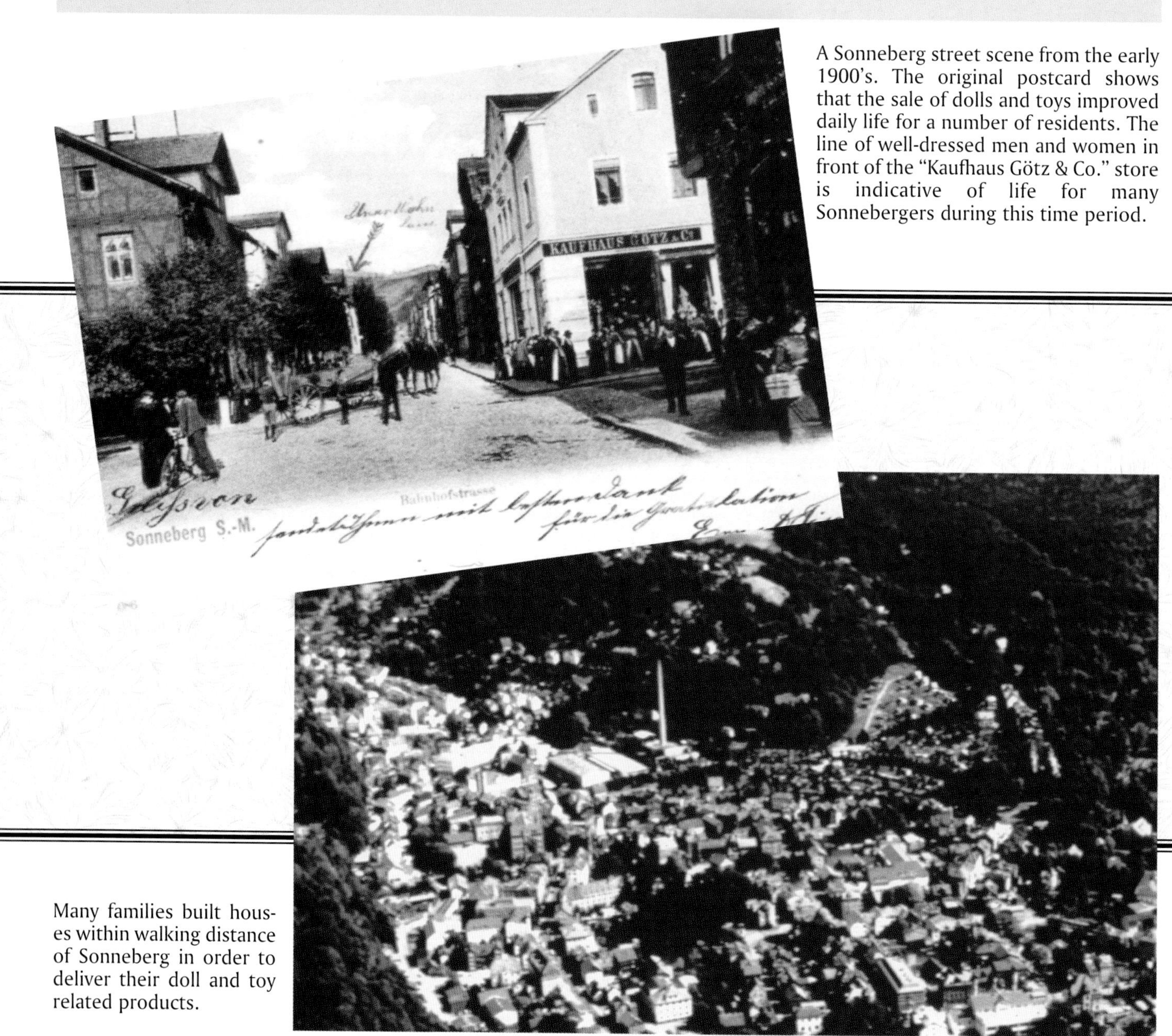

A Sonneberg street scene from the early 1900's. The original postcard shows that the sale of dolls and toys improved daily life for a number of residents. The line of well-dressed men and women in front of the "Kaufhaus Götz & Co." store is indicative of life for many Sonnebergers during this time period.

Many families built houses within walking distance of Sonneberg in order to deliver their doll and toy related products.

Chapter Three

Wooden Doll Making

Wooden dolls and toys were carved and turned on a lathe for hundreds of years in many parts of Germany as well as in Austria. Because they are unmarked as to maker, it is difficult to attribute a wooden doll to a specific wood carver or turner, or sometimes, even to a particular area of Germany. Early Sonneberg records indicate that many Grödner Tal and Oberammergau wooden dolls and toys were sold as "Sonneberg Wares." These early wooden dolls and toys were often sold unpainted to Sonneberg merchants, and then painted in Sonneberg before being exported. From Sonneberg, they were exported all over the world, adding confusion as to the origin of many early wooden dolls.

Wooden pull toys from Bestelmeier's Toy Catalogs are an interesting study. Georg Bestelmeier was a Nuremberg toy merchant from about 1793 to 1825. His catalogs are a very important source of information on German toys made during that era. The toys in the catalogs are dated from 1793 to 1808. Bestelmeier claimed that all of his toys were made in Nuremberg, but many of them appear to be the same as those shown in catalogs of the Sonneberg and Grödner Tal wood carvers and turners according to Karl Grober in *Children's Toys of Bygone Days*.

Three of the major early wooden doll-producing centers were the Sonneberg in Thuringia Grödner Tal in Austria, and Oberammergau in Bavaria. Before 1815, the Grödner Tal was also in Bavaria, Germany. However, from 1815 until 1919, it was part of Austria, and in 1919, this important doll producing area became part of Italy. Grödner Tal, Oberammergau, and Sonneberg each had ample supplies of wood from the surrounding forests. In addition, the severe winters in each area prevented farming and mining, which prompted residents to make dolls as a winter activity.

Wood was ideal for doll and toy making because it was readily available, inexpensive, and durable. One early Thuringian doll attests to the permanent nature of wood. According to the late Mary Hillier, in her

A 1760-80 "bustline" wooden doll from Southern Germany. The 15-inch doll has a jointed wooden body, a swivel neck, and a carved corset. The well-carved doll is indicative of the handwork created by early wooden doll makers. *Christiane Gräfnitz Collection.*

Right: A family of early wooden "bustline" dolls, circa 1790-1820, from Southern Germany. The 20-inch lady and the 7-inch child are dressed in original clothing. The lady has light-brown painted hair under her original black silk wig. The redressed man also has brown painted hair, under his longhaired sheepskin wig. The three dolls have fully jointed wooden bodies. *Christiane Gräfnitz Collection.*

An 18-inch German wooden doll with a well-defined profile, circa 1815-20. The fully articulated wooden body includes ball joints. *Christiane Gräfnitz Collection.*

The earliest documented Thuringian doll is on permanent display in the German National Museum in Nuremberg. The nine-inch doll, circa 1530, is carved from Lindenwood. *Original artwork by Hope Fjord.*

book *Dolls and Dollmakers*, this 9-inch treasure was found "behind some wooden paneling in a Rhenish (Rhine River) castle." This doll, the earliest documented Thuringian wooden doll, is on permanent display in the German National Museum in Nuremberg. The museum signage says, "Puppe, Lindenholz, gefasst, Thuringian, um 1530." The translation reads, "Doll, Lindenwood (also known as Basswood) made in Thuringia, circa 1530." It is remarkable that the doll is in such well-preserved, original condition after 470 years. Hillier describes the doll as:

> She has a tightly bodiced dress with long thin sleeves and a narrow pleated skirt reaching to the ground. The fine white folds of her linen shirt reach to the neck, where it is fastened with precious gold embroidery. A similar embroidered wider stomacher is worn over the narrow girdle and hides the opening of her dress. The original, wide wine-red cross strings of her skirt give a good idea of the colour that has been lost. A net cap drawn down each side over her ears has rounded points, and covering her head, reveals the high domed forehead.

In each wooden doll producing area, wood carvers began to make farming equipment and religious objects before they carved and turned household items, and ultimately dolls and toys. Woodcarving in the Grödner Tal (Valley) dates back to about 1500. This picturesque valley is located about half a mile from the Brenner Pass in the Dolomite Mountains of Italy. After the peace treaty of Saint Germain in 1919, this alpine region of west Austria became a part of Italy. The main villages in the Grödner Tal are St. Ulrich, St. Christina, and Wolkenstein. St. Ulrich is considered the center of Grödner Tal doll making.

The wood sculptors Friedrich and Michael Pacher were well known in the Grödner Tal area from about 1500. The first woodcarvings that can be traced to this area are religious carvings dating from about 1650. Even in the 1600's, forest management was important, and early wood carvers were cautioned against using too much wood.

By 1703, Johann De Metz employed over 40 wood carvers in the Grödner Valley. This factory made household items as well as wooden dolls and toys. By 1870, the Grödner area carvers were sending wooden dolls and toys to France, England, Russia, Australia, and America. In 1873, the population of the Grödner Tal was about 3,000. This number included 2,000 wood carvers, painters, and gilders. An order of 144,000 jointed wooden dolls was mentioned in a 1900 invoice.

The early Grödner dolls were carved and painted with a great deal of attention given to details. The dolls created by the early carvers were generally designed to represent ladies featuring carved and painted busts, as well as beautifully carved hair with painted temple ringlets, and hair ornamentation like carved combs and coronets. They ranged in size from 1 inch to about 40 inches. Some of the finely carved early wooden dolls had waist joints and occasionally, swivel necks. Even the 6-inch dolls were finished with a fine, translucent varnish that protected the painted surfaces. However, by the third quarter of the 19th century, the Grödner Tal wooden dolls were no longer carved and turned in the same meticulous way. The peg-wooden dolls from the late 1800's and 1900's were generally turned from one

A 20-inch German wooden doll, circa 1770-90, in original clothing. The slim wooden body with a pronounced hollow back and very slender waist is typical of a woman's body shape in the 18th Century, which was caused by wearing a corset from childhood on. The wooden limbs are ball jointed, and articulated at the shoulders, elbows, hips and knees. *Christiane Gräfnitz Collection.*

The carved wooden doll head features dark glass eyes, brown painted hair down to the neck, finely carved ears, a broad nose, and a well-modeled chin. *Christiane Gräfnitz Collection.*

Three Grödner Tal wooden dolls, circa 1815-20. The two larger dolls are about 6 inches tall. The dolls were made from a special tree that grows in the area. The wood, Zirbelholz, has a unique smell. The larger dolls have unusually large painted eyes and eyelashes. The dolls have jointed bodies with little waist definition. They are far earlier than the usual Grödner Tal dolls. The dolls show the broader bodies that were prevalent before corsets were fashionable. *Private Collection.*

An all-original 5-3/4-inch wooden doll, circa mid-1800's, exhibiting less detailed woodcarving, turning, and painting. The well-preserved patterned dress features a wide waist sash. The doll is possibly a Sonneberg doll created in the Grödner Tal manner.

piece of wood, and the torsos were much shorter. The hairstyles were no longer finely carved, and the heads were simple and round with very little painted hair detail. The body jointing also changed from ball and socket joints, to simple pivot joints.

Two wooden doll factories in St. Ulrich were known all over the world—the Insam & Prinoth Company and the Purger Company. The Insam & Prinoth doll factory (founded in 1820) had several warehouses continually filled with thousands of jointed wooden dolls in every size, painted and unpainted. According to the Colemans, "They bought 30,000 peg-woodens a week, all year long, thus buying a total of 1,560,000 a year as late as 1925." In 1887, these crudely made jointed wooden dolls were advertised at a price of 6¢ a dozen, wholesale. In the late 1800's, a good carver/turner could turn out 240 jointed dolls daily, and with the introduction of mechanical lathes, a wood carver/turner could make 1,200 dolls in 24 hours.

For over a hundred years, religious objects, dolls, and toys were the primary export items in Oberammergau as well. This picturesque Bavarian village is built on both

An 8-inch Grödner Tal wooden doll from the first quarter of the 19th Century. The original clothing features silk twisted cording over the neckline and waist.

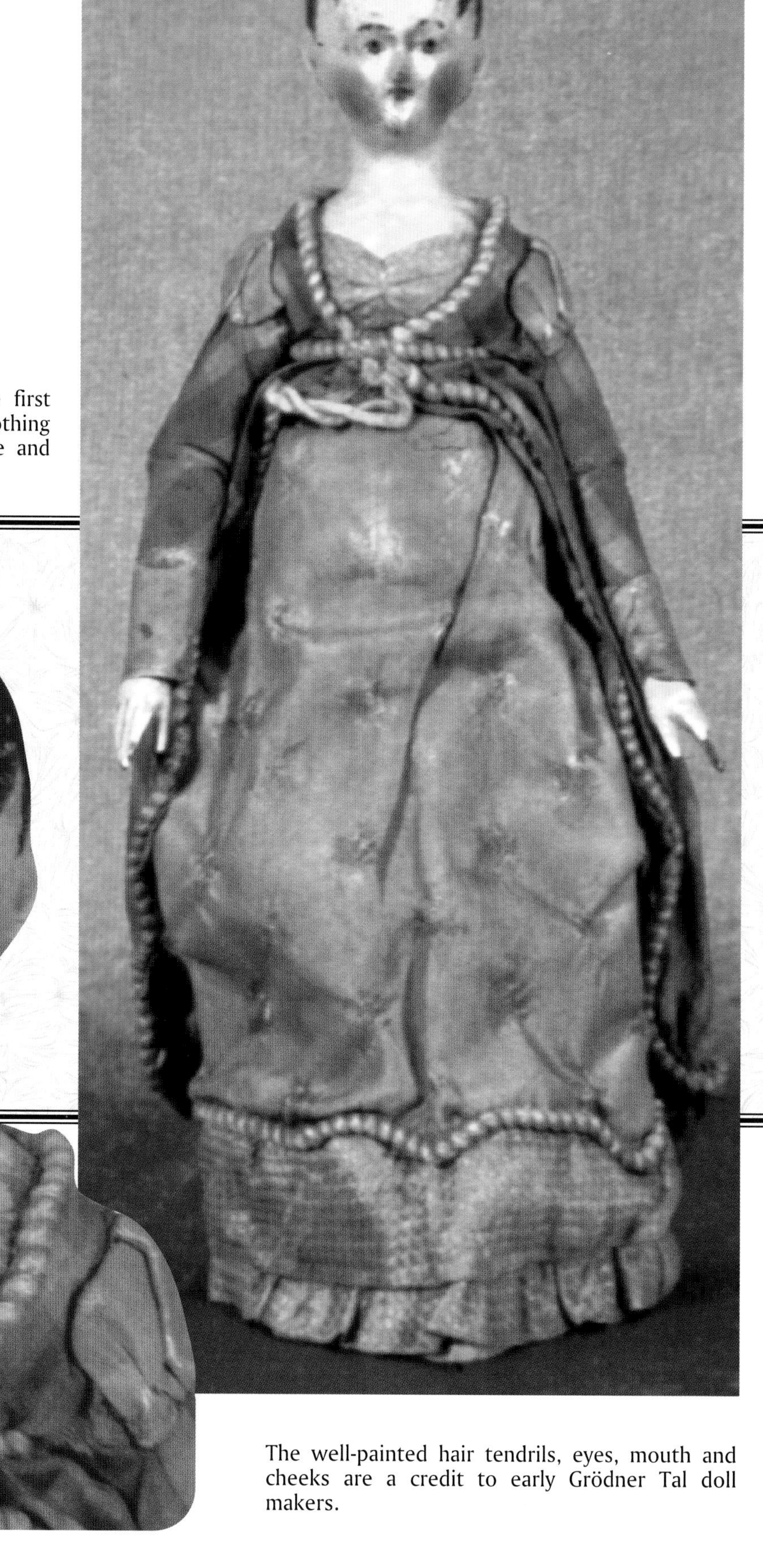

The well-painted hair tendrils, eyes, mouth and cheeks are a credit to early Grödner Tal doll makers.

This pair of later Grödner Tal "peg-woodens" made by the Purger Company measures 11-3/4 and 12 inches. By the 1900's, these cheap dolls had one-piece heads and torsos. The heads were simple and round with very little painted hair detail. The body jointing also changed from ball and socket joints to simple pivot joints.

A 2-1/4-inch 1800's Grödner Tal doll with simple face painting and an applied wooden nose wedge. The well-made pegged wooden body is jointed at the elbows and knees. The original clothing includes patterned trim at the waistline, hemline and lower edge of the pantaloons.

sides of the Ammer River. The name Oberammergau means "region on the upper Ammer." In 1961, the population was about 4,800. Today it is 5,350.

Only through woodcarving and turning, as well as the Passion Plays, did this Bavarian village become known around the world. The Passion Plays originated in 1634, and they continue to take place once every ten years. The community built its own art school from the profits of the Passion Plays in the years 1840 and 1850. Artistic talent is still very evident in Oberammergau today. Exteriors of several buildings are beautifully painted with scenes that depict stories from the Bible.

In 1520, Abbot Althammer in his *History of Ettal* describes the extraordinary skill of the Oberammergau woodcarvers who are able to "represent the passion of Christ in a half nutshell." It was a natural progression in Oberammergau to go from carved religious figures to simple wooden dolls that could be sold at town fairs. Carved shoulder heads of wood with a variety of hairstyles were considered a specialty of the Oberammergau carvers. The well-carved faces ranged in age from young to old, and the male shoulder heads often had very detailed mustaches and beards. In the late 1700's, toy makers from this area sold wooden jumping jacks, dolls, hobbyhorses, number games, bricks, ninepins, jig-saw puzzles and toy soldiers.

The Oberammergau Museum showcases a wide range of the town's wooden dolls and toys. One group is

An unusual 30-inch Oberammergau wooden doll, circa 1840-50. The man has carved hair that includes "comb marks," and a well-painted mustache and goatee. He has a jointed wooden body. The doll was found in an old storeroom in Oberammergau. *Christiane Gräfnitz Collection.*

made up of wooden "poupards" (babies dressed in swaddling clothes). Turned wooden "swaddled" babies were a specialty of area wood turners. An interesting variation in the museum is a carved wooden shoulder head that is attached to a kid "cone" body rather than a wooden body. A few of the Oberammergau wooden dolls in the museum closely resemble the early wooden dolls in the Sonneberg Doll and Toy Museum, which are credited to the Sonneberg wood carvers and turners.

As a child, Queen Victoria played with and helped dress her 132 small, jointed, early wooden dolls. The book, *Queen Victoria's Dolls,* includes a charming description of the "Tuck Combs" in her collection.

> There is the queerest mixture of infancy and matronliness in their little wooden faces due to the combination of their small sharp noses and bright vermilion cheeks (consisting of a dab of paint in one spot) with broad placid brows, over which neatly parted at each temple, are painted elaborate, elderly grayish curls. The remainder of the hair is coal black and is relieved by a tiny yellow comb perched upon the back of the head.

Before 1800, wooden dolls were often called "Docken." They were usually turned on a foot-powered lathe from one piece of wood, and the body proportions resembled an adult rather than a child. The first Docken were cone or "skittle" shaped and lacked arms. Later

A 7-1/2-inch Oberammergau wooden doll in original clothing. The well-carved hair and painted facial details are typical of the work credited to the area's skilled doll makers in the mid 1800's. The doll has a wooden body that is only jointed at the shoulders.

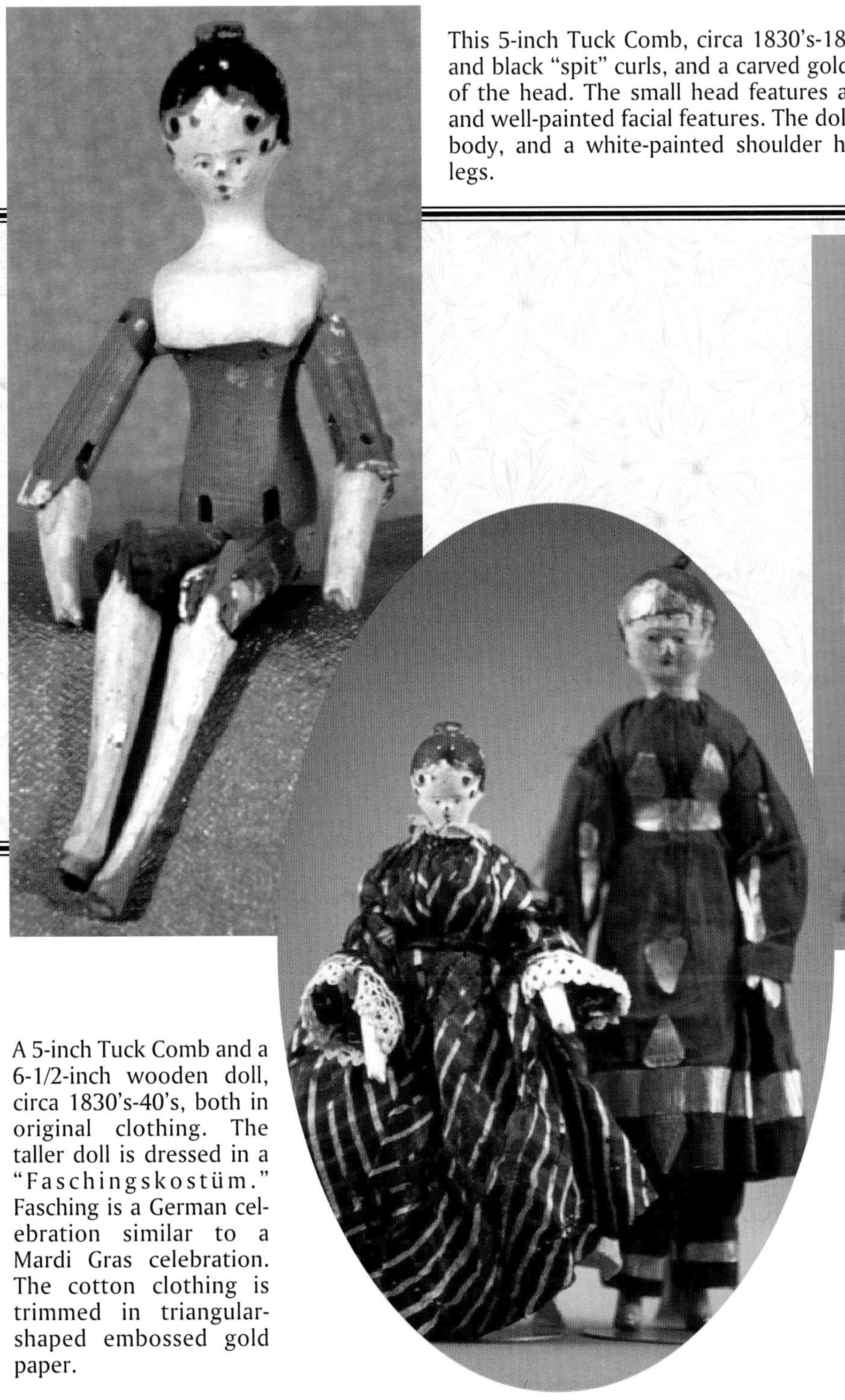

This 5-inch Tuck Comb, circa 1830's-1840's, has painted gray and black "spit" curls, and a carved gold painted comb on top of the head. The small head features a carved wooden nose and well-painted facial features. The doll has a turned wooden body, and a white-painted shoulder head, lower arms, and legs.

A 5-inch Tuck Comb and a 6-1/2-inch wooden doll, circa 1830's-40's, both in original clothing. The taller doll is dressed in a "Faschingskostüm." Fasching is a German celebration similar to a Mardi Gras celebration. The cotton clothing is trimmed in triangular-shaped embossed gold paper.

Above: A pair of 18th Century lathe-turned "skittle-shaped" dolls, similar to early wooden dolls currently on display in the Sonneberg Doll and Toy Museum. The dolls' bodies are painted with simple folk art designs. Before 1800, dolls were often called "Docken."

variations included the addition of hats made from round, flat pieces of wood, and small wood chips were glued to the bodies to emulate arms. Small triangular pieces of wood were sometimes added to the Docken to simulate a nose. Early wooden dolls and toys were seldom patented, and wood carvers and turners from many areas of Germany used the same designs.

By 1780, wooden exports from Sonneberg included Crown Docken, Dancing Docken, Clapping Docken, and Pulling Docken. A few Sonneberg Docken from the 1700's are on permanent display in the Sonneberg Doll and Toy Museum. Crown Docken wore gold painted wooden crowns. Clapping Docken were actually rattles that had hollow bodies and were filled with small seeds or rocks that rattled when shaken. Pulling Docken are not pull-toys. Rather, Pulling Docken were skittle-shaped dolls that held wooden babies in their outstretched wooden arms. When a string was pulled, the doll lifted the baby up and down in a rocking motion. Dancing Docken (Bristle Dolls) resembled walking dolls. They were only about two-inches tall with four small brushes attached to the bottom rim of their wooden skirts. The bodies were hollow, and the legs were attached to the inner body with strings. The legs hung freely inside the body allowing the legs to move when placed on a piano or drum. The doll appeared to "dance" when placed on a vibrating drum or piano.

Sonneberg wood turners were part of the home workers industry. Work was very specialized. A wood turner often made only one item such as a wooden doll limb. Forest management was established in Sonneberg by the early 1800's. Foresters auctioned trees that were cut into large rounds by lumbermen each year. The wood turners braced the large wooden pieces on a joiner's bench, and then split them into smaller pieces. The turner shaped the wooden dolls and toys on a lathe. Women and children family members "scoured off the rough edges with a very sharp knife."

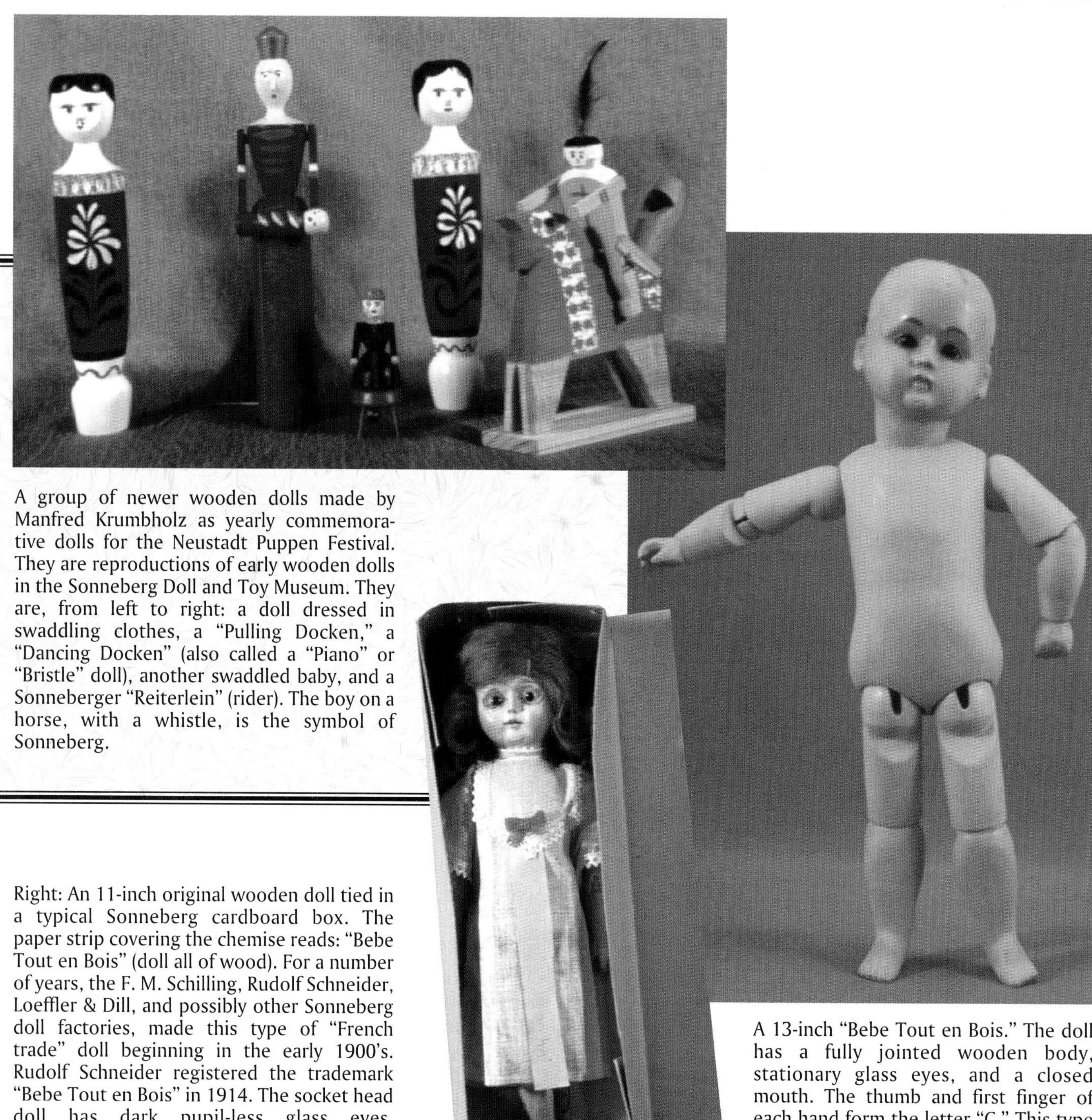

A group of newer wooden dolls made by Manfred Krumbholz as yearly commemorative dolls for the Neustadt Puppen Festival. They are reproductions of early wooden dolls in the Sonneberg Doll and Toy Museum. They are, from left to right: a doll dressed in swaddling clothes, a "Pulling Docken," a "Dancing Docken" (also called a "Piano" or "Bristle" doll), another swaddled baby, and a Sonneberger "Reiterlein" (rider). The boy on a horse, with a whistle, is the symbol of Sonneberg.

Right: An 11-inch original wooden doll tied in a typical Sonneberg cardboard box. The paper strip covering the chemise reads: "Bebe Tout en Bois" (doll all of wood). For a number of years, the F. M. Schilling, Rudolf Schneider, Loeffler & Dill, and possibly other Sonneberg doll factories, made this type of "French trade" doll beginning in the early 1900's. Rudolf Schneider registered the trademark "Bebe Tout en Bois" in 1914. The socket head doll has dark pupil-less glass eyes, multi-stroke eyebrows, exaggerated "French" eyelash painting, and a closed mouth with a darker red line painted between the lips.

A 13-inch "Bebe Tout en Bois." The doll has a fully jointed wooden body, stationary glass eyes, and a closed mouth. The thumb and first finger of each hand form the letter "C." This type of "curled" hand has been found on several "Bebe Tout en Bois" made by the F. M. Schilling doll factory.

Chapter Four

Papier-Mâché Doll Production

On July 16, 1805, Luise Leonore, the Duchess of Saxony, granted Johann Friedrich Müller and his brother, Gottfried, the license to manufacture and sell goods of papier-mâché in Sonneberg. The Müllers are credited with the introduction of papier-mâché in Sonneberg. By 1818, the Müller doll factory employed over 200 papier-mâché workers. In 1822, the *Allgemeiner Anzeiger fuer Bayern* read, "The largest manufacturer is Mr. Johann Friedrich Müller (seller and producer of papier-mâché). His store offers 58 different types of doll heads, excluding the semi-faces, masques and naturally hair styled heads." Although there is no current documentation concerning the exact date Müller began making papier-mâché dolls, we do know that papier-mâché revolutionized the Sonneberg doll industry. This was the first time that inexpensive mass

The Müller & Strasburger doll factory in Sonneberg.

A group of slate-sided home workers' houses in Sonneberg. Papier-mâché dolls and toys were a leading export item from the early 1800's to the early 1900's.

A 25-inch papier-mâché doll with a cloth body, circa 1840. The facial features include pupil-less glass eyes, a broad nose and a slightly smiling mouth. *Christiane Gräfnitz Collection.*

An 18-inch papier-mâché shoulder head doll, circa 1800. The doll, with a classic Greek hairstyle and painted hair tendrils, has exposed ears, a deeply molded bust and a leather body. *Christiane Gräfnitz Collection.*

production of doll heads was possible. Furthermore, every head coming out of a mold looked exactly like the previous one. Papier-mâché production was a major reason (along with the Great Sonneberg Privilege of Trade) that Sonneberg became the world's leading doll center. For many decades following 1805, papier-mâché products were the leading Sonneberg export items. By 1844, there were 750 papier-mâché workers in Sonneberg and the surrounding villages.

Papier-mâché dolls and doll parts were made by gluing sheets of paper together to form layered papier-mâché, or by adding various ingredients to paper pulp, thereby forming a type of composition. Papier-mâché recipes varied from factory to factory, and recipes were not shared. Each factory claimed to have the best recipe and the most indestructible. The recipes were based on one major ingredient: soaked and cooked paper.

Flour, paper pulp, and water made up the most basic recipe, but that mixture attracted insects and mice. Thousands of doll heads were eaten aboard the vessels transporting papier-mâché articles to the United States. The doll manufacturers tried repelling the vermin by adding tobacco leaves, parts of the bitter apple gourd, petroleum, sulfate of alum, or potash to their recipes. Some of these unusual ingredients remained in the papier-mâché recipes, while other ingredients were dropped in the following years. The typical recipe included three main additives to the paper pulp. They were ground chalk (whiting), plaster of Paris, and liquid glue. Over the years, many other ingredients were included in the recipes, and the proportions varied factory to factory. A few recipes included clay (soil), flour, sand, meal, and ashes. According to doll historians, Sonneberg papier-mâché was mostly chalk, with kaolin (porcelain clay) added. Combined with the shredded paper, this mixture, called "Masse" (mass), was extremely dense as well as durable. It was often identified as composition rather than papier-mâché.

The papier-mâché pressers received less pay than any other group of home workers. Every member of the family was an important part of the work unit. Children as young as age three trimmed and sanded the papier-mâché pieces after they were removed from the molds. Petroleum was sometimes used to coat the molds and as a dissolving medium. The odor from the sulfur molds, petroleum, and papier-mâché mixture was suffocating.

Emma Brewer wrote an important article in 1884 titled "Toydonia: Or the Land of Toys." Three paragraphs from this article are particularly interesting because of the inaccurate picture of Sonneberg doll making portrayed. They read as follows:

> Nearly the whole of the 8,000 inhabitants, men, women and children, are in some way engaged in toy making, and although it is in this manner they earn their living, and that oftimes but scanty, I do believe from what I see that they have as much pleasure from the toys as the children for whom they are destined.
>
> It is amazing to watch the young children hurrying home from school to obtain an empty chair at the worktable and see them imitate their elders. This is quite voluntarily done, and evidently affords them delight. In this way they are quite unconsciously learning the work from beginning to end, and enabling themselves to be themselves to be of assistance to their parents at an early age.
>
> The life of the workers in the toy house industry seems to me by no means unpleasant. Masters and helpers work into each other's hands; they chat and sing at the worktable without delaying the progress of the work or calling for rebuke, for a cheerful spirit is declared by the master to be a great help in the workroom.

This 16-inch papier-mâché shoulder head doll dressed in original clothing is representative of the fashions of the 1840's. The doll's wrists are tied with original blue wrist ribbons. The molded hairstyle features long curls over each ear and a braided bun in the back. The doll has a leather body with turned wooden limbs typically used on papier-mâché dolls made between 1820-1860.

The 1995 German book, titled in English, *Sonneberg Stories of Dolls, Slate Pencils and Cuckoo Whistles, From the Workaday World of Our Parents*, paints quite a different picture of the home workers' lives in Sonneberg. This important book is made up of separate articles that describe doll making in Sonneberg and the neighboring villages. The articles are actual memories or oral histories provided by the children of doll makers in this area. The lack of food, long hours of work and the absence of any of life's luxuries are the word pictures a reader receives from this important book. It is also clear that Thuringian children helped make dolls and toys their parents could never afford to buy for them.

Accurate descriptions of the work process provide information about each step relating to doll making. It was necessary for the home worker to keep his or her house as hot as possible in winter as well as in summer

Left: A typical Sonneberg doll factory. Doll limbs on drying racks fill every part of the large workroom. *Ana and Peter Kalinke Collection.*

Right: Women and children were an important part of the Sonneberg work force. *Ana and Peter Kalinke Collection.*

Left: Nineteen Sonneberg residents shown in an original early 1900's postcard. The man in the foreground is carrying a delivery basket on his back. A doll head is visible in the left corner of the basket. The group of men, women and children provide a graphic picture of the reality of life in Sonneberg that was endured by the majority of underpaid home workers.

in order to rapidly dry the papier-mâché products because slow drying caused the doll heads and body parts to warp. The papier-mâché doll-related articles were taken out of the molds while they were still slightly damp so that the air in the work area could circulate around each finished piece. Because there was so little space in the average home worker's house, the papier-mâché doll heads and body parts were placed on separate pegs attached to wooden drying racks. The drying racks were hung from hooks permanently mounted to the ceilings of rooms in a home worker's house, as close as possible to a fireplace or stove for maximum heat.

One Sonneberg oral history contains a description of a typical home worker's work place. It is as follows:

> There were many families who worked in the home industry. My parents had such a workshop in which they made dolls. Our seven-member family lived in a two-room flat, which had a bedroom and a large living-kitchen. In the bedroom, my parents had their marriage bed, and we four big children were together in one bed. My younger sister had her child's bed. Our large kitchen served as the kitchen, living room and workroom.

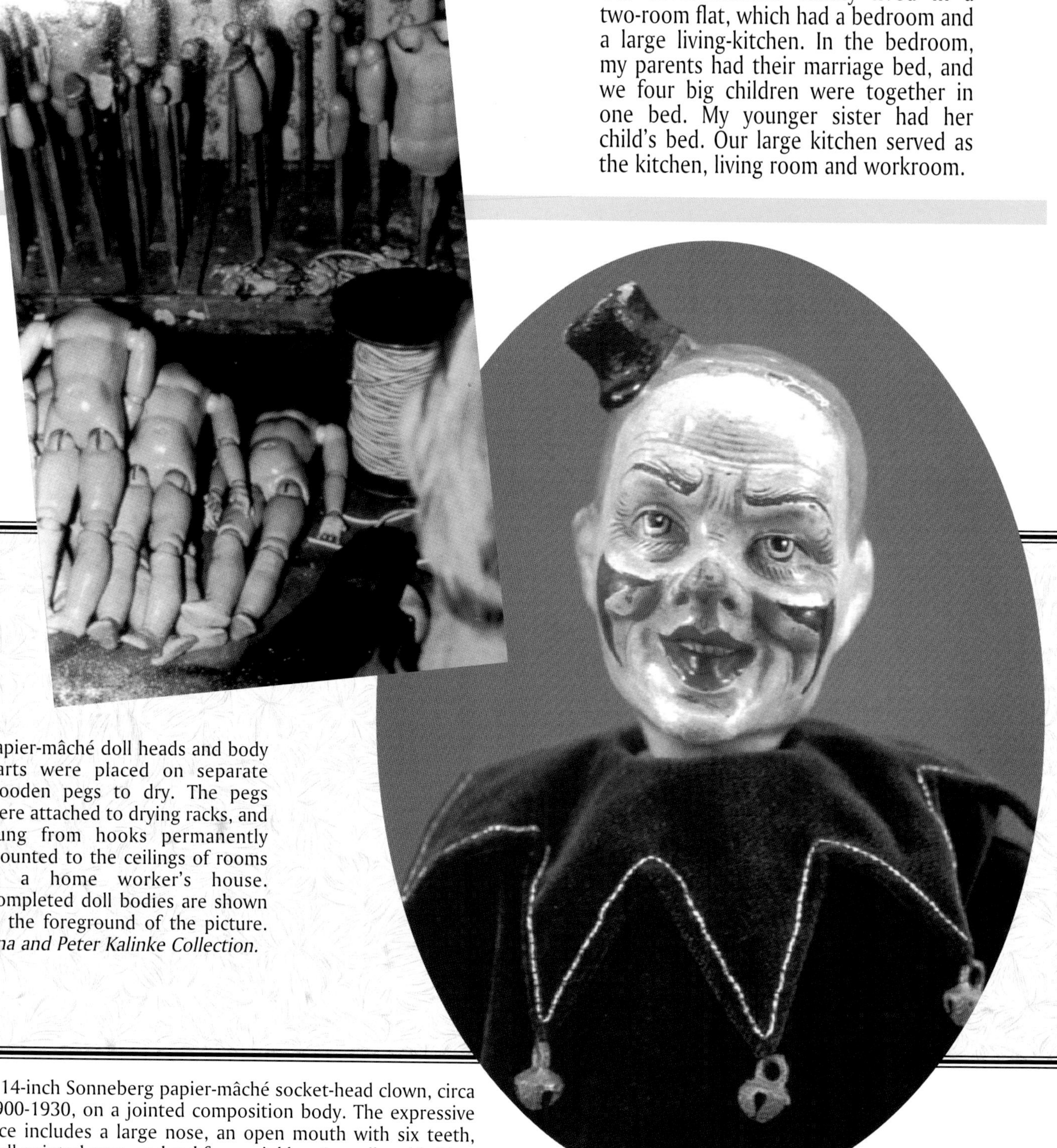

Papier-mâché doll heads and body parts were placed on separate wooden pegs to dry. The pegs were attached to drying racks, and hung from hooks permanently mounted to the ceilings of rooms in a home worker's house. Completed doll bodies are shown in the foreground of the picture. *Ana and Peter Kalinke Collection.*

A 14-inch Sonneberg papier-mâché socket-head clown, circa 1900-1930, on a jointed composition body. The expressive face includes a large nose, an open mouth with six teeth, well-painted eyes, and red face wrinkles. A small molded hat accentuates the clown-like effect.

Making Papier-Mâché Dolls in Sonneberg

Sonneberg doll factories often look more like large homes than actual factories. The family usually lived in the front of the house and dolls were made in work areas attached to the rear of the home/factory.

This 7-inch papier-mâché shoulder head doll, circa 1845-55, is dressed in original Alsace-Lorraine regional clothing. The body is cloth with leather arms that end in fringed leather stubs. The doll head includes painted blue eyes, a closed mouth, and molded hair that is pulled back into a braided bun and fastened with a molded comb.

C.L. Mateau wrote an article in 1898, titled "Wonderland of Work," that contained step-by-step descriptions of the papier-mâché work process. Papier-mâché doll heads were made in many small homes as well as in doll factories. The Sonneberg doll "factories" look more like large homes than factories. The doll factories were often made up of a number of "living" rooms in the front of the building and large "work" rooms were attached to the back of the house for doll manufacture and/or assembly work.

The article by the English writer C.L. Mateau states:

> Now come and look at that cauldron of uninviting paper pulp boiling away so steadily; yes, that is what your fine doll's face is to come out of. Just a lot of old scraps of torn paper; and soon a worker comes to peer and poke at the steaming paper pulp, and at last pronouncing it soft and clear enough for use, he squeezes and strains the water out of it. Then he mixes powered clay and a little glue in it until the whole is now like a great cake of baker's dough ready for making into loaves; indeed, it is soon rolled, and banged, and beaten into the semblance of long, cake-like shaped loaves, and laid on the ground by the side of another man, who picks them up one by one, and laying them on a board, flattens them out with a big rolling pin, exactly like cook does with a pie crust.
>
> This soft paste he then cuts into square pieces, which he places in piles, one on top of the other, taking care to scatter a little powdered clay-like flour between each piece, to hinder its sticking to its neighbor. Altogether it really is like cook's work, only instead of calling the dough 'pastry,' we must speak of it as 'papier-mâché,' and then the toy maker will understand us, for it is very much used in his trade.

But how is this papier-mâché to become a doll's head? We shall soon know, for a worker carries off a little pile of soft squares, and is busy in pressing down the paper dough into one of the hollow moulds we saw prepared just now. This done, he passes it on to another man, who, carefully flourishing a bit of soft wet sponge and a little bone tool, soon makes the soft paste fit neatly into every crevice of the mould, so that it must turn out an exact counterpart of its shape. Having made sure of this, he pares off all the rough edges of dough with a knife; exactly like a cook with her piecrust, then he gently slips the half head out of the mould, and lays it on a board to dry a little.

Poor fellows, how hot they all look here! The large room is so full of tobacco fumes, for every German workman smokes, and these doll makers more than others. Now we can scarcely see the dozens of wan little heads about us; but the workers declare they cannot keep awake in this heavy, oppressive atmosphere unless they do smoke. And, the room must not be allowed to cool, or the heads will not dry quickly enough, but be all dumpy, and lose their outline, like any other dough.

Above: A 1780 papier-mâché mask-face doll from Nuremberg, Germany. The 25-inch cloth-bodied doll, in original clothing, has a shoulder plate molded to indicate a bust. The painted facial features include dark eyebrows, expressive eyes, and bright red cheeks. *Christiane Gräfnitz Collection.*

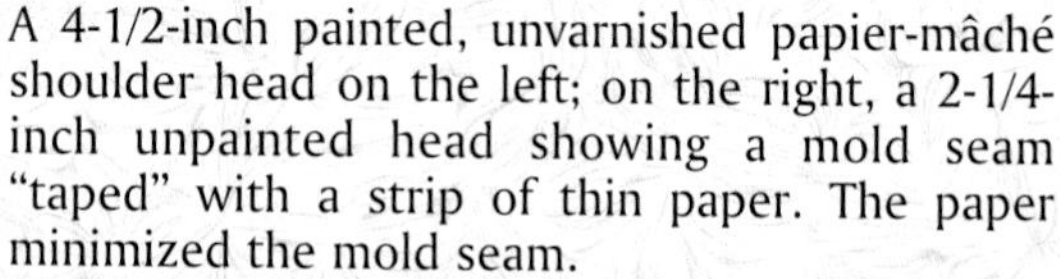

A 4-1/2-inch painted, unvarnished papier-mâché shoulder head on the left; on the right, a 2-1/4-inch unpainted head showing a mold seam "taped" with a strip of thin paper. The paper minimized the mold seam.

When the half heads are dry enough, the face halves are again squeezed in a mould to sharpen them up and make them perfect. Then, they are thoroughly dried; and the two halves are at last neatly glued together, and placed for the first time as perfect heads on a shelf, where they stand in a long row, side by side, cold and grim and gray, eyeless and hairless and colourless, in not by any means a pleasant stage of dollhood.

Now we follow our heads to the eye setter, a rough and heartless doctor, who seizes them one by one and quite unconcernedly cuts off the top of each cranium by running a sharp knife round it. He knocks the piece out by a sudden rap of a hammer, a startling operation, no doubt. But, one that must be gone through before Dolly can be possessed of eyes, lovely glass eyes, I mean, not mere painted ones, which any common doll has.

The unchanging orbs (stationary eyes) are much sooner fitted; for the worker, with a quick twirl of his sharp knife, cuts a couple of almond shaped holes and pops in the eyes which he first slightly warms, that they may hold still while he pours a little melted wax into the hollow skull to keep them fast in their places.

Let us hide away to the painting room, and watch their cheeks grow rosy, and their lips and eyebrows appear. This, at last, is a nice cool, comfortable room, with a long table running along its centre, and a great many busy people waiting to receive their batch of new heads, which will pass round from hand to hand, with each worker doing his or her own particular share at perfecting them.

The first doll's head being handed to worker number one, he will, with a stroke and a flourish, leave two little bowed, cherry-coloured lips, and pop it down on the other side ready for its next neighbor to catch up and decorate with eyebrows and outlines. Thus the heads proceed on their way, growing prettier at each step, until at last they are set down with blushing cheeks and pink lined nostrils.

A 14-inch papier-mâché shoulder head doll, circa 1845-1855, with a "Kinderkopf" (child's head) hairstyle. The doll is dressed in original regional clothing that includes a red wool vest and black velvet pants. The head is mounted on a cotton twill body with leather arms and wired fingers.

Below: This 11-inch Thuringian papier-mâché shoulder head doll, circa 1830's, has an elaborately molded hairstyle. The hairstyle features curls on each side of the head, and the hair is twisted over a form to create a Croiset-style topknot. The shoulder head is mounted on a kid body with wooden lathe-turned lower limbs.

Above: This 15-1/2-inch unusual 1860-70 "smiling" papier-mâché doll with softly curled blonde hair includes a molded papier-mâché rose. The doll has original bisque lower arms. *Christiane Gräfnitz Collection.*

A group of early Thuringian molded-hair papier-mâché dolls, circa 1830-1840. The dolls, measuring from 10-inches to 30-inches, show the variety of hairstyles popular during this time. *Christiane Gräfnitz Collection.*

An 1860's wax-over papier-mâché shoulder head doll with dark pupil-less glass eyes and a short curly hairstyle. The doll is wearing a red pillbox hat trimmed with a large molded black plume.

The 19-inch doll has a cloth body with leather arms and wooden lower legs. The original clothing includes a well-designed jacket trimmed in red—typical of the clothing worn by young girls in the 1860's.

The description of face painting described by C.L. Mateau provides clues to the uniformity found on papier-mâché heads. The eyes (painted) and eyebrows vary only in minor ways. Often, the same eyebrow painter painted day after day, year after year. Left-handed painters were better at painting left eyebrows and vice-versa, and women were better at painting lips. The heads were not always finished following the face-painting step. The papier-mâché heads were often given a coat of clear varnish or dipped in wax. Some doll makers sized the heads before the features were applied. Sizing was made from the gelatinous liquid from sheep or goat's skin. Sizing smoothed the rough papier-mâché surface, and provided a more even painting surface.

An average weekly wage in Sonneberg for a male factory worker in 1900 was about four dollars (in 1900, a U.S. dollar equaled 4.20 Mark. The German word "Mark" is singular and plural). A woman received the equivalent of three U.S. dollars for working in a factory for a week. One family of papier-mâché home workers received 50¢ for 16 hours of work in 1900. This same family of four completed 980 doll bodies for that salary. In 1880, the Sonneberg police were forced to close a six-room two-story worker's house, because 58 papier-mâché pressers lived and worked inside. In 1884, according to the United States Bureau of Labor Statistics, there were "60 wholesale houses in Sonneberg, and the toys sent out annually realize on an average 16,000,000 Mark" or $3,809,523.80 in U.S. dollars (1900 rate).

A few other papier-mâché doll factories from the Southern Circle provide an interesting study. They are the Andreas Voit/Ernst Conrad doll factory, the Müller & Strasburger doll factory, and the Heinrich Stier/Barbara Schilling doll factory.

Johann Andreas Voit (known as Andreas) was born on March 2, 1774. He was the son of a roofer. His first job was as a porcelain painter for the Kloster Veilsdorf porcelain factory. Voit founded his doll factory in 1806, and is credited with making his first papier-mâché doll heads in the town of Eisfeld in 1816. Voit moved from Eisfeld to Hildburghausen in 1822. Hildburghausen is in the Southern Doll Making Circle just 18.6 miles from Sonneberg. Voit employed about 50 workers, along with some home workers in 1822. He died at the age of 63, on February 18, 1837.

According to author Christiane Gräfnitz in her book *Papier-Mâché Dolls, 1760-1860*, "In 1837, Ernst Conrad joins the company, and the management is handled by

Left: A 30-inch Voit papier-mâché doll, circa 1820. The doll has a cloth body with papier-mâché arms and legs. Its dark brown hair is molded in a "Kinderkopf" hairstyle. *Christiane Gräfnitz Collection.*

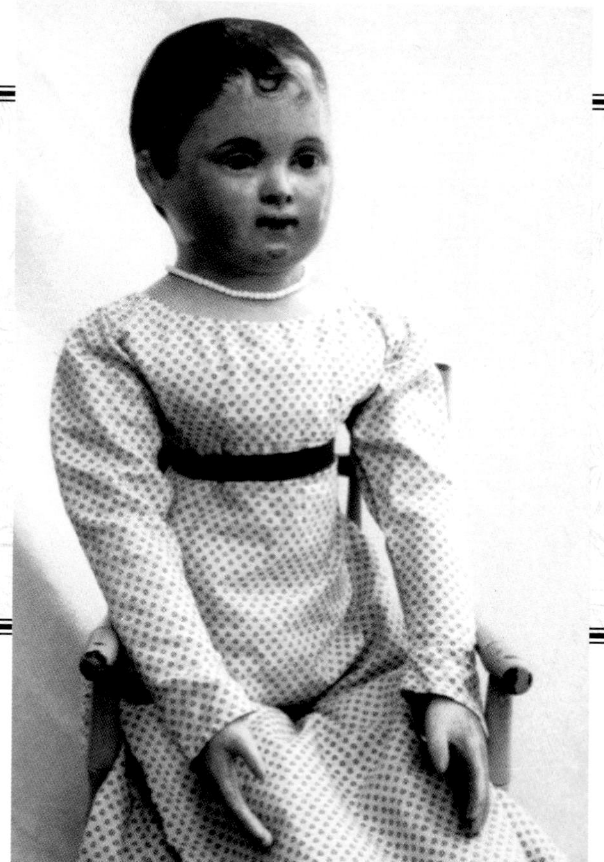

Right: This 16-3/4-inch papier-mâché shoulder head doll, circa 1840's-1850's, has an elaborate hairstyle featuring side poufs that roll back into a chignon encircled by a braid. The doll's face and hair was originally coated with a clear varnish in order to protect the painting details. Finely carved wooden hands are a typical feature of this type of doll.

An 18-inch papier-mâché shoulder head doll by Andreas Voit, circa 1830's. The doll has dark pupil-less eyes and a child's hairstyle. The cloth body includes well-molded papier-mâché arms that end at the shoulder, and papier-mâché lower legs.

A 20-inch papier-mâché boy, circa 1830. The doll has dark brown hair in "Kinderkopf" style, dark pupil-less eyes, and a leather body. The well-painted hair detail is a typical feature of early Voit dolls. *Christiane Gräfnitz Collection.*

Heinrich Christian Jacobi. From 1847-57, the company is jointly managed with Ernst Conrad." Voit's nephew and foster son, Ernst Conrad, studied art before he began working at the papier-mâché factory. Twelve Voit dolls were shown at the 1844 Berlin Trade Exhibition where they were awarded a Medal of Honor.

The Voit/Conrad papier-mâché dolls are often described as "French papier-mâchés." According to an article by the Ciesliks in their 1994 *Puppenmagazin*, "The papier-mâché dolls from Hildburghausen are today being erroneously classified as a French production. That is not true. The dolls were manufactured at the Voit factory, and assembled, and then sold undressed to Paris. There they were dressed according to the latest Paris fashion and shipped into the world as 'Paris Genre."

There is no question that a few Sonneberg papier-mâché manufacturers copied the Voit/Conrad dolls. The Sonneberg doll makers made copies of every "new" doll, including dolls made of wood, papier-mâché, wax, and porcelain. It is said that the competition tried to keep the Sonnebergers out of their sample rooms, to protect their new ideas. It is often difficult to differentiate between the authentic Voit/Conrad dolls and the Sonneberg copies.

Above: Four German papier-mâché shoulder head dolls made in the 3rd Quarter of the 19th Century. They are mounted on original bodies made by the Philip Goldsmith doll factory of Covington, Kentucky. The 25-inch Müller & Strasburger doll, with blonde hair, is marked with an original label edged in blue. It reads: "M & S Superior, 2015." The 23-inch doll, with black hair, is marked with the Ernst and Carl Dressel "winged trademark" of 1875. The smaller dolls, each measuring 13 inches, have hairstyles similar to the larger dolls.

Far Left: This A Voit/Conrad doll with a bald papier-mâché head, circa 1835-50, is dressed in an original cotton factory chemise.

The papier-mâché shoulder head with a large painted black spot and the pink kid body, and typical features of the Voit/Conrad dolls, sold as French dolls for many years. The 18-inch doll has a simple un-gusseted leather body with a defined waist and well-shaped limbs.

This 24-inch Voit/-Conrad papier-mâché doll has glass flirty eyes, a cloth body, and leather arms. The doll, circa 1840-1860, has a longer curly black hairstyle than is typical of the mid 19th Century time period. *Christiane Gräfnitz Collection.*

Right: An 18-inch Voit/Conrad papier-mâché doll described as a "Pauline-type." Dark pupil-less eyes and papier-mâché layered teeth are features of this doll, circa 1840-1860. The doll has a carton-type upper body and is dressed in original clothing depicting Marie Antoinette.

The Hildburghausen City Museum has an exceptional group of Voit/Conrad dolls in a permanent display. The exhibit includes examples of the rare red-wax doll-head models sculpted by Ernst Conrad. The Voit/Conrad factory is still standing in Hildburghausen. This historical building is located only a few feet from the original town walls that once surrounded Hildburghausen. Plaster head molds are visible on the deteriorating walls of the home/factory. The second floor of the building served as the living quarters. The original wall and ceiling detail remind one of the Voit/Conrad years of occupancy.

Johann Friedrich Müller's early years of production are poorly documented. More is known about Müller in 1844 when the Müller & Strasburger doll factory is listed in the Sonneberg commercial registers. We know that Müller admitted Strasburger as a partner between 1822 and 1844, and that Johann Friedrick Müller died in 1855.

The Müller & Strasburger doll factory is familiar to American collectors because of the large numbers of M&S "Superior" heads that were sold in the United States. One can conclude that many of these heads were sent overseas without bodies considering the frequency of finding the "Superior" head attached to an original Philip Goldsmith body. Goldsmith patented a doll's body, featuring a corset in 1885, but was in business for at least 10 years before that. He made and distributed dolls and

The Andreas Voit/Ernst Conrad doll factory in Hildburghausen. The plaque to the right of the doorway honors Conrad with the following inscription: "Hier wirkte Der Bildhauer Ernst Conrad 1818-1882." The German words on the plaque translate to "The sculptor Ernst Conrad worked here." The dates 1818 and 1882 are Conrad's dates of birth and death. Old doll molds are visible today on the deteriorating walls of the home/ factory.

The second floor of the Voit home served as the living quarters. The original wall and ceiling trim remind one of the Voit/Conrad years of occupancy.

A molded plaster wall scene over one doorway in the Voit/Conrad home/factory. The scene pictures a man and woman in the foreground and a house surrounded by evergreens in the background.

This papier-mâché shoulder head Schilling doll from about 1880 wears an original winged angel marked chemise. The doll has a cloth body with papier-mâché lower arms and legs. The "Mary Jane" one-strap shoes are painted an unusual purple color with a blue upper edge.

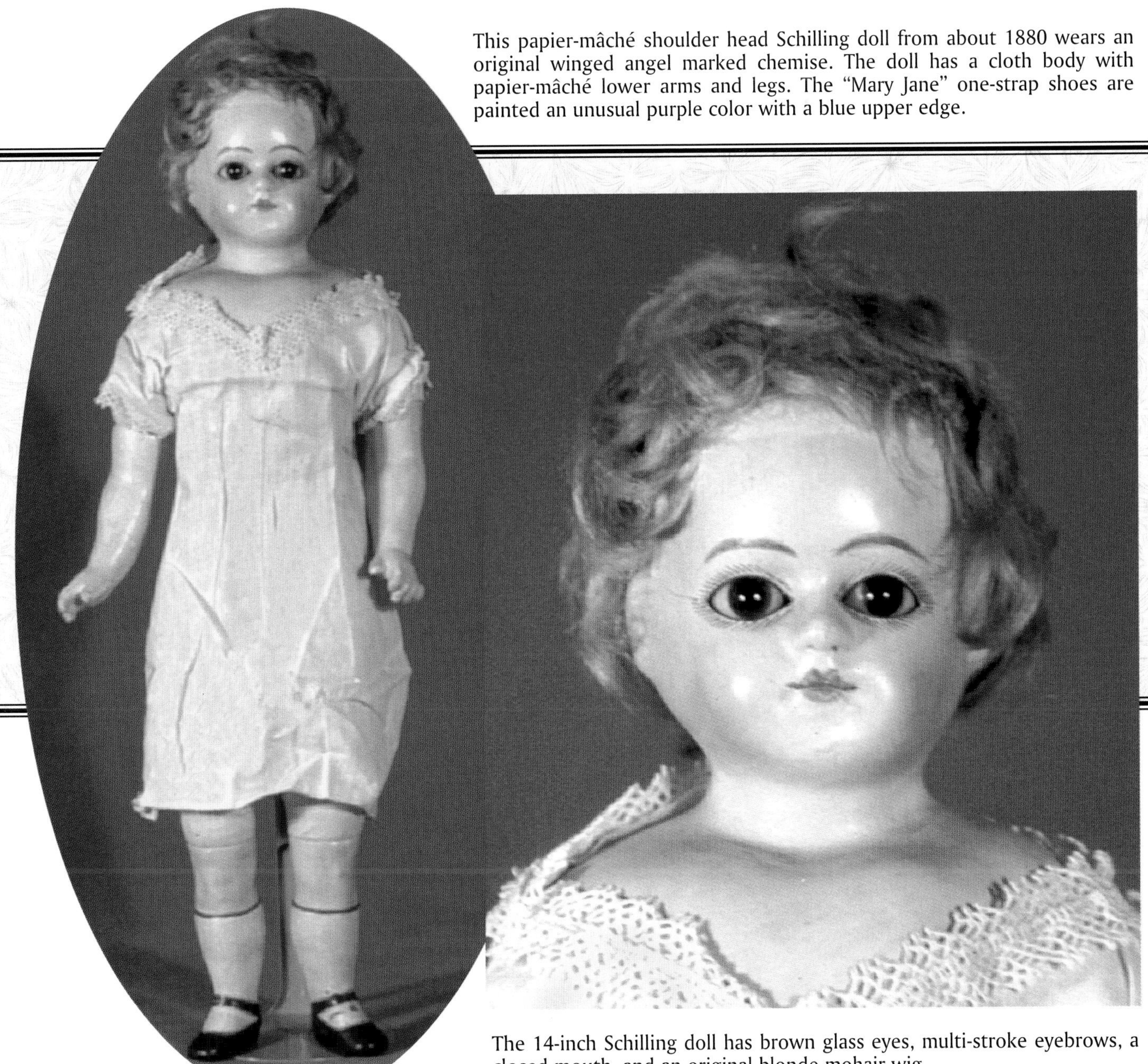

The 14-inch Schilling doll has brown glass eyes, multi-stroke eyebrows, a closed mouth, and an original blonde mohair wig.

dolls' bodies in Cincinnati, Ohio and across the Ohio River in Covington, Kentucky, according to the Dorothy Coleman article in "Spinning Wheel's Complete Book of Dolls."

The M&S papier-mâché shoulder heads are often marked with a rectangular paper label. The original labels are often edged in blue and contain the following blue lettering: "M&S, Superior, 2015." The Müller & Strasburger firm also used the numbers 1020, 2020, and 4515 on the company labels. The hairstyles vary, but generally, the hair is styled with a center part, and molded curls are arranged on each side of the head.

The Philip Goldsmith bodies are made of muslin and stuffed with cattle hair and sawdust. The lower arms are made of brown leather. A very identifiable Goldsmith hand feature is the use of a single stick inside each leather finger. The stockings were made of many types of patterned cotton. The Goldsmith stocking patterns vary, and stripes and checks in many colors have been found. Leather as well as cotton boots were made in a variety of colors. The Goldsmith boot is usually laced with crossed cotton threads, and two tassels trim the top of the lacing. In 1887, the Montgomery Ward catalog advertised the Goldsmith doll bodies as "Patent Corset Bodies (no head), entirely new, with seat, kid arms, colored stockings, shoes with tassels and adjustable lace corsets: 10 inches, 24¢ each and $2.50 a dozen; 16 inches, 48¢ each and $5.00 a dozen."

Barbara Schilling is unique because women doll factory owners were uncommon in Germany. In 1871,

Heinrich Stier, Barbara's uncle, founded the Barbara Schilling doll factory for his niece in Sonneberg. During the same year (1871), Stier retired and turned his successful doll business over to his brother Gustav.

The Schilling firm was established to produce "rubber Täuflinge and wax dolls," according to the Ciesliks in their January, 2000 issue of *Puppenmagazin.* A Schilling doll is pictured in the *Puppenmagazin* mentioned above. The papier-mâché head is "painted with a skin colored paint and then treated with a collodion lacquer, so that it can be washed/wiped off with soapy water without damaging the doll."

The Schilling "winged angel head" trademark was registered in 1879. In 1879, Barbara Schilling made Täuflinge (plural of Täufling) of composition, rubber, papier-mâché, and wax. Schilling directed her doll factory for only 12 years. In 1883, she turned the factory over to her son, Ferdinand Max Schilling. Under his direction, the company became the F. M. Schilling Company. The factory was still in business in 1924.

Today, many papier-mâché dolls and toys are still manufactured in the Sonneberg area. Papier-mâché holiday items like Easter rabbits, Halloween lanterns, and Father Christmas figures are a reminder of earlier dolls and toys.

This Schilling composition shoulder head doll, circa 1900, has glass sleep eyes, an open mouth with two lower teeth, cheek dimples, and a cloth body stuffed with straw. The composition lower arms and legs feature well-modeled hands and feet. The original mohair wig covers a dome-shaped head; the top of the head has been left unpainted. *Marguerite Hoffman Collection.*

Four 1920's papier-mâché rabbits measuring 5 to 7 inches. The two largest rabbits have original paper price stickers marked: "F. W. Woolworth, 15 cents."

Chapter Five

Adolf Fleischmann: "Verleger"

Adolf Fleischmann left an indelible impression on his hometown. Walking the streets of Sonneberg today, one is constantly reminded of his many contributions to the world of dolls. Fleischmann was born October 22, 1819. His baroque-style birthplace has been beautifully restored. The slate-roofed, yellow-painted building was his first place of business as well as his home. Fleischmann founded his doll and toy factory in 1844 when he was 25.

In 1848, Adolf Fleischmann married Amalie Engelhardt Lindner. Amalie's first husband was Eduard Lindner, brother of Johann Christoph and Louis Lindner, members of the Sonneberg Verleger group. Eduard committed suicide in 1847 and Amalie married Fleischmann the following year.

Adolf and Amalie moved into the *Villa Amalie* in 1848. Michael Schmidt, the well-known Sonneberg master builder, built Fleischmann's villa. Schmidt was the father of the Munich architect Albert Schmidt. Many foreign buyers and influential businessmen stayed at the *Villa Amalie*. The ruling duke, Duke Georg II of Sachsen-Meiningen, once spent three weeks at the villa during a trip to the area.

Adolf Fleischmann was the great-grandchild of Gotthelf Greiner, "Father of Thuringian Porcelain." As a boy, Adolf was sent to private schools for his early education. At the age of 15, he studied at the Leipzig School of Commerce. Following his business education in Leipzig, Fleischmann worked for an English trading company for two years. He was quoted in later years as saying that he learned "taste as well as manners" in England. Following his years in England, Fleischmann learned art from the painter Diez.

There is no question that Adolf was artistic. According to the Ciesliks, Fleischmann designed a scene from *Gulliver's Travels* for the 1844 Berlin Trade Exhibition. The large papier-mâché Gulliver was surrounded by dozens of small bread dough figures, representing the Lilliputians. In 1851, Fleischmann entered "Gulliver Among the Lilliputians" in the London International Trade Exhibition where he was awarded a medal. This exhibit is on permanent display in the Sonneberg Doll and Toy Museum.

Adolf Fleischmann's birthplace. The restored home/factory featuring neo-baroque styling was built in 1720. Fleischmann opened his first doll factory here in 1844.

In 1881, Carl Craemer became a co-owner of the Fleischmann doll and toy factory. Craemer was a very influential Sonneberg merchant. While he was President of the Sonneberg Chamber of Commerce, he was credited with many town improvements. In 1883, Adolf Fleischmann and Carl Craemer were among the founders of the Sonneberg Industrial School. Later, in 1908, Carl Craemer, along with F.E. Heron (Craemer's son-in-law) founded the Mengersgereuth porcelain factory.

Adolf Fleischmann produced 300,000 papier-mâché doll heads a year from 1844 to 1848. These figures are important because they represent orders from all over the world which is quite a feat considering the sort of communications used at the time. Imagine the efforts it took to take an order and ship a doll from the

Fleischmann factory to its final destination in America. The first Sonneberg post office was built in 1809. By 1880, letters were delivered twice a day. There were no telephones or railroads in Sonneberg during the 1840's. Telephones were not installed in Sonneberg until 1887; and the first phone line had 25 extensions. The transatlantic telegraph cable was not in place until 1866. The first train pulled into Sonneberg in 1858. Therefore, in the 1840's, Fleischmann transported his dolls and toys by horse and wagon, and his orders were placed through letters rather than over telephone or telegraph lines. The introduction of railroads and phones in Sonneberg greatly impacted the time required to place and deliver doll orders.

Left: The Villa Amalie in Sonneberg, named for Fleischmann's wife, Amalie Engelhardt.

The 1907 Sonneberg Railroad Station was once the center of Sonneberg doll and toy delivery. An original 1910 postcard pictures a boy with a "Schanzen" (delivery basket) on his back. A large delivery wagon is also pictured. The wagon is covered with cloth to protect the dolls and toys from damage due to changing weather conditions. In 1858, the first steam locomotive pulled into an earlier version of the Sonneberg Railroad Station.

Craemer's villa in Sonneberg, now a Music School. A 1910 original postcard shows the villa reflected in a pond, which was formerly located in front of Carl Craemer's home.

Cardboard Box Making

Once orders were placed and the completed dolls were ready to be sent to a buyer, they were packed in cardboard boxes. Box making was a very specialized craft. In a typical Sonneberg factory, men and boys, rather than women, made cardboard boxes because the large cardboard panels were so heavy. Furthermore, boxes were generally made in factories rather than in home workshops because of the space required to spread out the sheets and cut the cardboard.

A stack of cardboard boxes. A wide variety of sizes were needed to contain the myriad of dolls and toys shipped from Sonneberg.

A boxed set of 4-inch all-bisque dolls "stitched" into an original cardboard box. The box is lined with brightly colored tissue paper to attract buyers. The Hertwig dolls were destined for the Carl Horn doll factory in Dresden according to the original box label.

An original 22-inch bisque socket head Schoenau-Hoffmeister doll with a jointed composition body. The doll, tied in a cardboard box, is marked "Rosebud." The original box contains a paper mattress filled with straw. The stuffed paper mattress protected the doll during shipment to its final destination.

An original August 13, 1895 passenger list for the Norddeutscher Lloyd, Bremen. Two hundred and fifty four passengers listed by name and hometown in the booklet. The list includes the name: Herr D. J. Partello, U.S. Consul, Sonneberg. The main shipping ports during the early days of doll making were Bremen and Hamburg.

Below: An original 6-inch papier-mâché "Baker" doll, with stationary glass eyes and a wooden body. The original box is marked: "1889," along with the following translated message: "For The Birthday; for Emilie Schedel from B. Echert." The doll, dressed in a chef's hat and clothing, is holding a brass pan and spoon. *Jane Walker Collection.*

Rendering of a 1850 Adolf Fleischmann sample page from the doll factory's catalog. The sample page pictures 10 molded-hair papier-mâché shoulder head dolls on kid bodies with wooden turned lower arms and legs. It also shows 4 smaller papier-mâché shoulder heads on jointed wooden bodies. *Original artwork by Hope Fjord.*

Many boxes were lined with brightly colored paper to "enhance" the dolls. The majority of Thuringian dolls were packaged in cardboard boxes with white paper linings edged with paper lace. In addition, cloth or paper "mattresses" were often added to the boxes of expensive dolls. Early cardboard boxes were made by hand. The box makers in the 1900's used a large stamping machine to cut the outline of a box out of cardboard. A stapling machine inserted metal staples into the sides of each box to complete the corners.

A Verleger like Adolf Fleischmann was responsible for all shipping arrangements. In order to minimize breakage during delivery, dolls and toys were often stitched into their cardboard boxes. Women in the factory's finishing department used needles and heavy thread to securely attach the dolls to the bottoms of the cardboard boxes. It was very important to the buyer and seller that the doll's hair, clothes, and eye mechanisms remain in place during transit.

Once the dolls were stitched into their boxes, the cardboard boxes were stacked in wooden crates for delivery across the ocean. The wooden crates were lined with oiled paper to keep out moisture while traveling in the hold of the ship. Dolls and toys were generally shipped from the German ports of Bremen or Hamburg. The large sailing vessel *Norddeutscher Lloyd* sailed from Bremen to New York weekly in 1880.

Adolf Fleischmann's dolls are seldom marked. The 1991 German book, titled in English, *Toy Making and Handwork in Thuringia and Erzgebirge* includes a sample page from Fleischmann's 1850 manufacturer's catalog. The sample page featured a group of Fleischmann's milliners' model-type dolls. The black and white picture showcases 14 dolls in various sizes. The hairstyles reflect the simple hairstyles of the 1850's. The curls are arranged close to each doll's face. Ten of the papier-mâché shoulder plates are attached to the so-called "milliners' model-type" body which are kid bodies with wooden limbs. The smallest papier-mâché shoulder heads are attached to jointed wooden bodies. The doll faces on Fleischmann sample page look like portraits of women. Two of the groups of dolls are identified with the numbers 6050 and 6040.

Fleischmann's papier-mâché shoulder heads are occasionally marked with a rectangular paper label that reads: "A.F.&C.; Superior; 2018." A similar label marked: "M&S; Superior; 2015," has been found on Müller & Strasburger papier-mâché dolls from the same era. It is possible that the Müller & Strasburger doll factory made some heads for Adolf Fleischmann.

Adolf Fleischmann's *Villa Amalie* was considered a "social center" of Sonneberg. As a member of the Town Council, Fleischmann was well respected by his peers. On his 70th birthday, in 1889, the townspeople arranged a torchlight parade in front of his villa. Fleischmann died on March 28, 1895 at the age of 76. He is buried in the Lutheran Church Cemetery across the street from his villa. His grave is a fitting tribute to one of Sonneberg's "favorite sons." No one will ever forget his face because it is featured as a portrait medallion on his gravestone.

Following his death, his widow Amalie donated her husband's business journals, his personal journals, and samples of his dolls and toys to the Sonneberg Doll and Toy Museum. Fleischmann's love of Sonneberg is reflected in his historical journals describing "the early days in the town of toys."

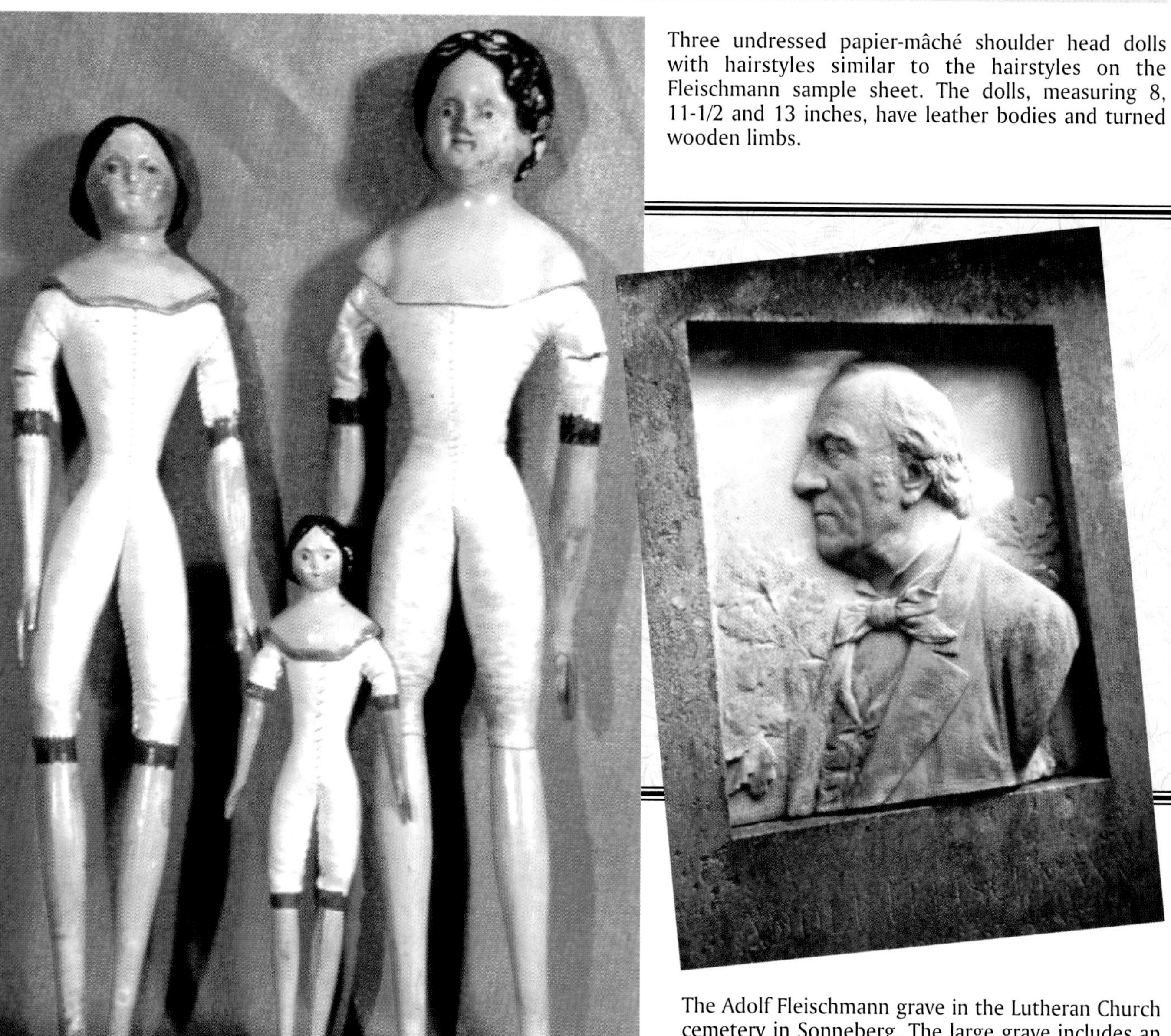

Three undressed papier-mâché shoulder head dolls with hairstyles similar to the hairstyles on the Fleischmann sample sheet. The dolls, measuring 8, 11-1/2 and 13 inches, have leather bodies and turned wooden limbs.

The Adolf Fleischmann grave in the Lutheran Church cemetery in Sonneberg. The large grave includes an obelisk over the Fleischmann portrait medallion. The dates of birth and death on the grave are: October 22, 1819 and March 25, 1895.

Chapter Six

The Dressel Doll Factory

The Dressel doll factory is the oldest German doll factory for which continuous records have been found. It was the largest doll factory in Sonneberg for hundreds of years. Many generations of Dressels were financially successful because of their contacts all over the world.

The first Dressel mentioned in Sonneberg records was Killian Dressel. Killian was the Nuremberg woodcarver who moved to Sonneberg in the late 1500's and brought with him the "secret" of bismuth colors. The first Sonneberg reference concerning the Dressels is from Meyers *Orts und Verkehrs Lexikon, Volume II*, Microfilm #496,641. This particular film provides an historical account of the 1596 Sonneberg fire, which left the castle/fortress and a large portion of the town in ruins. One Lexikon (Encyclopedia) entry states, "In 1596, Sonneberg has 309 houses and 2400 residents. Among the buildings distinguished by size and position are the upper district house, the Dressel farm, and some private homes." The Dressel farm probably belonged to the Killian Dressel family who lived in Sonneberg in the late 1500's.

One of several former Dressel doll factories in Sonneberg. The large building is marked "Herko" today. Fire destroyed an earlier Dressel doll factory.

According to the Colemans, Johann Georg Dressel founded the Dressel trading house in 1700. The trading house later became the Dressel doll factory. The Dressel doll and toy factory remained in the family for 245 years until 1945, when the company and the property were nationalized. Six generations of Dressels owned the family business during its 245-year history. It is difficult to sort out all the Dressels. They all made important contributions to Sonneberg and to the company that had such a major impact on doll production throughout the world. During that entire 245-year period, the Dressels sold the dolls and toys that were popular at the time including dolls made of wood, papier-mâché, wax, glazed and unglazed porcelain, celluloid, and plastic. Unfortunately, the majority of Dressel dolls were not marked with a Dressel trademark. The Dressel trademark was not registered until 1875, and by then, the company had been selling dolls and toys for 118 years.

This 33-inch Simon & Halbig bisque socket head doll with a jointed composition body, circa 1910, is marked: "1348//Jutta//SH//16." Countess Jutta von Henneberg was the patroness of Sonneberg. She granted "city rights" to the town in 1349. *Jane Walker Collection.*

A 1920's original boxed set of wooden animals, farmer, trees and fence sections from the Erzgebirge area. The "hoop" animals were a specialty of Seiffen and surrounding towns. The animals were made by turning a round section of wood on a lathe to indicate a particular animal. The individual animals were then "sliced" from each circle of wood. As late as 1924, the Dressel doll factory advertised Erzgebirge wooden dolls and toys.

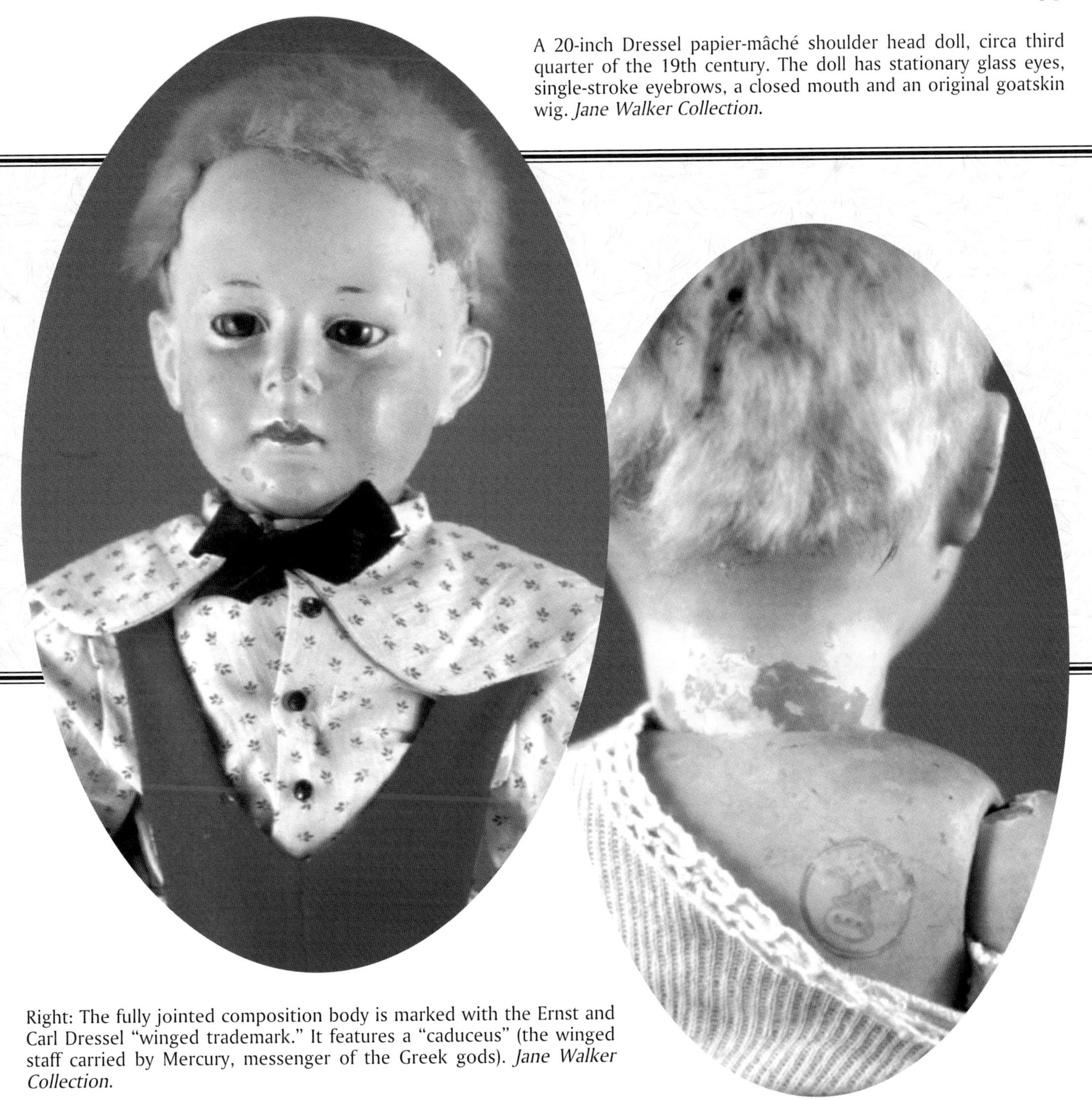

A 20-inch Dressel papier-mâché shoulder head doll, circa third quarter of the 19th century. The doll has stationary glass eyes, single-stroke eyebrows, a closed mouth and an original goatskin wig. *Jane Walker Collection.*

Right: The fully jointed composition body is marked with the Ernst and Carl Dressel "winged trademark." It features a "caduceus" (the winged staff carried by Mercury, messenger of the Greek gods). *Jane Walker Collection.*

Johann Georg Dressel was a ducal court actor and member of the municipal council. He was also acting mayor of Sonneberg, a guild master, and Lord Mayor from 1735 to 1740. Johann Georg Dressel's son was Johann Paul Dressel who died at the young age of 29. Both of these men formed key connections to several other doll-making families through marriage. Johann Georg Dressel married Anna Margaretha Heubach and his son Johann Paul Dressel married Sophia Fleischmann.

In 1757, Johann Paul's son, Johann Philipp Dressel, inherited the business that had been his father's and grandfather's. Johann Philipp Dressel is credited with founding the Dressel Verlag House and Factory in 1789, and he received the title of Verleger from the ruling duke, Georg the First in that same year. Johann Philipp Dressel's handwritten 567-page book from the year 1790 to 1793 lists 60 types of "superfine" doll wares and trading stock. The first company records indicating toy production was from 1757. A few of the toys listed include a teacher with children, a group of soldiers, a horse stable with six horses and a coachman, a sheep farm, Turks, joggers, priests, miners, princes, Moors and Hungarians. These bread dough figures were formed free hand on a core of wood.

The Cuno and Otto Dressel villas are still standing in Sonneberg today. The street sign at the bottom of the hill below the villas reads: "Gaststätte Ellerhütte."

A 1935 Cuno and Otto Dressel original postcard advertising a group of dolls and toys including clowns. This type of advertising postcard was used for years to encourage buyers to come to the Leipzig Fairs.

In 1764, Johann Philipp bought the Dressel Courtyard, the factory complex that once was owned and used as a residence by Duke Heinrich VII and Duke Wilhelm the Brave. In 1804, the Dressel Company used the name Johann Philipp Dressel Son. Later in 1830, the company name changed to Ernst & Carl Dressel, with Ernst Friedrich Dressel Sr. listed as the owner. In 1830, the company listed "wooden jointed dolls supplied from Gröden" as an export item.

Ernst Friedrich Dressel, Sr. married Henriette Bischoff with whom he had eight children. Two of the children are well known to doll collectors—Cuno and Otto Dressel. They became owners of the Dressel doll factory in 1873. Cuno and Otto Dressel were well respected in Sonneberg and throughout the world. Because of their international connections, the guest suites in their homes served as "luxury hotels" for German royalty as well as representatives from the world of art and industry.

Cuno Dressel died in 1893. Because Cuno had no children, his brother, Otto Dressel, ran the doll factory with his two sons, Otto Jr. and Ernst Friedrich. When Otto Dressel, Sr. died in 1907, his sons became the owners of the doll factory. Otto Dressel, Jr. retired in 1914. The last group of owners included Otto Junior's son, Dr. Hans Dressel, and Otto Junior's son-in-law, Hermann Ortelli. The Ortelli family directed the Bank of Thuringia, which later became the Deutsche Bank.

Hermann Ortelli died in 1939, and Dr. Hans Dressel ran the business until he died in 1942. Like the Fleischmanns, the Dressels were interested in Sonneberg and its history as a doll and toy-producing center. In 1909, Dr. Hans Dressel wrote his doctoral thesis titled "Development of Hand Skills and Industry in Sonneberg."

Many of the Dressel villas and factories are still standing in Sonneberg today. They reflect the Dressel success story. Three of the Dressel villas were built near the Lutheran Church that the Dressels attended. Cuno and Otto's villas are located across a footbridge directly behind the church. Otto's son, Ernst Friedrich Dressel, Jr.'s, villa still stands across the street from the 1845 Lutheran Church.

The Dressels maintained a permanent sample room in the "Three Kings" building at the Leipzig Spring Show. Foreign buyers named it the most beautiful display at the show. The Leipzig Fairs were held twice a year—one in spring and again in autumn. The Spring Fair started the first Sunday before Easter and ended three weeks later. The Autumn Fair opened the last Sunday in August.

Buyers came to Leipzig from all over the world to see and order the latest dolls and toys. Doll buyers often stopped in Sonneberg to place advance orders before traveling to the spring and autumn Leipzig Fairs. Many local and foreign buyers stayed at the Krug's Hotel in Sonneberg. A guest list from the hotel guest registry in 1881 included Goebel from Oeslau; Strobel and family from Cincinnati; and Zetsche, Ilmenau and Louis Wolf from Boston.

Foreign buyers were always pleased with the dolls offered by the Sonnebergers because they were inexpensive and well made. According to the Ciesliks, "In 1797, there were 16 producers from Sonneberg listed at the

An original 1920's postcard of a Leipzig Fair booth. The color illustration shows a young boy behind a draped table filled with dolls and toys. The outdoor booth is typical of the booths that filled the town during the many spring and fall Leipzig Fairs.

A pair of papier-mâché dolls known as "Patent Washables" measuring 13 and 16 inches. The inexpensive dolls, circa 1880's-1915, were a typical Dressel export. The dolls have multi-stroke eyebrows, stationary glass eyes, and cloth bodies stuffed with excelsior. The taller doll has six painted teeth while the smaller doll has a closed mouth with a darker line painted between the lips.

A pair of bisque head dolls, 5-1/2 and 7 inches tall, dressed in original clothing as pictured in a 1915 Butler Brothers catalog. The bisque heads include single-stroke eyebrows and stationary glass eyes. The five-piece composition bodies feature white socks and black one-strap shoes. The New York importing firm, Butler Brothers, was the most important customer of the Dressel doll factory during the years Cuno and Otto Dressel ran the company.

Leipzig Fair, amongst others, 5 with dolls, 17 with Thuringian porcelain." The Leipzig Fairs must have been an exciting time for buyers as well as sellers. The exhibitors rented space in many buildings all over town including restaurants and hotels. They also rented outdoor spaces. As late as 1926, over 8,000 exhibitors were listed and 758 merchants sold dolls and toys.

Not only did the Dressels exhibit at the Leipzig Fairs, but they also traveled world wide to sell their products. Cuno and Otto Dressel were listed as exhibitors at the 1876 Philadelphia Exposition shortly after they became owners of the company. The Dressel ad for the show is interesting because it provides information on the Dressel exports in 1876. The advertisement reads, "Cuno & Otto Dressel, Manufacturers and Exporters of German Toys and Dolls, Sonneberg, Thuringia (Germany). Toys and Dolls of every description: Wood, Papier-mâché, Solid Paste, Glass, Wax, China, etc. Baskets, Glass Beads, Musical Instruments, Masks, Slates, Slate Pencils and Marbles."

Exposure through local as well as international trade fairs created important links between German manufacturers and foreign buyers. Furthermore, good communication between the manufacturer and the American importer was crucial because a remote center of production like Sonneberg had little chance for survival unless there were close contacts with customers through the importers. Manufacturers like the Dressels studied American history as well as current events so that their dolls would appeal to the American market. Otto Dressel, Sr. made yearly trips abroad establishing strong business relations with the representatives of major American stores.

The Dressels' most important customer was the New York importing firm Butler Brothers. According to the Coleman doll research, three brothers, George, Charles H., and Edward B. Butler, founded Butler Brothers in 1877. They were factory agents, importers, and jobbers. Butler Brothers had branches in Sonneberg, St. Louis, Chicago, Minneapolis, Dallas, San Francisco, and Boston. We are able to recognize a number of Dressel dolls imported by Butler Brothers thanks to the ads in *Playthings* and the Butler Brothers Wholesale Catalogs.

Cuno & Otto's cousin, Wilhelm Dressel, also had ties to an American company. F. W. Woolworth bought Wilhelm's export business in 1913. Relationships between importers and manufacturers were often "strictly business," but sometimes friendships emerged that lasted a lifetime. Such was the case with Wilhelm Dressel and F. W. Woolworth. They shared their lives with one another through letters and visits.

The Woolworth Importing Company turned the former Dressel business into another Woolworth branch with Wilhelm's son Fritz as the general director. With

A Simon & Halbig bisque character socket head marked "S-1" on a jointed composition body. The doll has multi-stroke eyebrows, brown stationary eyes, a closed smiling mouth, large molded ears, and red painted face wrinkles. The all-original 12-1/2 inch "Uncle Sam" doll was sold as part of the Dressel 1896 Portrait Series.

This Simon & Halbig bisque socket head, marked "Old Rip//12/0," was made for the Dressel doll factory. The 1896 original Dressel doll has stationary glass eyes, painted face wrinkles, and a closed mouth. The 11-1/2-inch portrait doll represents Rip Van Winkle.

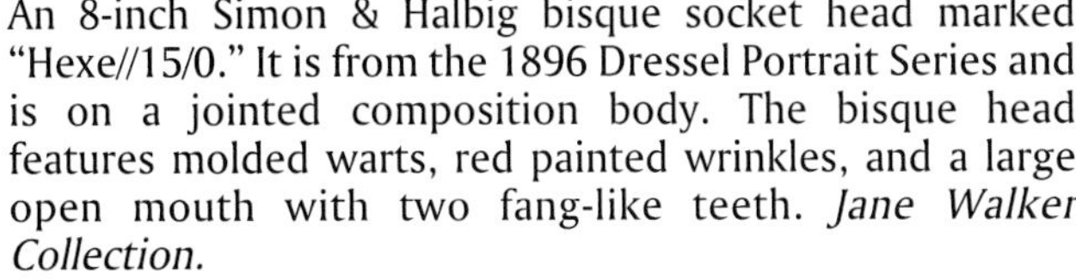

An 8-inch Simon & Halbig bisque socket head marked "Hexe//15/0." It is from the 1896 Dressel Portrait Series and is on a jointed composition body. The bisque head features molded warts, red painted wrinkles, and a large open mouth with two fang-like teeth. *Jane Walker Collection.*

An 8-1/2-inch Simon & Halbig bisque socket head doll marked "17-SP." The original portrait doll, sold by the Dressel doll factory, represents William Thomas Sampson. Sampson, commander of the Western Atlantic Squadron, is credited with establishing the blockade of Cuba during the Spanish American War. The doll has single-stroke eyebrows, stationary glass eyes, and a molded beard. The original uniform includes a metal belt buckle and sword as well as metal epaulets and buttons. Thuringian doll factories concentrated on important American historical events in order to sell dolls.

Woolworth's financial backing, the branch in Sonneberg was substantial. The building, which was located directly across the street from the railroad station, was five stories tall and contained 3,530,000 cubic feet of enclosed space. It was the largest building in Sonneberg. The Sonneberg architect Walter Buchholz was credited with the design of the steel and concrete building. It took 16 months to build, and was completed in 1926. Each floor was made up of different units that served a specific purpose. A large area of storage was provided in the warehouse division. Other floors housed the goods receiving department, office space, a packaging department, and a bank. In 1930, Woolworth had 800 to 900 Sonneberg suppliers and home trade workers.

In 1929, the Berlin native Carl Weiss became director of the Woolworth branch, and later in 1934, Oscar Dressel replaced Weiss as director. During World War II, on April 11, 1945, the retreating German army put explosives around the building so that it wouldn't fall into American hands. The huge building was almost completely destroyed. The gutted remains were not removed until 1958. The property remained in the Woolworth family throughout the war years and as late as 1991. The Woolworth Company has closed its five-and-dime stores in the United States, but continues to operate Foot Locker and other athletic gear stores under the new name Venator Group.

The 1940 book *Five and Ten: The Fabulous Life of F.W. Woolworth* by John K. Winkler includes many letters from Woolworth on his toy-buying expedition in 1890. Woolworth traveled with B. J. Hunt, Jr., a buyer and partner of Horace Partridge & Company, a very large toy

A 1930 original postcard pictures the large Woolworth building to the right of City Hall in Sonneberg. Both buildings were located across the street from the Railroad Station. The German troops blew up the Woolworth Building in 1945.

Krug's Hotel in Sonneberg. Many important doll and toy buyers stayed in Krug's Hotel while they were in town to place orders. In 1881, the hotel register listed American buyers from Boston, New York, San Francisco, Louisville, Cincinnati, Philadelphia, and Chicago.

Children of all ages delivered dolls and doll parts in Sonneberg and other doll making areas of Thuringia.

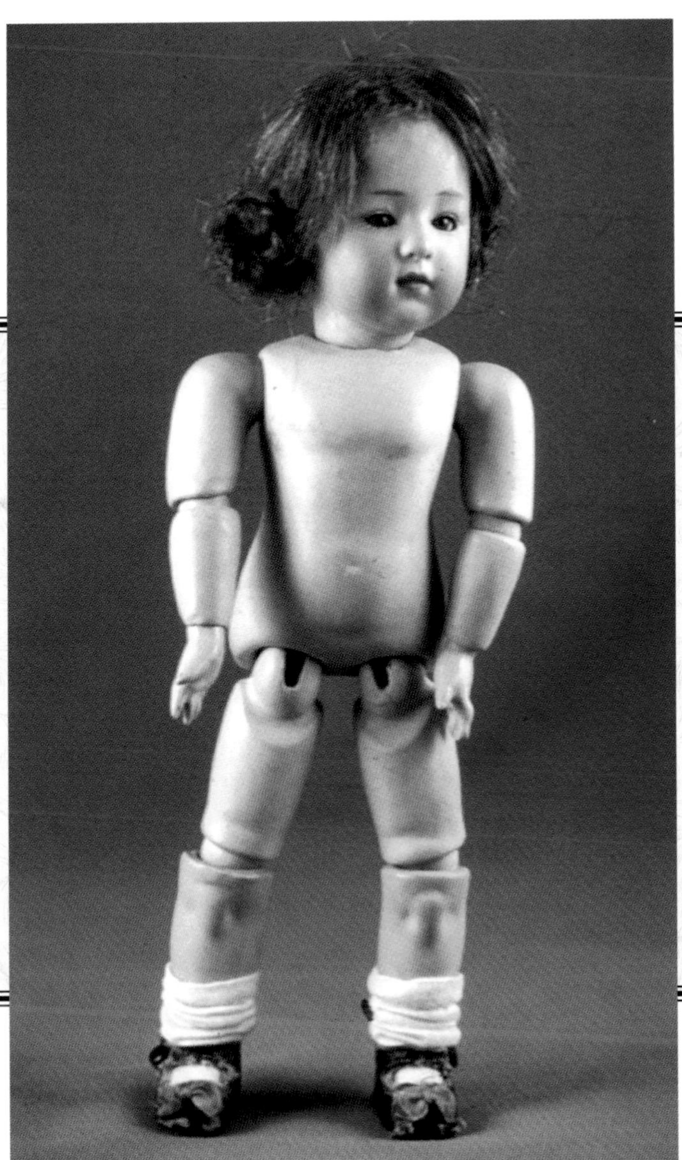

This 11-inch Gebrüder Heubach bisque head doll, circa 1912, is marked "Germany 1." The doll head has blue sleep eyes, multi-stroke eyebrows, and a closed mouth. The Heubach head was made for the Dressel doll factory according to an identical doll found in an original Dressel box marked: "Bebe Jutta-Puppe//Doll//Paper Pulp//Body//Light and Durable//No. 29B." *Marguerite Hoffman Collection.*

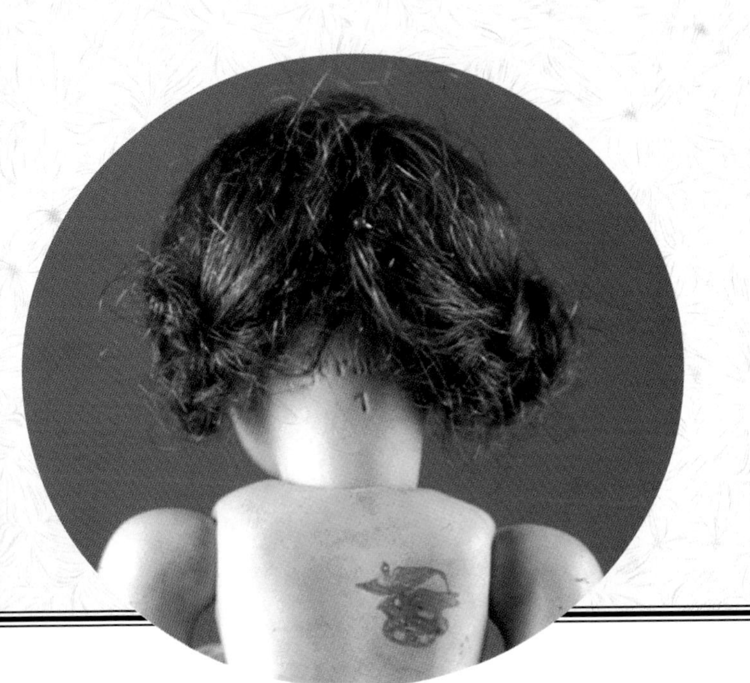

The Dressel winged trademark is stamped in red on the doll's jointed composition body. *Marguerite Hoffman Collection.*

importer in the United States. Several letters from Sonneberg provide a fascinating insight into the "town of toys." The letters read as follows:

> On our arrival at Sonneberg, we took the bus to Krug's Hotel, where we shall stay for several days. Sonneberg is headquarters for dolls for the whole world, as nearly every doll of every description is made here or within a few miles from here, and this is the market. It is a place of about 15,000 people.
>
> It seems as though the whole trade of America is represented here. As we walked along the streets, we could look in the windows of the houses and see the women and children at work making dolls while the men drink beer. We could see some of the women and children molding the legs, others the head, some putting the hair on, another making the shirts, others putting in the eyes, and one would be painting the finished doll. After they are finished they are put in long baskets and taken to the packers where they are put into large cases and shipped to all parts of the world. The poor women do most of the work, even to lugging them to the packing houses.
>
> It is no longer a mystery to me how they make dolls and toys so cheap, for most of it is done by women and children at their homes anywhere within 20 miles of this place. Some of the women in America think they have hard work to do, but it is far different than the poor women here, that work night and day on toys, and strap them onto their backs, and go 10 or 20 miles through the mud with 75 pounds on their backs, to sell them. The usual price they get for a good 10 cent

doll is about 3¢ here, and they are obliged to buy the hair, shirts and other materials, to put them together, and they probably get about 1 cent each for the labor they put on them.

The streets are filled with women with baskets on their backs filled with dolls and toys, and they walk in the middle of the street where the mud is ankle deep in preference to the clean sidewalk. We saw a poor little girl that could not have been over four years old with a basket strapped on her back larger than herself and Mr. Hunt asked her where she lived, and she told us a place about five miles from here, and she came alone.

Child labor conditions improved in 1904, when the "Act On The Work Of Children" went into effect. According to this Act, the following work was officially allowed for children from eight years old on: "Painting and brushing of doll joints, sorting and inserting of doll eyes, blowing of doll eyes by bellows, sewing, crocheting and knitting of doll dresses, sewing of doll bodies, making curls for the doll wigs as long as cleaned hair of wool or mohair are used and packing the dolls in paper boxes."

During the many years porcelain dolls were a chief Thuringian export, the Dressel doll factory purchased doll heads and parts from a number of Thuringian porcelain factories. Heads from the following porcelain factories have been found on original marked Dressel composition bodies: Simon & Halbig, Ernst Heubach, Gebrüder Heubach, Armand Marseille, Hertwig, F. & W. Goebel, and Schoenau-Hoffmeister. An "American School Boy" bisque head marked 30 B 3 is credited to the F. & W. Goebel porcelain factory in the 1999/2000 Ciesliks' *Puppen* price guide. Many "American School Boys" have been found on original marked Dressel "Poppy" bodies.

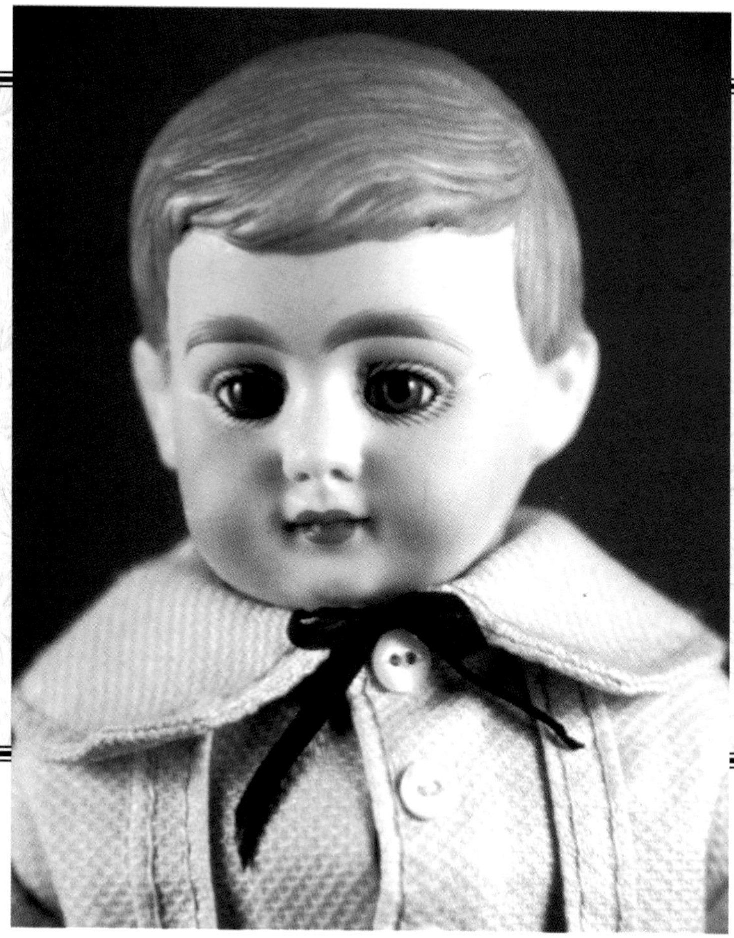

A 13-inch "American Schoolboy." The F. & W. Goebel porcelain factory made the bisque shoulder head, marked "Germany// 30/B3-1/2," for the Dressel doll factory. The doll, circa 1900 on, has molded hair, stationary blue eyes, multi-stroke eyebrows, a closed mouth, and cloth body with composition lower arms and legs. *Jane Walker Collection.*

An 11-1/2 "American Schoolboy" with a Dressel cloth body marked "Poppy." The pink cotton body features composition arms and lower legs. The Dressel doll factory registered the trademark "Poppy Doll" in 1912.

Chapter Seven

The Sonneberg "Täufling"

The Sonneberg Täufling has been described and pictured in numerous doll books and magazines over the years. The German word "Täufling" is defined in the *Oxford Duden's German Dictionary* as "a child to be baptised," but the word "Täufling" was more often used by German doll makers to mean a doll representing a baby or young child under the age of six.

It was first referred to as an "enigma" because the maker or makers were unknown. Around 1965, the American doll researcher, Jo Elizabeth Gerkin, went to Sonneberg and found a Täufling marked with the patent stamp of Ch. Motschmann. Many years later, doll researchers discovered that Christoph Motschmann only made the voice box for the doll, not the entire doll. The Ciesliks state, "Dolls with this (the Ch. Motschmann patent) stamp were made between 1857 and 1859. The patent

A 13-1/2-inch wax-over papier-mâché Sonneberg Täufling with black pupil-less eyes, single-stroke eyebrows, a closed mouth, and a dome-shaped head with painted curls over each ear. The typical Täufling body includes a cloth midsection with a voice box, a papier-mâché lower body, twill covered upper joints, wooden lower arms and legs, and string suspended papier-mâché hands and feet.

The Lindner family villa in Sonneberg.

had a validity of two years, which means that the stamp might be applied for only these two years." Many other theories have surfaced concerning the origin of the Sonneberg Täufling. The most widely accepted theory focuses on the visit of Sonneberg resident Edmund Lindner to the 1851 London World Exposition. It was here, many believe, that Lindner first saw a Japanese "mitsuore-ningyo" (3-bend doll). Some researchers have speculated that he found a similar doll in a London shop and others feel he bought the Japanese doll Cologne, Germany on his way home with the intention of having the doll copied.

In March of 1992, an article by Wolfgang Kuebart appeared in the Ciesliks' *Puppenmagazin.* This article sheds even more light on the origin of the Sonneberg Täufling. The Kuebart research contains entries from the chronicles of the city of Sonneberg. Deacon Friedrich wrote these important historical chronicles. Two pages from the chronicles contain the letterhead "Louis Lindner & Sons, Sonneberg." These handwritten pages contain a paragraph that describes the origin of the Sonneberg Täufling as follows:

> In 1850, on one of his business trips, Edmund Lindner saw a doll in the shop of a customer in Brussels with limbs which was from Japan. It was nude, dressed only in a little shirt. He liked it and thought it would be good to manufacture it in Sonneberg. He bought the item, took it to Sonneberg, and had it made by one of his people (Finger), 10-1/2 inches tall, it was an unusual piece. Its head not wax coated and with still eyes 9 fl. per dozen. The price a little high compared to the store in Brussels. But the demand at the trading company Louis Lindner & Sons (the only company selling the Täufling in 1850) was so great, manufacture could not keep up. From 1851, the item was often copied and also improved. So did Heinrich Stier, who manufactured the dolls with a wax-coated head and moveable eyes. Later those were replaced with ball eyes. Not only were they improved, they were also made in very poor quality.

According to the Kuebart article, Johann Georg Finger was born in Steinach in 1813. He began as a trading employee/helper, and later worked for the Lindner export company. Church registers listed his two sons as Täufling manufacturers. Kuebart also notes that in 1850, Finger delivered dozens of dolls to Lindner, which suggests that he was already a manufacturer at that time. Johann Georg Finger died in 1872

A 1998 article in the German *Spiel & Zeug* magazine provides clues about the origin of the waxed Täuflinge. The 1998 article on waxed Täuflinge (Täuflinge is the plural form of Täufling) written by Gerhard Stier describes the life of Sonneberg doll maker, Heinrich Stier. Gerhard Stier states that Heinrich Stier was the son of a Bossierer (bread dough modeler). Stier went to the United States with a friend from Sonneberg to open a wax doll factory in 1848. Apparently, the Sonneberg doll makers had trouble working out the right formula to make wax dolls. Therefore, Stier decided to learn the "secrets" of wax doll manufacture from a London manufacturer. Some doll researchers believe he worked for Montanari. Later, Stier went back to the United States with his Sonneberg friend to try again. Still, the two men had little success, so Stier went back to Sonneberg where he opened his doll factory in 1852. Shortly after opening his factory, he received special permission from the ruling duke to make wax papier-mâché Täuflinge.

The Lindner doll factory located across the street from the Lindner villa.

In the German *Spiel & Zeug* magazine article, Gerhard Stier states, "His (Heinrich Stier's) first big order he received thanks to Sonneberg businessman Edmund Lindner. Lindner commissioned the Sonneberg doll manufacturer to copy such a doll. Heinrich achieved the best results and received his first big order. His first waxed papier-mâché Täuflinge were made with 'Masse' (mass) heads and a flesh-colored coating. Stier turned out to be a real inventor—sleep eyes, 'mama' voices, new

A Sonneberg Täufling identical to a Täufling pictured on an 1860 sample page in Lindner's doll and toy catalog. The Täufling on the sample page has an identical open mouth with upper and lower teeth, curly wig, stationary glass eyes, painted single-stroke eyebrows, and well-defined, painted cheeks.

The typical Täufling cloth upper arm, wooden lower arm and papier-mâché hand.

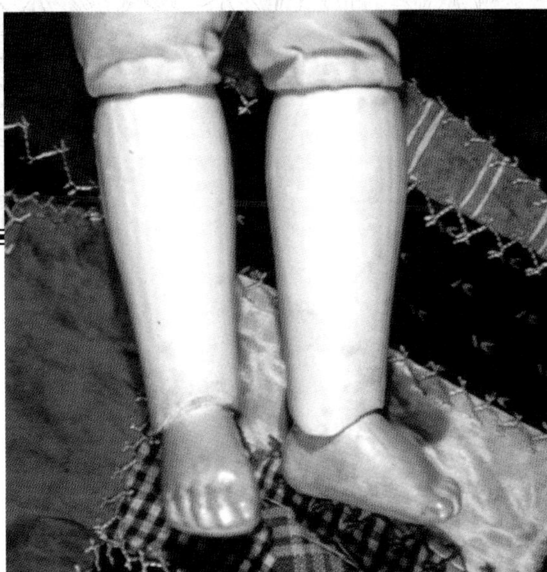

Täufling wooden lower legs and papier-mâché feet.

hair-dos made from human hair, later made from mohair, are credited to him." A page from the 1860 Lindner sample book is pictured with the Stier article. The Täuflinge have open mouths with teeth. A few wear curly wigs. Two of the dolls on the sample page have "voice" strings hanging below their simple chemises.

The 1880 Louis Lindner & Söhne manufacturer's catalog is preserved in the archives of the Sonneberg Doll and Toy Museum. The Täuflinge shown on two pages of the 1880 Lindner catalog are very different in appearance from the 1860 Täuflinge. The later Täuflinge have closed mouths, and all of the dolls wear lace-edged baby bonnets rather than wigs. Three of the 1880 Täuflinge have moveable jaws. One of the Täuflinge has an Asian appearance. The Lindner family was instrumental in creating ties to American customers. In 1851, Louis was chosen to direct the first American consulate in Sonneberg. He acted as honorary consul until 1865.

Making Wax-Over Papier-Mâché Doll Heads

Called waxovers, these dolls were made in Sonneberg for decades. The 1898 article titled "The Wonderland of Work" by C. L. Mateau offers descriptive information on the manufacture of wax-over papier-mâché dolls. The article is as follows:

> The dolls' heads are handed over to a man standing before a big vessel of boiling wax, clear and white and steaming wax. He takes them one by one, and gives each one or more dips; the more dips the better the lady's position as a "wax" doll is likely to be. Now we can understand why that ugly red wash was put on first, for it shines lightly through the clear, pure, white wax, and makes it look lovely pink, delicate and proper for all waxen babies, especially when they are next dusted over with that sweet-scented bloom of violet powder, which makes them look like fresh-gathered peaches, and which will also make their waxen skins still easier to beautify, for as yet they are very wan and white, and as nobody ever saw a pale-faced new doll, it would not look right somehow. No little girl would care to buy it, I fancy.

A less expensive version of the Sonneberg Täufling was made for a number of years. These Täuflinge may be described as "Half-Täuflinge" because the upper and lower arms are the standard Täufling type, but the one-piece legs are made of turned wood. The legs feature painted boots, trimmed with painted gold buttons. The boots are painted in a number of colors including pink, blue, maroon, gray, or black. The "sack" bodies do not have a lower hip section made of papier-mâché. Instead, the bodies are made of a type of open weave cotton that looks like fine cheesecloth with an inserted rectangular voice box (bellows). One face type seems to be prevalent appearing on many bonnet wax-over papier-mâché dolls.

Many of these inexpensive Sonneberg wax-over papier-mâché dolls are marked on the lower right side of the shoulder plate. The mark looks like three separate letter indentations. It is difficult to decipher the letters, but it is possible that the three letters spell "M & S."

A 13-inch wax-over papier-mâché shoulder head doll, circa 1860-1870, with Täufling-type arms and painted boots. The shoulder head is mounted on an open-weave cotton "sack" body, which includes a bellows-type voice box. The doll's shoulder plate is marked with three separate letter indentations that could be "M & S" (Müller & Strasburger).

A wax-over papier-mâché head with flat blonde mohair curls glued to the dome-shaped head. The 14-1/2-inch doll, circa 1860-1870's, has the typical Täufling-type body and arms. In place of Täufling legs, the doll has lathe-turned wooden lower legs that include black painted boots. The boots feature a red painted top line and a double row of painted buttons.

Chapter Eight

The Limbach Porcelain Factory

The small town of Limbach resembles many other Thuringian doll-making towns. It is located in a valley surrounded by dense forests. Limbach was part of the Duchy Sachsen-Meiningen, which was established in 1680 resulting from a land division in the Gotha area. Gotthelf Greiner, the "Father of Thuringian Porcelain," was born in Limbach. The Greiner birthplace is a well-restored, gray slate-sided house that now contains the town's tourist information office. The Greiner family mausoleum is located on the nearby hillside.

In 1761, the glass master, Gotthelf Greiner, along with glass painter, Gottfried Greiner and pottery master, Georg Dümmler, produced Thuringian hard paste porcelain. Gotthelf Greiner converted the former glass factory in Limbach into a porcelain factory. Because of the natural resources available such as wood, water, kaolin, as well as capable workers, success was practically guaranteed.

The Limbach porcelain factory first produced porcelain dishes, pipe heads, and small figurines. The early Limbach products were "simple in form and colorful, often covered with folk art designs," according to author Renate Gauss in the German book, titled in English, *Gotthelf Greiner and Christian Fleischmann - Manufacturer and Salary Worker at the Porcelain Manufacture Limbach.*

Gotthelf Greiner came from an old Thuringian glassmaking family, according to Gauss. He was born on February 22, 1732 in Alsbach. Gotthelf's father and three other glass masters built the first glass factory in Limbach. It was also the first building in the newly founded village according to Renate Gauss. By age 12,

Gotthelf Greiner's birthplace in Limbach. Greiner, known as "The Father of Thuringian Porcelain," is credited with founding the Greiner porcelain dynasty.

Gotthelf was working in the glass hut where he "made little glasses and perfected them until his father was happy."

His father let Gotthelf keep the money he made from the sale of his glasses, which encouraged even further productivity. By the age of 16, Gotthelf mastered his craft to the extent that he became a "Garmacher" or finisher. When he was 18, Gotthelf took over the management of the glass factory from his alcoholic father. In 1754, Gotthelf Greiner married Dorothea Sophia Fröbel from Lichtewith whom he had eleven children. Dorothea's dowry helped Gotthelf pay off the loan on the Limbach glass factory.

The glass factory became quite successful in the following years and Greiner was soon known as "owner of a glass factory, publisher, businessman, money exchanger and money lender." Unfortunately, the Seven-Years-War resulted in a decreased demand for glass products. In an effort to stay profitable, Gotthelf became interested in copying Chinese porcelain, which had been eagerly collected by German royalty for many years.

The Chinese are credited with the discovery of porcelain. According to General Editor David Battie in the book, *Sotheby's Concise Encyclopedia of Porcelain*, the first porcelain was probably made during the Sui Dynasty (AD 581–617) or the early Tang Dynasty (AD 618–906). Marco Polo brought back information about this new modeling product in the 13th Century after a trip to the Far East. In the 16th Century, Portuguese and Dutch sailors returned home with pieces of Chinese porcelain. Soon, work began in Europe in an effort to produce this valuable product.

Porcelain is approximately half white china clay (kaolin) that does not discolor under high temperatures, a quarter quartz (a mineral that is the chief constituent of sand and many other rocks), and a quarter feldspar (also a mineral found in certain rocks formed under conditions of intense heat). One recipe for Thuringian hard paste porcelain is 40–60% kaolin, 20–30% quartz, and 20–30% feldspar. The ingredients are finely ground, water is added, and the mixture is stirred to make a thick liquid.

The quarries in Steinach and Neuhaus provided most of the kaolin used in the Thuringian porcelain factories. Steinach is located a few miles south of Lauscha, and Neuhaus is located a few miles south of Katzhütte. The quality of a porcelain article depends upon the quality of the kaolin and the fineness to which it has been ground. Both Thuringian quarries had large deposits of kaolin described as exceptionally high quality. When exposed to the heat of the kiln, feldspar not only melts and fills the pores of the kaolin, but it fuses with the quartz, which is

A 2-inch Limbach bisque head shard featuring a molded mustache, a goatee, and a Sailor hat. The head, buried for over a hundred years, is reminiscent of the 16th Century Sailors who transported Chinese porcelain to Europe.

This unmarked bald shoulder head doll from the 1850's has a painted black "wig spot" and an original human hair wig. The china shoulder plate measures 3-3/4 inches. The Limbach porcelain factory made a number of early unmarked china dolls. One Limbach china shoulder head in the Sonneberg Doll and Toy Museum is dated 1840.

harder than steel. Porcelain is durable because of the fusing of its components. The main difference between soft and hard paste porcelain is the higher firing temperature required for hard paste porcelain. Hard paste porcelain is fired at over 2,515 degrees Fahrenheit.

In about 1675, Count Ehrenfried Walter von Tschirnhausen began experimenting with radiant heat and a reflective mirror to find the melting points of refractory substances such as kaolin. Though Von Tschirnhausen may have produced a form of soft paste porcelain, but he was not successful in finding the secret of hard-paste porcelain.

Called "The Father of *German* Porcelain," Johann Friedrich Böttger (1682-1719) first worked as an alchemist for Frederick the First of Prussia. Alchemy is defined as a form of chemistry and speculative philosophy practiced in the Middle Ages and the Renaissance. Alchemists concentrated on discovering methods of transforming baser metals into gold. They also tried to find a universal solvent and an "elixir of life."

Böttger diligently tried to please Frederick the First by succeeding in the impossible task of turning baser metals into gold. Failing in this assignment, Böttger left Berlin in 1700. August the Strong, King of Poland, captured Böttger and ordered Böttger to produce "white gold" (porcelain). In 1708, Böttger was successful in producing his first samples in Dresden. In 1710, his "proper production" was achieved at the Saxonian Porcelain Manufactory at Meissen.

Unaware of the Böttger discovery, which was kept very secret, Gotthelf Greiner tried to imitate the beautiful Chinese porcelain. The original idea (to manufacture porcelain) came from Gotthelf's relative Gottfried Greiner. Gottfried was a successful glass painter prior to becoming a porcelain maker. The other member of the Thuringian team was Georg Dümmler, a Coburg potter and turner. These three men worked together for several years trying to make hard paste porcelain. According to author Renate Gauss, Gotthelf decided to leave his two co-workers and discover the "secret" on his own. He had his own kiln built in which his first Thuringian hard paste porcelain was fired. The first pieces turned out "pretty good" and "white" according to Gotthelf. However, Gotthelf was not satisfied with the glaze, so he went to his former partners, Gottfried Greiner and Georg Dümmler, and asked for their help. He bought their individual porcelain recipes and combined them. Finally, he succeeded in discovering hard paste porcelain along with the perfect glaze.

According to a quote in the Gauss book, Gotthelf Greiner stated, "It looked just like the Meissen porcelain." Greiner first made a porcelain cup and then tobacco heads (the porcelain bowls at the end of long wooden smoking pipes). The Greiner porcelain was made in the summer of 1761, according to Gauss. She also states, "George Heinrich Macheleid also discovered the secret of the 'Arkanum' (hard paste porcelain) shortly before Greiner made porcelain."

In 1762, Greiner's "privilege to produce porcelain" was cancelled. Thus, in 1764, he was forced to become a partner of Johann Wolfgang Hammann from Katzhütte. In 1772, Greiner finally received "a new concession from the Court's Chamber." This court approval enabled Greiner to turn the Limbach glass factory into a porcelain factory. He fired his first Limbach porcelain on November 14, 1772.

The sale of the first Limbach porcelain was to the brothers Bischoff from Sonneberg. They purchased the entire production for cash. Afterward, Greiner quickly returned to the factory to make more porcelain—as much as his wood allowance could tolerate. The quarry in Steinheid supplied the necessary kaolin. It wasn't until 1788 that Greiner first used the clover trademark.

The "Irish Queen" shoulder plate is marked with the Limbach three-leaf clover following the numbers "8552." The Limbach porcelain factory used the clover trademark from 1788 on.

This 19-1/2-inch "Irish Queen" untinted bisque shoulder head doll has molded curly black hair trimmed with a blue molded bow. The doll has blue intaglio eyes, single-stroke eyebrows, and an open/closed mouth with molded upper teeth. A special feature of the doll is an elaborately molded blouse with rows of blue-trimmed ruffles and a high collar, which is typical of clothing styles from the turn of the last century.

This Limbach bisque socket head doll, circa 1919 on, has multi-stroke eyebrows, brown sleep eyes, and painted heart-shaped open mouth with four upper teeth. The 17-inch doll is on a jointed composition body with a voice mechanism controlled by two pull cords. *Jane Walker Collection.*

The bisque head is marked: "NORMA// (the Limbach crown over a three-leaf clover)// Limbach//1." *Jane Walker Collection.*

In 1781, author Kessler von Sprengeysen wrote the following of the Limbach porcelain factory:

> About 50 fabricators work here all the time, not counting the craftsmen, wood makers and workers. So far, they are not making much else than tea and coffee services; because they sell so much they can hardly keep up. Parts of the factory are: Greiner's living and storage quarters; the pretty factory building, which employs turners, modelers and painters; the Wirtshaus pub/guest house; two kilns (firing ovens); the 'hut' to prepare the material; different 'home economy' buildings and the glazing mill in 'Theurer Grund.' There are a total of 7 houses with 47 adults and 22 children, 69 persons.

By 1782, Greiner's porcelain holdings were expanding with the purchase of the porcelain factory in Grossbreitenbach. Gotthelf Greiner also rented the porcelain factory in Ilmenau from 1786 until 1793. He stopped renting the factory shortly after his wife's death in 1793. The death of his wife affected Greiner both physically and mentally. He closed his factory ledgers and rented his porcelain factories to his sons.

Gotthelf Greiner died on August 12, 1797 leaving his children a large inheritance of property, cash, outstanding loans, and factory inventories. The Limbach sons continued the business, and in 1797, shortly after Gotthelf's death, the family bought the Kloster Veilsdorf porcelain factory. The number of Thuringian porcelain factories from these early Greiner foundings increased to about 100 in the 1920's. At the turn of the last century, the Thuringian porcelain factories employed 22,839 workers. The factories continued to produce large

This 14-1/2-inch bisque socket head doll, circa 1911 on, has blue sleep eyes, multi-stroke eyebrows, a closed mouth, and a fully jointed composition body. The head is marked with the Limbach three-leaf clover following the numbers "8679." *Mary Beard Collection.*

A pair of Limbach all-bisque dolls, measuring 7 and 7-1/2 inches, with blonde molded hair, white socks edged in blue, and brown one-strap shoes. *Jane Walker Collection.*

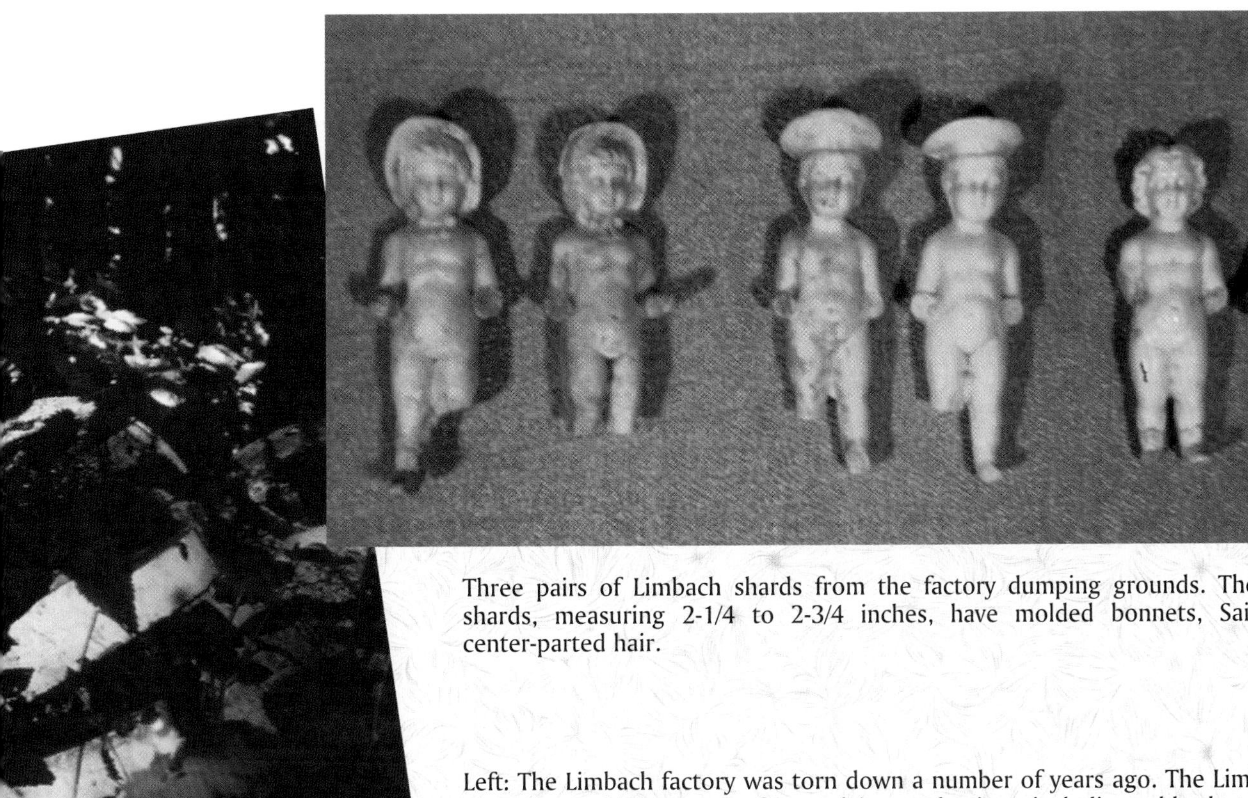

Three pairs of Limbach shards from the factory dumping grounds. The bisque dolls shards, measuring 2-1/4 to 2-3/4 inches, have molded bonnets, Sailor hats, and center-parted hair.

Left: The Limbach factory was torn down a number of years ago. The Limbach dumping ground provides traces of porcelain production, including old plaster doll molds and shards.

amounts of porcelain after World War I employing over 20,000 workers during the decade after the war.

Greiner is called "The Father of *Thuringian* Porcelain" because he is credited with founding the Greiner porcelain dynasty. The Greiner family owned the following early Thuringian porcelain factories: Sitzendorf-Volkstedt, Kloster Veilsdorf, Gera, Wallendorf, Grossbreitenbach, Rauenstein, Tettau and Limbach. These important Thuringian porcelain factories were all founded in the 1700's, and nearly all of the early Greiner family porcelain factories made doll-related articles during the 1800's and early 1900's. Unfortunately, because the majority of the dolls are unmarked as to factory or date produced, it is impossible to attribute a particular factory or even a date produced to the majority of Thuringian early porcelain dolls.

The Limbach porcelain factory was torn down several years ago. The Limbach dumping grounds contain thousands of broken pieces relating to porcelain doll production. The Limbach porcelain factory rejects that are still buried in the ground on the original factory site offer important clues concerning factory production.

The modeling of the hands and bare feet on many of the all-bisque dolls is quite detailed. Some of the pieces are marked with the Limbach clover as well as a mold number while others are marked with a "P," a number, and "Germany" followed by the Roman numeral I or II. One group of 120 similar all-bisque dolls without arms and legs is a particularly interesting study. The porcelain slip composition or the firing temperatures must have been incorrect because all of the dolls have dark gray sections running through their faces and bodies.

It is possible to create a Limbach porcelain inventory from the dumping ground shards. The factory made a number of all-bisque dolls with molded clothing. Many of the nude examples of "Frozen Charlottes" have molded hats or bonnets. The doll's house dolls are made of tinted, unglazed porcelain. Some of the seated all-bisque dolls fit into porcelain tubs painted with a blue or gold rim.

Limbach dolls are occasionally found on mechanical pull-toys. One pull-toy doll's head is incised with the typical Limbach three-leaf clover. The doll is herding a group of chickens made out of a plaster-like material. When the wheels turn, the doll "runs" and moves her right arm up and down. The chickens turn in a circle as the pull-toy moves. The label on the base of the toy reads, "Aussteller der Leipziger Messe." This means

"Exhibitor at the Leipzig Fair." The Limbach doll head was painted to look like a French doll. Her eyelashes and eyebrows are very exaggerated as compared to the face painting usually found on German dolly-face dolls.

According to an entry in the *German Doll Encyclopedia*, the Limbach porcelain factory listed doll production in 1893 and was still producing jointed bathing dolls in 1930. The products included doll's house dolls, bathing dolls, nanking dolls, bisque doll heads, and jointed dolls. In 1918, the factory listed an inventory of 16,000 porcelain products. Martin Wendl and Ernst Schäfer wrote the German book, titled in English, *The Joy of Collecting Old Thuringian Porcelain*. It contains the following list of Limbach porcelain products: Little gold knick-knacks, small figures, animal families, single free standing animals, bathing children, jointed dolls (with or without dress), Negroes, Indians, Easter items, hanging figures, mirror figures and still lives. The Limbach porcelain factory employed over 500 workers according to the Wendl/Schäfer book. One Limbach china shoulder head, circa 1840, is on permanent display in the Sonneberg Doll and Toy Museum. It is indicative of the quality found in the early Limbach doll-related porcelain products.

A pair of all-bisque Limbach dolls measuring 3 and 4-1/2 inches. The seated baby in the tub and the boy wearing a "flocked" dress match shards from the Limbach dumping grounds. Butler Brothers catalogs pictured seated all-bisque dolls in porcelain tubs from 1908 until 1925.

Right: This 8-inch bisque socket head doll, marked with the Limbach three-leaf clover, is mounted on a pull-toy. The doll has exaggerated "French" face painting and a wooden body with articulated arms and legs. As the wooden pull toy rolls forward, the doll moves her right arm and the chickens turn in a circle.

Chapter Nine

The A.W. Fr. Kister Porcelain Factory

The A.W. Fr. Kister porcelain factory was founded in the small town of Scheibe-Alsbach in 1835. The large factory complex is made up of a number of buildings that vary in age and appearance. A visit to the factory site provides the visitor with an insight into factory production. The oldest factory building was flooded due to spring rains, and the floors in part of this building were covered with mud. A stream ran under this part of the factory.

The largest building had three floors built of red brick. The many windows in this building provided much-needed light for the factory work done inside. Another building had a stone foundation and painted slate siding, while the third large building had an outdoor walkway on the second floor. The fourth large building was a separate storage shed made up of discarded molds supported by wooden timbers. The steps leading to the second floor of the storage building were in very poor condition.

A large hand-powered "Holzwolle" machine was still located on the second floor of the storage building. "Holzwolle" translates to "wood wool" in English. We

The A.W. Fr. Kister porcelain factory in Scheibe-Alsbach.

One Kister factory building is built of stone and sided with painted slate.

call wood wool "excelsior". The machine turned pieces of wood into fine wood shavings, which were often used to stuff doll bodies. Excelsior was primarily used as a packing material. Dolls and other porcelain products were very fragile. Excelsior protected the products of a porcelain factory during shipment.

The rooms in the porcelain factory were still marked with signs indicating the activity that took place in each room such as the "molding room." A large room on the top floor once held thousands of molds. Porcelain number ovals were still attached to each shelf. The two-inch blue and white plaques served as an accurate reference as to the location of each Kister mold.

The stairways in the factory contained an interesting assortment of wooden turned handrails. A large wooden shipping trunk was still in an attic room on the third floor of the oldest factory building. The wooden trunk was lined in red felt and held separate wooden sections that could be lifted out of the trunk. It must have been made to hold specific porcelain samples made by the porcelain factory.

A hand-powered "snow" machine was still bolted to a long counter in one factory room. Imperfect porcelain products were carried to the machine and ground into very fine particles. The fine porcelain, called grog, was applied to dolls and figures to indicate snow. A variety of "Snow Babies" were made in the Kister porcelain factory.

Kister "Snow Babies" were often attached to sleds and skis. Some of the sleds were marked with the mold numbers 5542 and 5574. The larger Kister "Snow Babies", standing on skis with their hands on their hips, have a definite "character" look. They have molded eyelids and open/closed mouths.

An interior room of one factory building contained several huge vats of yellow glazed brick attached to a cement platform. The vats were used to mix porcelain slip, which was then poured into the plaster molds. The Kister porcelain factory produced a wide assortment of porcelain products including a large number of doll shoulder heads and limbs as well as all-bisque dolls. The Kister inventory also included half dolls in a variety of poses and flat porcelain articles that were used as

Doll-related porcelain shards washed to the surface of the ground in a stream that ran under one factory building.

The walls of a detached Kister storage building are made of stacked plaster molds supported by wooden crossbeams.

An old "Holzwolle" machine stored on the second floor of the storage building. The machine turned pieces of wood into fine wood shavings called "wood wool" (excelsior). It was used primarily as a packing material and to stuff doll bodies.

A snow machine attached to a counter in one room of the factory. The machine crushed unusable porcelain pieces into small pieces, which were applied to Snow Babies and porcelain figurines to simulate snow. Workers carried wooden boxes filled with factory "seconds" to the snow machine.

Flat decorative pieces of Kister porcelain originally used as jewelry broaches.

jewelry broaches. The porcelain articles produced by this factory appealed to a wide variety of customers. The Wendl and Schäfer book on Thuringian porcelain includes the following list of Kister porcelain products: White biscuit figures, groups, busts, decorated fantasy figures, flower holders, table decorations, chandeliers (for electrical use), clocks, mirrors, writing utensils, Easter items, bonbonniers, night lights, birds, toothpick holders, boxes, holy figures, containers for holy water, crucifixes made from porcelain or parian masse, mounting items for gas and electrical lighting, freestanding animals, bathing, jointed dolls, doll heads, handles for walking sticks and umbrellas made of imitation ivory. One specialty of the Kister factory was "figures, busts and groups with old-ivory and colored ivory decoration, only in the finest 'Old Sevres Manner' and under glaze decor."

Many doll-related porcelain pieces were discarded under the floorboards in the oldest section of the factory. It was difficult to dispose of damaged or poor quality porcelain in the winter, when the ground was frozen, and the imperfect items, called seconds, could not be buried. The shards under the floorboards in the

Kister factory included black as well as white "Frozen Charlottes" in sitting as well as standing positions. There were beautiful early shoulder heads with the gray-streaked hair so typical of Dressel & Kister doll heads. Other glazed porcelain pieces included flesh-tinted as well as untinted body parts such as arms, legs, and Täufling-type lower torsos.

Some of the most beautiful shards were Parian-type doll-related pieces of untinted, unglazed porcelain. Parian may be defined as the finely textured, unglazed porcelain that resembles the marble from the Island of Paros in the Aegean Sea. It was mainly used in the manufacture of classical style busts as well as the figure groups so popular during the Victorian era. Parian is characterized by a special property—light penetrates the porcelain to a certain depth thus creating a beautiful glow. Doll historians have concluded that doll heads were never made of Parian; they only resembled Parian. One large piece found under the factory floor had a blue ruffled coronet molded into the doll head. A black patterned snood was attached to the coronet. A few porcelain lower legs had blue painted garter bows and short black boots laced with rose-colored crossed painted laces. From the number of Parian shards still located under the floorboards in the Kister factory, it is apparent that this factory made a number of untinted bisque doll shoulder heads.

Untinted, unglazed porcelain heads, like those made by the Kister factory, are known for their hair, hat, and shoulder detail. The shoulder plates and hair are often

Broken porcelain pieces under the floorboards of the oldest factory building include black bathing dolls as well as china Täufling lower bodies, heads, arms, and legs.

An untinted bisque Kister lower leg from under the factory floorboards contains several factory features including a blue garter bow and rose-colored laces painted on a flat tan-soled black boot.

A 27-inch Kister untinted bisque shoulder head doll, circa 1860's. A Kister face shard found under the floorboards of the factory matches the face painting on the doll.

The deep molding of the hair is a common feature on many Kister shards.

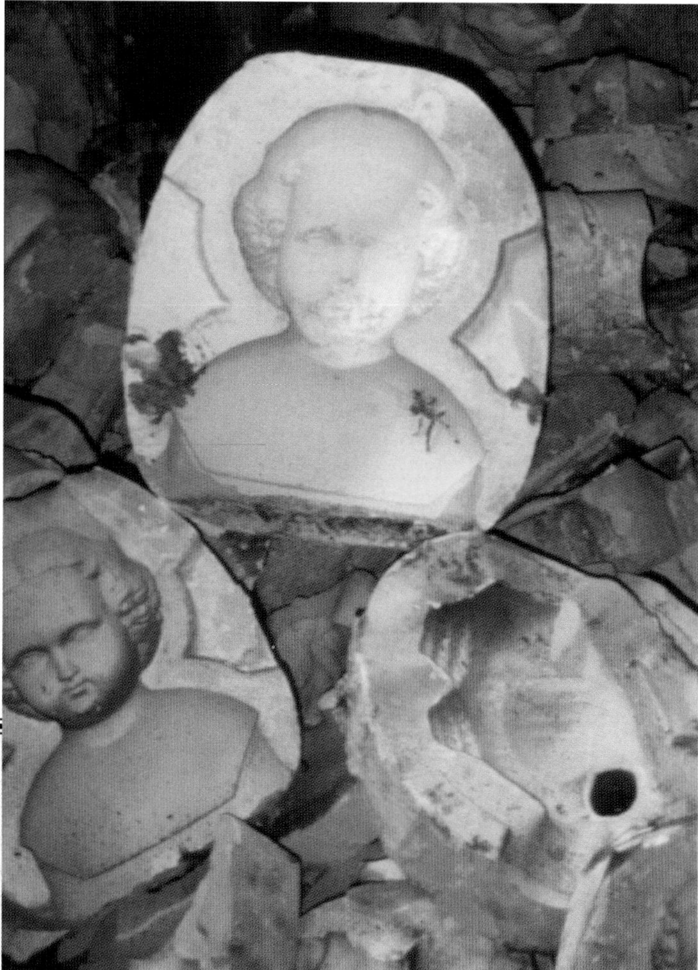

Old molds stacked in a corner of a factory mold room provide clues to factory porcelain production.

A Kister face shard provides important clues to the origin of many early unmarked china dolls.

An 1850's 14-inch Täufling china boy with a flange swivel neck attached to a china shoulder plate. The lower section of the body, arms, and legs are also made of glazed porcelain. The doll has a cloth midsection, upper arms, and upper legs. The Täufling is strung with a knotted cord attached to a cork piece that fits into the head through the neck. The stringing cord goes through a hole in the shoulder piece where it is tied to a small piece of wood. The doll's head, lower body, arms, and legs match the Kister factory shards. *Tim Dyar Collection.*

A 20-inch unmarked china shoulder head doll, circa 1840-50, with molded, brown-painted hair. The molded hair, painted eyes, and mouth with flat lower lip and upturned corners are similar to painting details found on early Kister doll head shards. *Christiane Gräfnitz Collection.*

Shards of five china shoulder heads with molded hair, measuring 1-1/4 to 1-3/4 inches, show the variety of early Kister hairstyles.

elaborately decorated with colored ribbons, flowers, scarves, combs, and feathers. The shoulder plates also contain molded ruffles, collars with ribbon ties, as well as beads and ornate jewelry.

Parian-type shoulder head dolls usually have blonde hair, but some are brunettes. Blue eyes are more common than brown eyes. Identical glazed and unglazed porcelain heads have been found leading to the conclusion that the same plaster molds were used for china, Parian-type, and bisque doll heads.

The first Kister porcelain doll heads and figurines were shown at the 1854 Industrial Exhibition in Munich. The 25th Anniversary booklet published by the Armand Marseille porcelain factory includes the notation that the porcelain factory in Scheibe-Alsbach (A. W. Fr. Kister) was "one of the earliest" to make Thuringian porcelain doll heads.

An original Kister factory booklet, titled "Porzellanmanufaktur Scheibe-Alsbach GmbH," provides accurate information concerning this important Thuringian porcelain factory. It was published a few years before the Kister porcelain factory closed in 1996. The factory trademark on the booklet is of a fancy script "S" over two crossed bars. It reads as follows:

> The porcelain factory was founded in 1835 by Louis Oels. In a short period of time, starting only as a pipe head painting business, it established itself to a world famous manufacture. In 1847, Dressel and Kister were the new owners and, they employed 148 specialty workers. The incredible craftsmanship and quality of their porcelain figurines at that time was so great and the sales so good, that in 1850, Scheibe-Alsbach was the only Thuringian manufacture to produce in large numbers. Special raw materials, special 'Masse' and perfect glazing techniques allowed sculpting of even the smallest details. This craft, as well as the masterly achievements of the modelers and the painters gave Scheibe-Alsbach its unique position on the market.

In the 1860's, the manufacture broadened their inventory from devotional items and toys to busts of poets and composers, aiming for exact perfection of the portraits. Artistic masterpieces were manufactured in the 1880's and 1890's. They made live busts from bisquit porcelain and painted them with soft, dull colors. The unusual size of the busts and design of the renaissance costumes demanded the highest craftsmanship of the modelers, firers and painters.

In the 1890's, Kister's son, August Wilhelm Friedolin, discovered a new genre. It was the depiction of details of famous paintings in the form of a porcelain group. Favored subjects were the paintings of David Watteau and other French painters and famous ladies like Madame Reclamier, Madame Pompadour and Marie Antoinette. Dancing pairs, lady dancers and scenes from society are also models of the 1890's into the 20th Century. A study of the hairstyles provides proof that a wide variety of early china doll heads were made by this porcelain factory.

Many medals and prizes fetched at international and national exhibits are proof of the artistic value of the Scheibe-Alsbach products. In 1873, they fetched the "Grand Prize" medal of the Vienna World Fair. This was followed by almost yearly achievements from Melbourne to Chicago, Brussels to Turin.

A large china shoulder head doll with all of the Kister trademark face features including the 1860's hairstyle. The shoulder head measures 7-1/2 inches.

Eight Kister china shoulder heads that range in size from 2 to 6 inches. A "Jenny Lind" doll head is on the top row and a "Mary Todd Lincoln" doll head is in the middle of the bottom row.

An unpainted glazed porcelain shard from the factory grounds matches the molded dress of a 5-inch barefoot Kister "Frozen Charlotte."

This 15-inch china "covered wagon" shoulder head doll from the 1850's shares the same face, lower arms, and legs as Kister shards found under the floorboards in the factory.

The slightly tinted china shoulder head exhibits several early Kister features such as the flat lower eyebrow edge, and the flat edge on the lower lip with very finely painted upturned lines on the corners of the mouth.

The models for the well-guarded mold treasures were mostly designed by Professor Otto Möller, Professor Otto Poertzel, Professor Carl Lysek and the modelers Felix Zeh, Carl Fuchs, and Heinz Schober. At the beginning of the 20th Century, Professor Poertzel and modeler Felix Zeh (1869-1937) were the busiest artists in the Scheibe-Alsbach manufacture. Felix Zeh specialized in rococo and "Biedermeier" figures and the depiction of historical scenes. He made the "Marshal" figures of Napoleon's Army. He was eager to create perfect portraits and paid great detail to the authenticity of the uniforms. He also was intrigued to make a model of the "Great Corsican" himself, crossing the Beresina, a battle leader, a loser fleeing Russia, and being banned on St. Helena.

All uniforms are still intact at the manufacturer's "fundus" and are well guarded. They are the base for the broad spectrum, which reaches from folk-like scenes, depiction of historical personalities to the variety of Napoleon figures and his post of General. Even today, the treasury of mold models is constantly being expanded, by the handwork of young talented craftsmen.

Like other manufactures that belong to the "Thuringian Porcelain Culture Circle," porcelain figures have always been hand-made in Scheibe-Alsbach. Since the famous manufacture was taken over by the "Royally Privileged Porcelain Factory Tettau" in Upper Frankonia in 1991, nothing has changed. Even the independence of this factory was not touched. The only thing the take-over assures is that the business conditions for perfect manufacturing will be secured for the future.

Many examples of Parian-type dolls have been attributed to the Simon & Halbig, C.F. Kling, Alt, Beck & Gottschalck and Dornheim, Koch & Fischer porcelain factories. The early dolls often have deep shoulder plates that slope downward exposing a long, well-modeled neck. The earlier porcelain hands are often spoon-shaped. Some early Kister lower arms are slightly cupped, and feature red outlining between each finger. Many early doll heads share the same distinctive facial features such as a very unusual mouth. It has a flat edge on the lower lip, and the mouth is turned up at each corner with a very finely painted line. In addition, quite a few early Kister doll heads have a very flat lower eyebrow line. The eyebrow is painted in two colors on a number of large Kister china dolls.

The Kister porcelain factory made glazed and unglazed lower arms with large, well-modeled hands. A dimple is evident over each finger on some porcelain hands, and these hands include very realistic hand lines. The factory also made a variety of lower legs. Some legs have flat-heeled black boots with tan soles, and a raised tassel in the center of the top (pointed) boot. Others have high heels with pink upper spats also tasseled at the point. Stockings are often ribbed, and the shoes are laced in gold. One Kister shoe is a typical black one-strap "Mary Jane," while another light blue shoe contains a large raised blue buckle.

The Kister porcelain factory exhibit at the 1854 Munich Trade Exhibition featured porcelain shoulder heads and figurines. The Kister factory also had an exhibition at the 1893 Chicago World's Fair that included jointed dolls, cloth dolls, and bathing dolls. According to the *German Doll Encyclopedia*, "In 1893, the company employed 170 factory workers and 340 in home trade; and in 1949 the Kister porcelain factory was still making jointed dolls, doll heads and tea-cozy dolls."

According to author Robert E. Röntgen, in his 1997 book, *Marks on German, Bohemian and Austrian Porcelain*, the A.W.Fr. Kister Porzellanmanufaktur made decorative porcelain, figurines and religious articles until 1972. In 1972, the company was nationalized and named VEB Porzellanmanufaktur Scheibe-Alsbach (VEB Porcelain Manufactory Scheibe-Alsbach). In 1996, the Kister porcelain factory was advertised for sale for the total price of one Mark. A buyer was not found, and the factory closed.

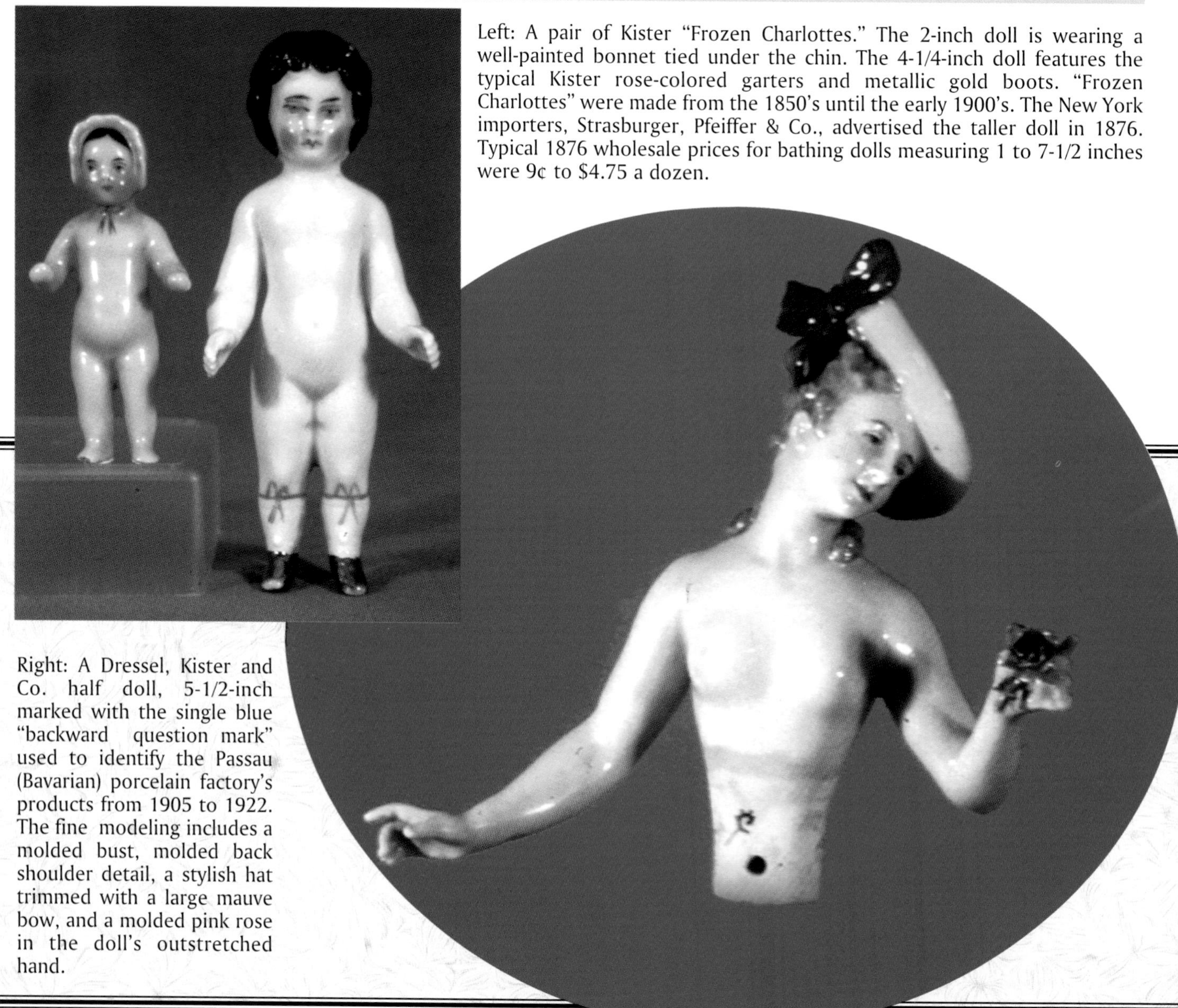

Left: A pair of Kister "Frozen Charlottes." The 2-inch doll is wearing a well-painted bonnet tied under the chin. The 4-1/4-inch doll features the typical Kister rose-colored garters and metallic gold boots. "Frozen Charlottes" were made from the 1850's until the early 1900's. The New York importers, Strasburger, Pfeiffer & Co., advertised the taller doll in 1876. Typical 1876 wholesale prices for bathing dolls measuring 1 to 7-1/2 inches were 9¢ to $4.75 a dozen.

Right: A Dressel, Kister and Co. half doll, 5-1/2-inch marked with the single blue "backward question mark" used to identify the Passau (Bavarian) porcelain factory's products from 1905 to 1922. The fine modeling includes a molded bust, molded back shoulder detail, a stylish hat trimmed with a large mauve bow, and a molded pink rose in the doll's outstretched hand.

Chapter Ten

The Hertwig Porcelain Factory

The Hertwig porcelain factory was founded in 1864. It is still standing in Katzhütte. "Katz" means "cat" in English, and "hütte" translates to the word "hut." The Hertwig factory symbol is a cat on a roof. A number of Hertwig figurines are marked with the "cat on a roof" trademark. The Hertwig factory is located next to a stream like many other Thuringian porcelain factories.

The original handwritten factory ledger was discovered in 1995 along with a number of other books pertaining to the factory. An entry in the ledger lists doll head production as early as in 1865, just one year after the company began producing porcelain products. The contents of the factory were auctioned in September of 1995. The cubicles in one of the storage rooms were

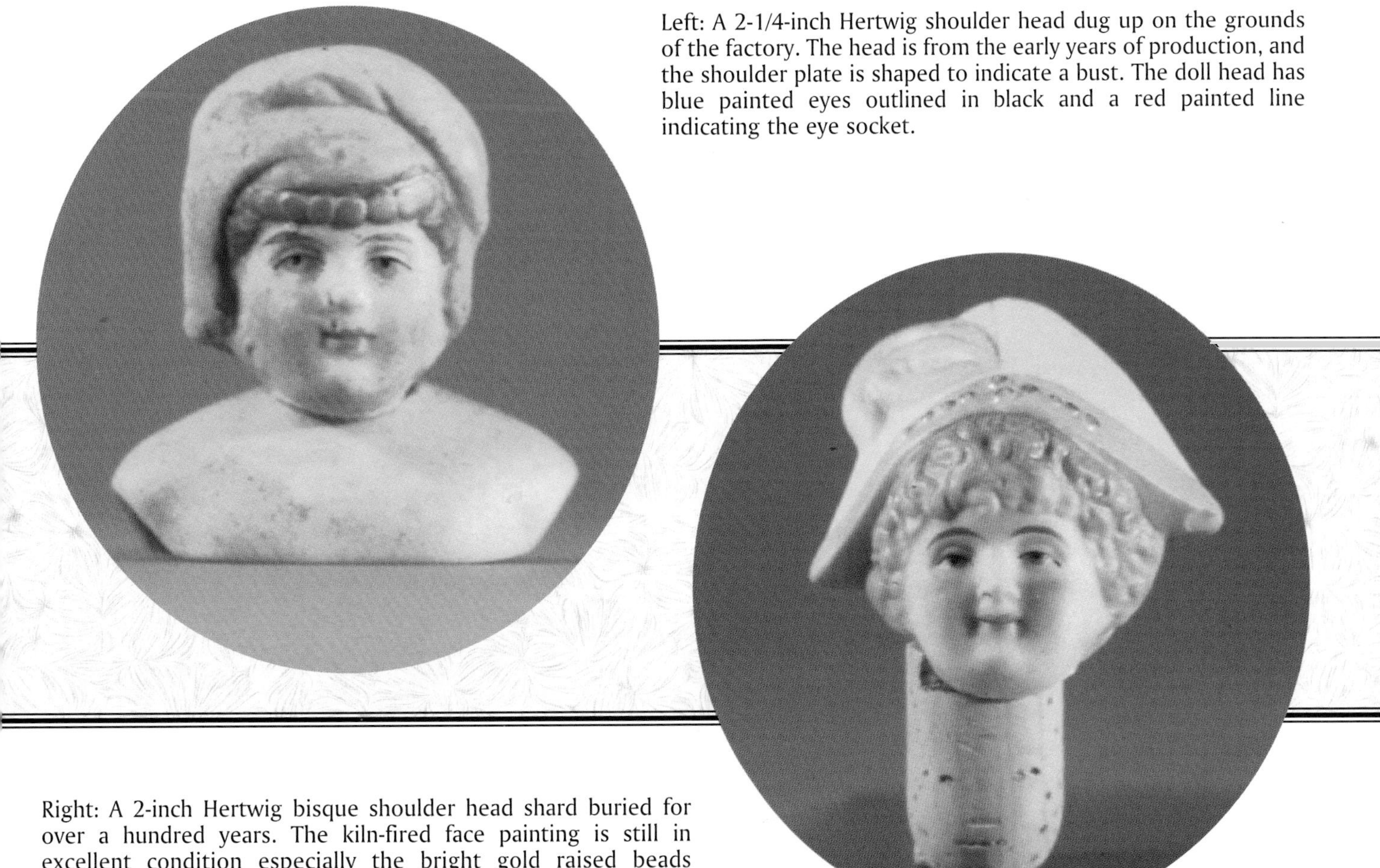

Left: A 2-1/4-inch Hertwig shoulder head dug up on the grounds of the factory. The head is from the early years of production, and the shoulder plate is shaped to indicate a bust. The doll head has blue painted eyes outlined in black and a red painted line indicating the eye socket.

Right: A 2-inch Hertwig bisque shoulder head shard buried for over a hundred years. The kiln-fired face painting is still in excellent condition especially the bright gold raised beads trimming the Napoleon-style molded hat.

filled with hundreds of unpainted "Snow Babies" and all-bisque doll parts. The Hertwig sewing room contained sewing machines that were still bolted to the floor. The cardboard patterns used for doll clothes were neatly stacked in small wooden cubicles next to the sewing machines.

A tour of the factory complex offered clues to the history of doll making in this prolific factory. The Hertwig factory complex was made up of at least five large two-and three-story buildings. The buildings varied in size and appearance. Some of the buildings were made of red brick while other buildings were made of yellow brick. One building was covered with stucco applied over the brick. Another building looked like it was one of the earliest factory buildings. This interesting building was used as an artist's studio according to a factory employee. Another building was used as a medical facility. The cabinets were still filled with medical equipment.

The President's office was located in an octagonal tower. Clocks were still attached to the sides of the

Above: In 1983, the Sonneberg Doll and Toy Museum purchased a number of original Hertwig sample boards from the company's historical collection. A Hertwig "ring bearer" and "flower girl" are dressed in original clothing and accessories. The dolls match a group of all bisque dolls on a Hertwig sample board.

The Hertwig porcelain factory in Katzhütte.

The Hertwig porcelain factory complex is made up of a number of buildings that vary in age and construction style.

Two shards from the Hertwig factory. The bonneted shoulder head on the right, measuring 2-1/2-inches, was never painted. The 2-inch shoulder head on the left is marked with the typical Hertwig "Germany." The letter "G" has a unique downward curl and the down stroke on the letter "Y" turns up in a curl.

building just under the roof. Long building wings were part of the tower. One section of the tower contained a beautiful room with walls still covered in dark blue-flowered wallpaper. A large steamer trunk was still standing in the corner of this room. The gold lettering on the trunk spelled: "Hertwig, Katzhütte, Germany."

The largest building had a large central hall and curved steps that led to the upper floors. The Hertwig factory buildings had been totally vandalized, and even the stair railings had been taken out of the buildings. Papers, most of which dated back to the DDR (German Democratic Republic) period covered many of the floors. An upstairs room was filled with transfer patterns. They were stenciled onto many porcelain articles especially tableware. Some of the Hertwig transfers still in the factory were used to mark canisters of spices. The top floor of the main building had narrow steps that led to a large floored attic. In one corner of the attic, a large table

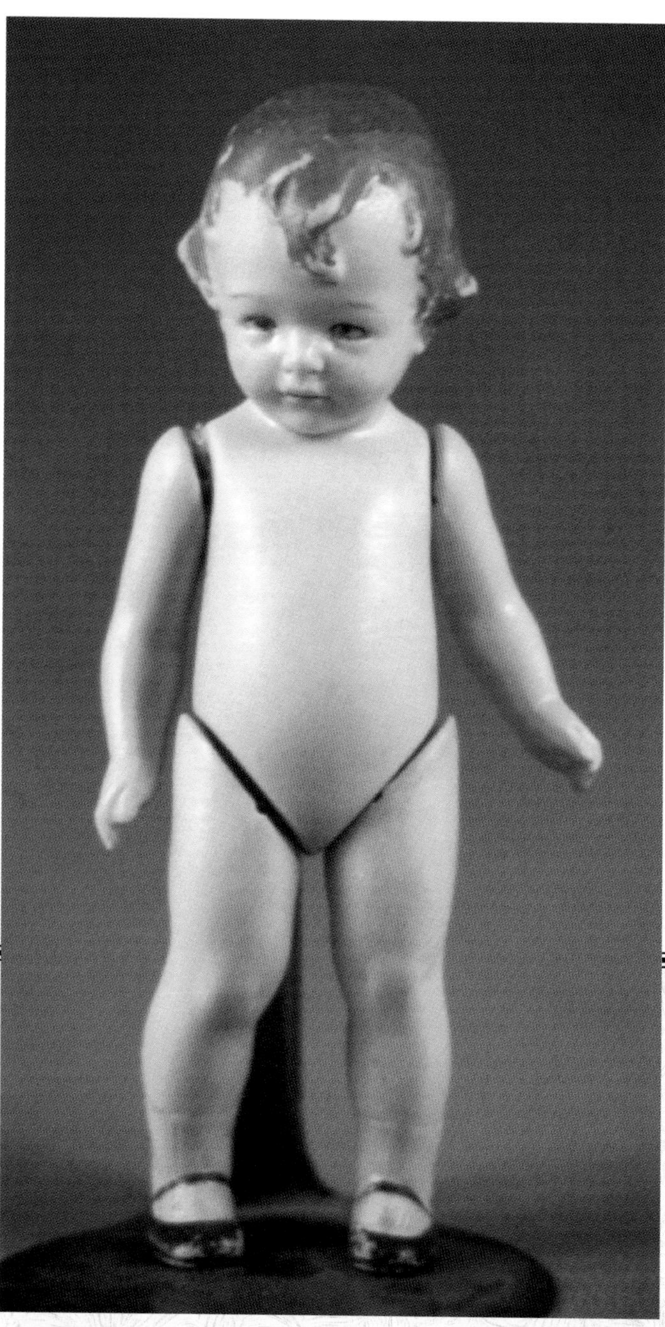

rested against a wall. This ten-foot table with a well-designed scrolled top was used as a display table at the 1926 Leipzig Fair according to the attached placard.

One small room, which had black shades covering the windows, was used as a photographer's studio. Catalogs were still on one table showing the Hertwig products for that year. Nearby rooms were used to create and store molds. The shelves in the largest mold storage rooms were numbered using cardboard rectangles, unlike the beautiful porcelain ovals used to mark the mold storage shelves in the A.W. Fr. Kister factory.

A road divided the factory complex. There were cobblestone paths between some of the buildings. Many of the cobblestones were lifted in hopes of finding Hertwig "buried treasure." Broken porcelain doll parts could be found all over the factory grounds. Behind one smaller building was a hydraulic loading ramp. The three open sheds next to the loading ramp were in very bad condition.

The Hertwig porcelain factory had a very large inventory of doll-related articles including doll heads, half dolls, and all-bisque dolls. Along with the porcelain production, factory and home workers made doll bodies. Nanking dolls were a major export item from about 1870 until the 1940's.

Left: A pre-tinted Hertwig 6-inch doll with a turned head marked: "L A & S -1921//Germany//Mibs." Louis Amberg and Son commissioned the doll. An original paper label on the chest of an identical doll reads, "Please Love Me—I'm Mibs." Helen Drukker designed the Mibs dolls. *Jane Walker Collection.*

Nine Hertwig shoulder head shards measuring from 2-1/4 to 2-3/4 inches and wearing molded bisque "straw" hats. The original painted flowers and raised dots on the hat brims vary in color and quality of hand painted details.

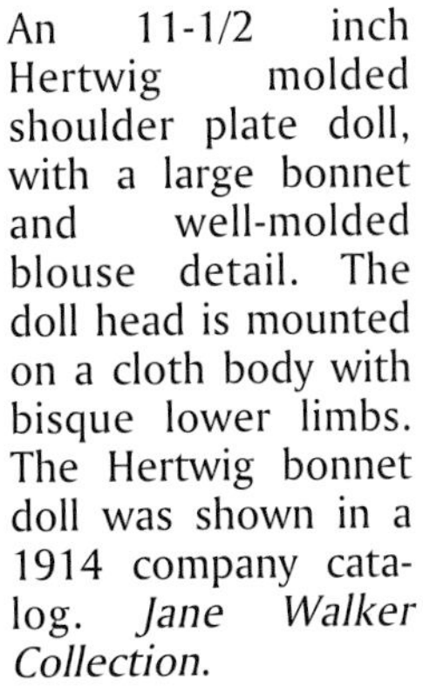

An 11-1/2 inch Hertwig molded shoulder plate doll, with a large bonnet and well-molded blouse detail. The doll head is mounted on a cloth body with bisque lower limbs. The Hertwig bonnet doll was shown in a 1914 company catalog. *Jane Walker Collection.*

Above: This 5-1/2-inch all-bisque Hertwig doll is wearing a molded coat featuring pink lapels and a long green belt fastened with a molded rosette. The arms are attached to the body with coiled wire. *Jane Walker Collection.*

Left: The Hertwig porcelain factory made a number of dolls with molded half-torsos. A 9-inch doll, with a cloth body and bisque arms, is wearing a molded blouse featuring blue buttons and neck edging. *Jane Walker Collection.*

Left: This 7-inch Hertwig boy is wearing molded clothing in the dropped waistline style often worn by children during the early 1900's. The boy's white suit is trimmed in blue, and his orange tie matches his molded, laced boots. *Jane Walker Collection.*

This seated 8-1/2-inch Hertwig china shoulder head doll with a "nanking" body has original "stitched" lower legs used to prevent damage during shipment. A 6-3/4-inch #1160 Simon & Halbig shoulder head doll, with stationary glass eyes and an original wig, has the same type of "nanking" body. The word "nanking" indicates the type of cotton used to make the cloth doll bodies from about 1870 until the 1940's. The Hertwig factory often produced 120,000 "nanking" dolls a day with the help of a large home work force.

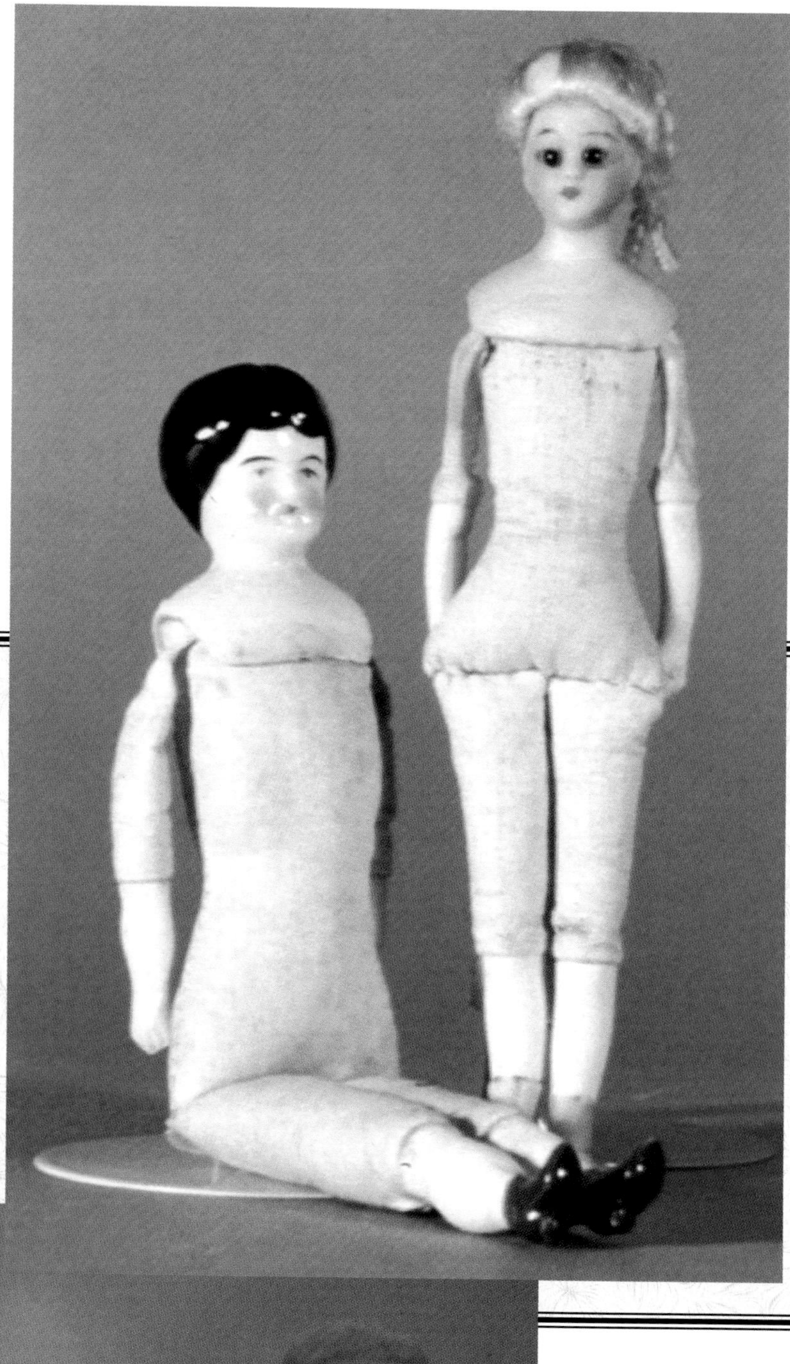

Below: A group of Hertwig all-bisque dolls measuring from 2 to 3 inches. Two are in original clothing. The girl on the left, wearing a flower headband, is shown in several different sizes on a Hertwig sample board in the Sonneberg Museum.

An 1888 entry in the *German Doll Encyclopedia* describes these cheap dolls under the Hertwig & Company heading as follows:

> In addition to knick-knacks and household pottery, they made "nanking" dolls, i.e. dolls with stuffed bodies of cotton ("nanking"), and heads and joints of porcelain. Three machines punched out the material that needed to be sewn together and stuffed with sawdust, including the body, the upper arms and the upper thighs of the doll body.
>
> Each punch produces 10 dozen parts. 600 workers, most of them in home trade, and 45 sewing machines are employed for sewing, stuffing and finishing the production. By this method, they produced in summer 1000 to 1200 dozen per day, and in winter 2000 dozen dolls a day. The "nanking" doll was mainly made for the American and Australian markets, and was the most preferred doll type. They were available in sizes 3.90 to 29.25 inches. In 1939, "nanking" dolls sold for 35¢ in the 6-inch size and up to $2.50 for the 18-inch doll size.

An interesting quote concerning the total number of dolls made by a porcelain factory like the Hertwig factory comes from an 1884 *Harper's Bazaar* article and reads, "A single oven contains 5,000 dolls, and thirty ovens are often full in one factory. One German factory has been running about one hundred and thirty years, and has produced about one billion dolls." It is doubtful that any of the Thuringian porcelain factories had thirty ovens (kilns) in one factory, but each kiln was often filled with 5,000 doll heads at one time. The Armand Marseille porcelain factory was probably the largest Thuringian factory, as far as overall doll production. The Marseille porcelain factory had 10 kilns in the Köppelsdorf factory.

In 1983, the Sonneberg Doll and Toy Museum purchased a number of dated sample boards from the historical collection of the Hertwig porcelain factory. The glazed and unglazed porcelain dolls are still firmly tied to their individual sample boards. These important doll samples document Hertwig porcelain production from the late 1800's to the 1930's. Some of the original Hertwig sample boards are now in private collections. A few have been pictured in doll books and magazines.

The Hertwig factory made a vast array of doll heads as well as all-bisque dolls. One group of dolls well known to American collectors is the so-called Hertwig "Pet Name" dolls patented in 1895 and introduced in the 1889 Butler Brothers' catalog. The first group of "name" dolls had names on their front shoulder plates. Their names were Edith, Esther, Florence, Mabel, Pauline and Ruth. The second group of "name" dolls was offered in 1910. They were Marion, Dorothy, Helen, Bertha, Agnes and Ethel. Hertwig also made this second group of dolls for

A 12-inch "Bertha" Hertwig "pet name" shoulder head doll from the 1910 name series. The popular dolls, with names on the shoulder plates, were on the market for over 25 years. In 1931, Butler Brothers advertised a 12-1/2-inch doll for $2.00.

Butler Brothers, and the bodies were printed with "A. B. C." and other patterned bodies. The second group of dolls is similar to the first group of "name" dolls by Hertwig, and many from the second group have been dug up at the Hertwig factory. The Hertwig "name" dolls were well received and were on the market for at least 25 years. Butler Brothers advertised the 12-inch size for $2.00 as late as 1931.

Small Hertwig all-bisque dolls and toys were sold at a variety of American stores like Woolworth and Kresge. They were also shown in catalogs like Sears, Roebuck and Co. and Marshall Field. "Snow Babies" were offered at Christmas, Easter rabbits in the spring, and Halloween novelty items were stocked during the fall season.

One group of Hertwig all-bisque dolls is popular with doll as well as toy collectors. These small dolls represent characters from American comic strips. They are called "knotters" because they are strung with knotted elastic cord. The cord is knotted at the top of the doll's head and goes through the body where it is tied in another knot. One set of these dolls is designed to represent the comic strip "Gasoline Alley" by Frank King.

Many other all-bisque Hertwig sets are popular with collectors including the "Our Gang" group. Hal Roach introduced this group of charismatic comedic child actors in the 1920's. The comedy series was so popular that it continued for several decades, enchanting movie attendees. One pair of Hertwig "Our Gang" knotters are quite appealing. The boy represents "Jackie Cooper" and the girl represents "Mary Ann Jackson." Each all-bisque doll is marked with the actor's full name and the word "Germany" under the name.

In 1891, a United States trade law mandated that all imports must be marked with a "country of origin" mark. In other words, "Germany" was a required mark on all dolls and toys made in Germany, but the marking was often a label made of paper or a hangtag attached to the arm of a doll. It is fortunate for collectors that the Hertwig "country of origin" mark is so distinctive. The letters "G" and "Y" are unique and quite identifiable. The Hertwig "G" in "Germany" has a downward tail and the bottom of the "Y" curls up at the end. Although the hundreds of different Hertwig doll molds vary in size and in modeling, the incised "Germany" remains the same on each marked bisque doll.

Some Hertwig all-bisque dolls are not marked including "Snow Babies" and dolls with molded clothing. "Snow Babies", called "Schneekinder" in German, originated as sugar and then marzipan "Babies" in Lübeck, Germany according to one historian. The old confectionery firm, Johann Moll, commissioned the Hertwig porcelain factory to create the popular edible sweet treat as a group of bisque snow figures. The Hertwig sample boards in the Sonneberg Museum feature a jointed standing "Snow Baby" as well as a shoulder head "Snow Baby."

The Sonneberg Museum sample boards also serve to identify another group of unmarked Hertwig all-bisque dolls. Hertwig made a number of unusual dolls with molded clothing. One doll, dressed as a sailor, was

A pair of 3-1/2-inch Hertwig pre-tinted pigeon-toed all-bisque boys dressed in painted bathing suits. *Jane Walker Collection.*

Below: Six all-bisque 1-1/2-inch Hertwig "Snowmen" with red molded top hats. The novelty dolls are still stitched to an original red-trimmed piece of cardboard.

Left: Two Hertwig all-bisque "knotter" dolls. The 3-1/2-inch boy has the following markings on his back: "Jackie Cooper//Germany." The 3-inch girl is marked: "Mary Ann Jackson//Germany." The dolls represent child actors in the Hal Roach "Our Gang" series (1924-1944). *Jane Walker Collection.*

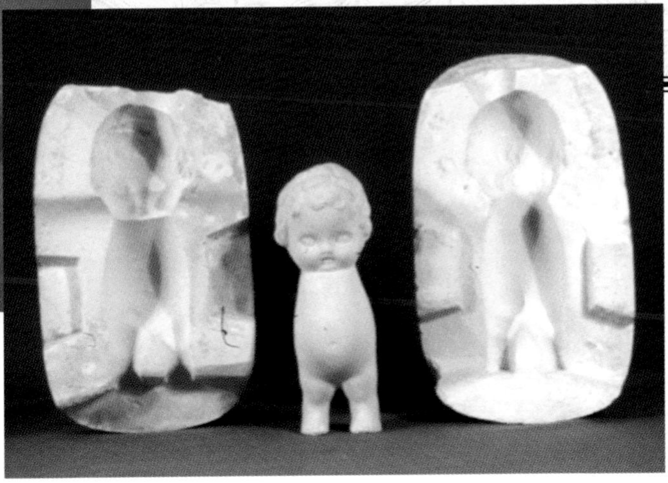

A 5-inch Hertwig "pigeon-toed" all-bisque doll is identical to a number of dolls tied to original sample boards in the Sonneberg Museum. The original Hertwig plaster mold is shown with the unfired doll.

available in at least three sizes including 4-1/2-inches, 6-inches, and 7-inches. The Hertwig doll is dressed in a molded sailor suit with separate arms attached to the body with coiled wire. The molded hair is blonde, and the white suit is trimmed in either pale blue or pink.

Author Genevieve Angione describes and pictures these "Sailor Dolls" in her book, *All Bisque & Half Bisque Dolls.* The Angione book states, "In 1908, the Butler Brothers Wholesale Catalog for Fall lists these dolls in a bordered display box as follows: 'Sailor Boy' Bisque Dolls; Big Value, 5 and 10¢; F 4072-4 1/8 in., flesh tinted faces, hands and legs, painted features and hair, white costume and hat, blue and pink painted trimmings, shoes and socks; 1 dozen in box per dozen, 41¢."

The second half of the 20th Century since World War II has not been kind to many of the Thuringian porcelain factories. The Hertwig factory is a prime example. Many of the factory windows are broken, and birds are flying in and out. Maintenance costs are high due to the number and size of the factory buildings. Most of the Thuringian porcelain factories were located in small towns, and the majority of the towns' residents worked in the factory for most of their lives. Factory closings have had a major economic impact on these small German towns. Today, the closed Thuringian porcelain factories stand as silent sentinels to the past. One by one, many doll-related porcelain factories will be torn down in the years ahead.

But, not all of the Thuringian porcelain factories are scheduled for the wrecking ball in the near future. Several years ago, signs went up in Thuringia to mark the "Thuringian Porcelain Road." Many old porcelain factories have been remodeled and now feature museums, porcelain demonstrations, and salesrooms showcasing current products to allow a tourist to take part in the "Life of White Gold" in the present.

A pair of Hertwig all-bisque Sailor dolls measuring 2-1/4 and 2-1/2 inches. The doll on the left was pictured in the 1908 Butler Brothers Wholesale Catalog. One dozen dolls were packed in a box, which sold for 41¢.

Below: A group of Hertwig Snow Babies. The 2-1/2-inch Snow Babies, sitting on an original candy container, are playing with a cotton snowball that has been covered with finely ground porcelain. The 5-inch standing Snow Baby has wire-jointed arms and legs. The doll on the sled measures 1-1/2-inches, and the smallest doll measures 1-1/4-inches. Snow Babies were made from the late 1800's until World War II. A similar group of Snow Babies was advertised in a 1914 Marshall Field catalog as "Alaska Tots."

Chapter Eleven

The Weiss, Kühnert & Co. Porcelain Factory

According to an original company document, Christian Weiss (capsule turner); Theodor Kühnert (mold pourer); Johann Fischer (porcelain painter); Carl Scheidig (porcelain painter) and E. Baumann (porcelain painter) founded the Weiss, Kühnert & Co. porcelain factory in 1891. The early factory burned to the ground twice during the early years. The reconstructed factory was built of steel framing with concrete ceilings. The factory originally had two kilns. The hot air from these firing ovens heated the entire factory. Generally, 250 to 300 workers were listed as employees of the porcelain factory during their many years of porcelain production. When coal was not available during World War I, a sawmill was built on the grounds of the factory. After World War I, a massive three-story building was built. There was also a building on the factory grounds that contained living quarters for workers.

The Weiss, Kühnert & Co. porcelain factory exported 95% of their products. Very few German sales were listed. Their products were shipped internationally. Robert Weiss and Kühnert's son-in-law, Carl Scharich, led the company after World War I and Otto Weiss, the third generation descendant, directed the company during the following few decades.

In 1972, the porcelain factory was nationalized and named the VEB Utility Porcelain Company. The factory

The Weiss, Kühnert & Co. porcelain factory in Gräfenthal.

A group of bathing beauties currently being made from old WKC molds by the German Doll Company. The dolls are marked with a kiln-fired blue roly-poly clown trademark. The mermaids and mermen are between 2-1/2 to 4 inches long and 2-1/2 to 3 inches tall. The dolls on the bottom row are identified and marked as follows: The boy "centaurs" (with the head, trunk and arms of a boy and the legs of an animal) on a porpoise, is marked with the mold number: "8127." The merboy on the right with a double tail, sitting on a big fish, is marked: "Germany//8128." The middle row dolls are as follows: The double-tailed mermaid, sitting on an alligator, is marked: "8108." The merboy with a double tail, sitting on a sea horse, is marked: "Germany//8125." The double-tailed mermaid with long blonde hair, sitting on a seashell, is marked: "7022//Germany." The double-tailed mermaid, on the top row, is sitting on an alligator with a curled tail. The doll is marked: "Germany//7240." *Bickert and Schlegel Collection.*

Old WKC molds are stacked in a large room on the third floor of the factory.

A 3-inch pair of WKC bisque Snow Babies, riding on a sled marked "Germany," and an illegible mold number that begins with "7." A number of Snow Baby molds were found at the factory. *Bickert and Schlegel Collection.*

A WKC sample page from an original 1920's factory catalog. Forty-four porcelain products are pictured in color. A few of the items pictured on the sample sheet include a bathing beauty, half dolls, clocks with matching vases, religious articles, figurines, dressing table accessories, a wall pocket, animal and bird figures and an ashtray.

continued to produce decorative porcelain, including lamps, candlesticks, and beer mugs until 1990. In 1990, the company was privatized and the name was changed to Porcelain Manufactory Gräfenthal. The factory closed in 1995.

In 1999, a young Ohio woman bought the entire contents of the Weiss, Kühnert & Co. porcelain factory. With the help of a German partner, she founded The German Doll Company. The German Doll Company is currently producing dolls including Rose O'Neill's Kewpie as well as other porcelain products from original factory molds. The dolls are marked with a kiln-fired blue roly-poly clown.

A tour of the old Weiss, Kühnert factory in Gräfenthal was like stepping back in time. The factory equipment, molds, and packing boxes were still in place as if the employees had taken a lunch break. The huge red brick factory was four stories high in one area. The 82-foot original beehive kiln was built into the factory extending through several floors. Each room was used for a different purpose. Porcelain slip was still clinging to the mixing vats. Cardboard boxes were bound together and stacked all the way to the ceiling in a small storage room. Bales of excelsior were still stacked in another room. The molds stacked in an upstairs room looked like gray ghosts rising out of the mist.

One large room stood out from all the others. Long wooden tables filled the room. The 22 windows on two walls provided excellent natural light. A large porcelain pipe was suspended high above the windows. A number of separate rubber hoses with metal spigots were attached at three-foot intervals from the porcelain pipe. Each individual hose ended in a trough that drained into another large pipe. The workers poured porcelain slip into plaster molds at the long wooden tables.

A study of 36 original sample pages dating from about 1915 through the 1930's from the Weiss, Kühnert & Co. manufacturer's catalogs provides accurate information on the company's porcelain products. Through these original sample pages, the Weiss, Kühnert & Co. porcelain factory reveals information about the entire German porcelain industry. The mold detail and the types of designs are indicative of the variety of porcelain products made by many Thuringian porcelain factories. Considering the number of molds needed for each piece, it is understandable why so much storage space was necessary for the molds in a porcelain factory.

The WKC sample sheets illustrate dozens of items, sometimes over 75, on a single page. In just this group of 36 separate sample sheets, over 2,000 different articles are pictured in detail. Some of the ornate porcelain clocks, with scenes attached required ten or more separate molds to make the entire piece. Many figurines and vases were made in several sizes. Each size of a figurine was given a separate mold number on the sample page.

Mantelpiece "trivia" was in vogue when these sample sheets were made. Many of the clocks with matching vases were used to decorate a mantel. The company made a number of religious articles including large elaborate crosses decorated with molded palm leaves. Dressing table containers are pictured as well as perfume

The study of Thuringian porcelain is possible because of the porcelain factories still standing today. Unlike many other areas of Germany, few Thuringian porcelain factories were destroyed during the two World Wars. Often, original equipment used in early production has not been removed. Such is the case concerning the Weiss, Kühnert and Co. porcelain factory. The original beehive kiln, the foot-powered potter's wheel, and the original molds are still in the factory. The original 3 x 4 foot book listing the location of every mold is still bolted to a wall in the factory.

After spending several days and nights in the factory, you are able to substantiate the daily role a worker plays in a Thuringian porcelain factory. As the early morning mist blanketed the narrow road leading to the factory, you could almost make out the shadowy figures of the workers reporting for work. Following their ghostly footprints into the factory allows you to study the individual work areas. The concrete steps on each floor of the main factory building were very worn from over a hundred years of wear and tear. The long wooden worktables had deep grooves and notches reflecting years of daily use. The tall rolling metal carts were still filled with uncompleted porcelain articles, which were never sold. The sides of the mixing vats were still coated with plaster. A large bag of plaster rested against the wall next to the mixing vat. The time clocks had all stopped at the same time. As the majority of old Thuringian porcelain factories disappear year after year, it is fortunate that factory photographs and records, as well as dolls, remain as reminders of the past.

Two WKC doll heads representing a small sampling of the doll-related articles originally made by the porcelain factory. The 5-inch bisque socket head on the left is marked: "4703//Weiss Kühnert//&//Co.//Gräfenthal//6//Made in//Germany." The character doll head has multi-stroke eyebrows, an open mouth with two upper teeth, and a deep dimple in each cheek. The unpainted "Badekinder" (bathing child) head shard on the right measures 5 inches.

A WKC "Badekinder" mold model marked: "Germany//6042." The bathing dolls, known as "Frozen Charlies," were very popular during the 3rd Quarter of the 19th Century.

Chapter Twelve

The Gebrüder Heubach Porcelain Factory

The Gebrüder Heubach porcelain factory is well known to doll collectors because of the wide range of expressive character dolls made since 1910. Before doll heads were produced, the factory made decorative and household porcelain as well as figurines. Johann Heinrich Leder founded the Lichte porcelain factory in 1822. The Lauscha brothers, Christoph and Philipp Heubach, bought the porcelain factory on September 16, 1843. Like so many other small doll-making towns, the majority of Lichte's residents worked at the porcelain factory.

A pair of marked Gebrüder Heubach figurines measuring 7-3/4 and 8-1/4 inches. The boy and girl figurines have molded trim on their clothing that is painted to look like fur. The porcelain factory, founded in 1840, made figurines and other porcelain products before doll heads were introduced in 1910. *Jane Walker Collection.*

Left: A 9-1/2 inch expressive Heubach "Screamer" character doll marked: "Germany// 7134." The mold design was registered in 1910. The doll has squinting intaglio eyes, single-stroke eyebrows, forehead frown creases, and a large open/closed mouth with a realistic molded tongue.

Descendants of many of the same families work there today. Only the name of the porcelain factory has changed.

A collection of Heubach dolls is always a delight. The doll head mold numbers begin with 5625 and end with the mold number 12,386. The faces portray a wide range of human emotion. A Heubach house is still standing across the street from the porcelain factory in Lichte. The porcelain factory made a large number of figurines and other porcelain products before doll heads were produced in 1910. Some of the same molds were used for doll heads as well as figurines. The figurines and doll heads often have well-molded intaglio eyes. Intaglio eyes are painted eyes that have semi-spherical impressed or incised pupils. Heubach intaglio eyes are very realistic.

The mold number 6969 Heubach "Pouty" was often made for the Cuno & Otto Dressel Company in Sonneberg. Although the Heubach porcelain factory was in Lichte, Gebrüder Heubach had a large assembly factory in Sonneberg. Heubach sold dolls to a number of Thuringian doll factories. The bisque head doll, "Whistling Jim" (mold number 8774), was advertised by the Neustadt doll makers A. Bechthold and Christian Förster. The Sonneberg doll makers Matthias Müller, Carl Scharfenberg, and Oskar Liebermann also sold these Heubach heads. Gebrüder Heubach doll heads were advertised in a number of catalogs including the 1911 Louis Lindner & Sons Catalog and the Marshall Field & Company Catalog for the year 1914.

Many other German doll companies bought Gebrüder Heubach heads including: Otto Schamberger (Sonneberg); Emil Bauersachs (Sonneberg); Hamburger & Co. (Berlin); Eisenmann & Co. (Furth); A. Luge & Co. (Sonneberg); Gebrüder Ohlhaver (Sonneberg); Wagner & Zetsche (Ilmenau) and Gottlieb Zinner & Söhne (Schalkau). The Zinner firm was well known for its mechanical dolls and toys, which were often credited to French doll makers. Before 1916, the Wagner & Zetsche doll factory in Ilmenau bought most of their doll heads from the Gebrüder Heubach porcelain factory. The well-made Wagner & Zetsche kid doll bodies contrast with the poor quality five-piece Neustadt composition doll bodies often found on Heubach dolls.

A Heubach family home in Lichte.

The Gebrüder Heubach porcelain factory now operating as the "Lichte Porcelain Factory." It stands across the street from the Heubach home.

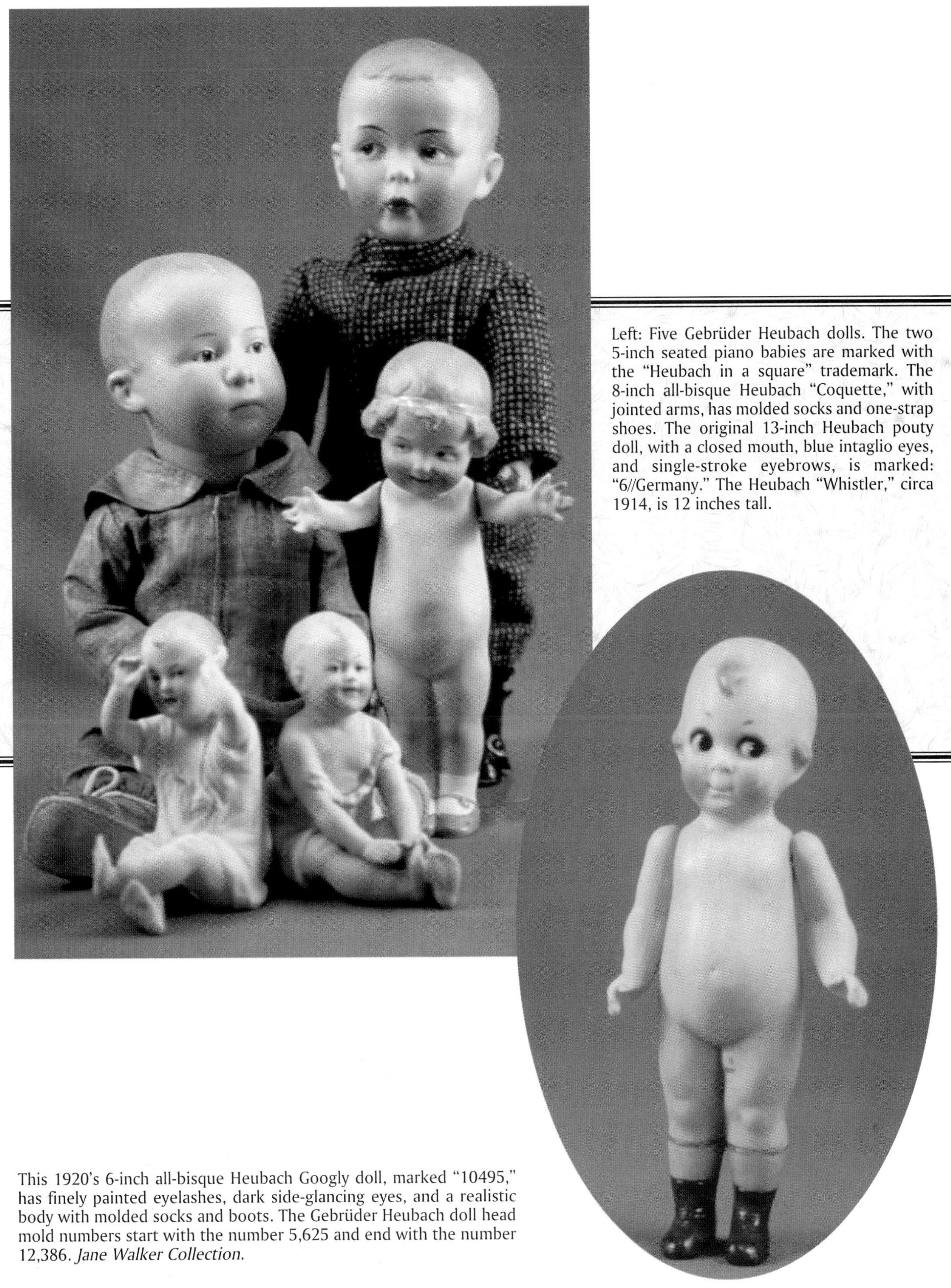

Left: Five Gebrüder Heubach dolls. The two 5-inch seated piano babies are marked with the "Heubach in a square" trademark. The 8-inch all-bisque Heubach "Coquette," with jointed arms, has molded socks and one-strap shoes. The original 13-inch Heubach pouty doll, with a closed mouth, blue intaglio eyes, and single-stroke eyebrows, is marked: "6//Germany." The Heubach "Whistler," circa 1914, is 12 inches tall.

This 1920's 6-inch all-bisque Heubach Googly doll, marked "10495," has finely painted eyelashes, dark side-glancing eyes, and a realistic body with molded socks and boots. The Gebrüder Heubach doll head mold numbers start with the number 5,625 and end with the number 12,386. *Jane Walker Collection.*

A Heubach 19-inch "Coquette" shoulder head doll, circa 1912, on a kid body with bisque lower arms. It is marked: "(Heubach in a square)//Germany." The doll has side-glancing blue eyes intaglio with white highlights, single-stroke eyebrows, and an open/closed mouth with a row of tiny painted teeth. The molded curly hair features a ribbon headband tied in a bow. *Jane Walker Collection.*

The Heubach porcelain factory made "Whistling Jim" doll heads for a number of Thuringian doll factories. A 12-inch doll, circa 1914, is marked "8774" and features a bellows-type voice box inserted into the cloth body. The doll, with side-glancing intaglio eyes, single-stroke eyebrows, and a pursed open/closed mouth emits a very realistic sounding whistle when the voice mechanism is pushed. "Whistling Jim" was advertised in a 1924 Montgomery Ward catalog for 89¢, plus 6¢ postage.

A pair of Gebrüder Heubach dolls. The 15-inch Gebrüder Heubach bisque socket head doll, circa 1912, is marked: "5636//3-1/2//Germany// (Heubach rising sun trademark)." The appealing face includes blue sleep eyes, an open/closed mouth with two lower teeth, and cheek dimples. The small Heubach shoulder head doll, circa 1912, is marked: "7345//14/0 (Heubach in a square) //Germany." *Jane Walker Collection.*

An 11-inch Heubach bisque socket head doll, circa 1912. The doll, marked "6970," has intaglio eyes, multi-stroke eyebrows, a closed mouth, and a jointed composition body.

The Gebrüder Heubach assembly factory in Sonneberg was a busy place especially when Christmas orders were due. Doll bodies, shoes, wigs, voice boxes, and clothing were made and delivered by home workers who lived in the many small villages that surrounded Sonneberg. The small village of Neufang, located on the outskirts of Sonneberg, was home to a number of families whose lives depended upon the manufacture of voice boxes. The Neufang voice box makers perfected the art of sound using wood, small springs, brass foil, paper strips, goat leather, cardboard, rubber, and animal glue.

The voice boxes often utilized a bellows principle. The Neufang families of home workers were well known for their unusual voice boxes. At first, animals and dolls made the same indistinct sound. In the following years, as the voice box mechanisms were perfected, birds "sang," lions "roared," and cows said "moo." Dolls soon "whistled" and said "ma-ma" and "pa-pa."

Many of these sophisticated voice boxes used brass plates over flat pieces of iron. The sound traveled through the space created between the iron and brass. The bellows forced the air through the space. By bending the top brass piece carefully, various noises were created. The voice box was usually enclosed in cardboard. The form and length of the cardboard covering also contributed to the quality of the sound. Voice box makers turned out about 500–600 voice boxes a week. One family received $8.35 for living expenses for a week's work in 1900. Every Saturday, the Neufang voice boxes were delivered to doll makers including Martin Eichhorn, H. Josef Leven, and others in Sonneberg.

The Heubachs established a school for sculptors at the porcelain factory in Lichte in 1862. The range of character heads reflects the artistic abilities of the many porcelain sculptors in the Thuringian Forest. At the Heubach porcelain factory, the sculptors not only designed doll heads, but children's tea sets, vases, inkwells, match holders (using doll heads), animal figures, figurines, and half dolls. One outstanding Heubach design is of a realistic bisque basket complete with lid and molded lock. Peeking out from under the basket lid are four beautiful Heubach character babies, two with molded bonnets.

One group of Gebrüder Heubach novelty dolls emerged from realistic cracked eggs much like chickens hatch. The largest egg in this series featured a seated

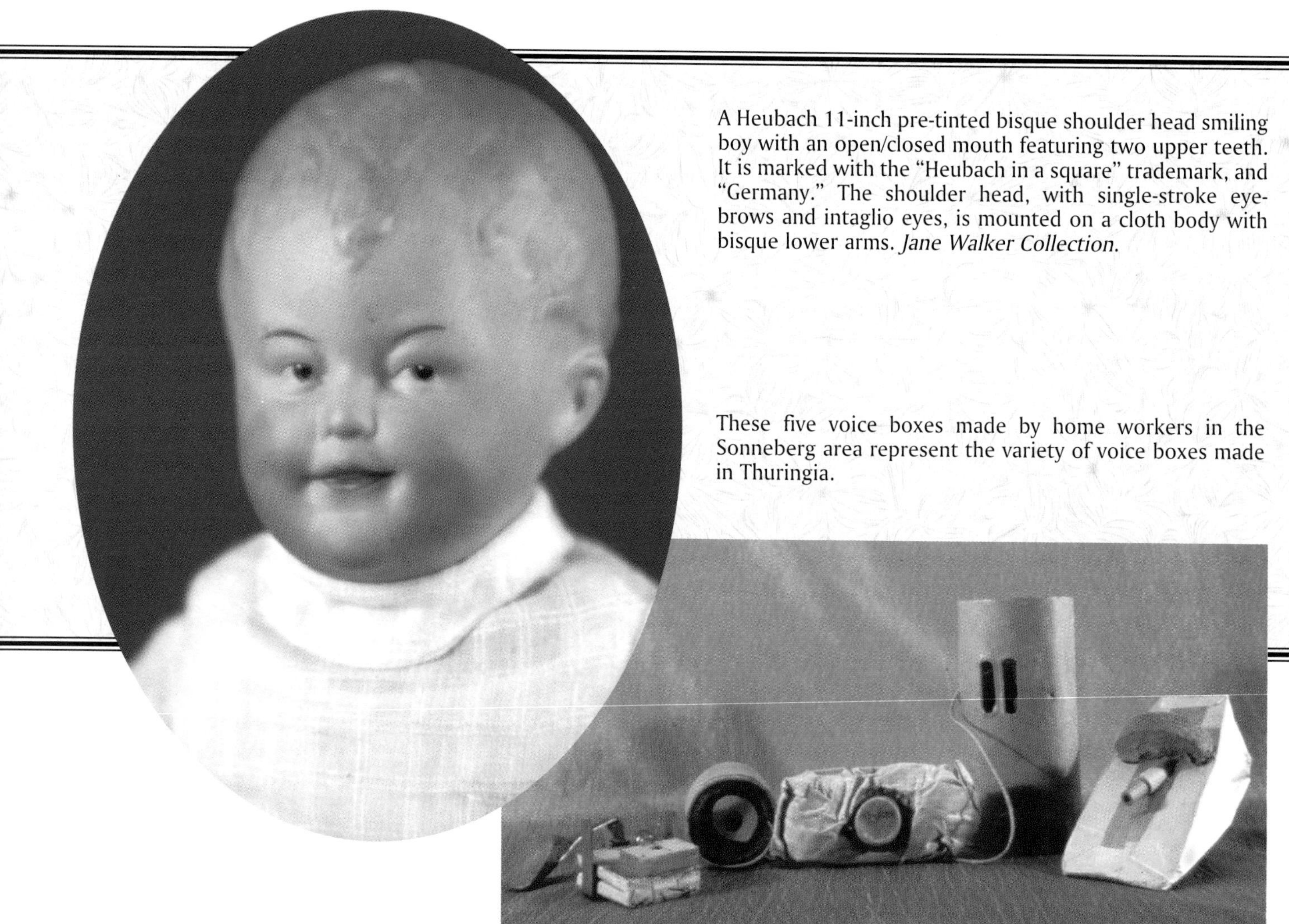

A Heubach 11-inch pre-tinted bisque shoulder head smiling boy with an open/closed mouth featuring two upper teeth. It is marked with the "Heubach in a square" trademark, and "Germany." The shoulder head, with single-stroke eyebrows and intaglio eyes, is mounted on a cloth body with bisque lower arms. *Jane Walker Collection.*

These five voice boxes made by home workers in the Sonneberg area represent the variety of voice boxes made in Thuringia.

A Heubach "pouty" doll, marked "7602," is tied in an original box. The boy doll, circa 1912, is 10 inches tall and dressed in a felt uniform that matches the picture of the boy on the box lid. An English translation of the German words on the box are: "Think of Our War Orphans!" and "We Have Only One Will: To Win or Die."

baby dressed in black holding the 5-inch egg. Three other black babies are "hatching" from the egg. Single eggs featuring both black and white babies were also part of this series. The 2-inch porcelain eggs have the face and hands of the baby on one side of the egg and the seat and feet emerge from the opposite side of the cracked egg. Sculptors trained at schools like the Sonneberg School of Industry and the Lichte Trade School depended on town fairs, as well as the Leipzig and Frankfurt Trade Fairs, to provide new modeling ideas. Throughout doll history, there have always been individual dolls with "portrait" faces, which exhibit human emotion, but in 1908, the Munich Art Dolls gave sculptors a completely new focus—the realistic "children of the street." The Munich Art Dolls are credited with starting the German character doll movement.

Large porcelain factories like the Armand Marseille, Simon & Halbig and Gebrüder Heubach factories, had their own factory sculptors who worked full time for the porcelain factory. Smaller porcelain factories hired free-lance artists and sculptors who created doll head designs for that particular factory.

The *German Doll Encyclopedia* provides information on the role of a porcelain factory sculptor. It states, "When discussing models, it was therefore quite common to have the porcelain workers, turners, and masters of firing participate in the discussions. Using his own ideas or for a special order, the sculptor freely modeled the model of a doll head or doll body. The clay model was poured in molds of sulfur, gypsum or metal."

The Ciesliks also provide the following important information on a sculptor's pay scale:

> One series of doll heads created by a famous artist was between 200 and 600 Mark at the turn of the century. (In 1900, a U.S. dollar equaled 4.20 Mark. Therefore, 600 Mark converts to $142.86). According to the size of the factory, one needed for manufacturing from two up to more than one hundred molds for each series, for a standard series of doll heads in general consisted of about ten to twelve sizes. Heavy penalties were given to sculptors who 'sold' model heads to other companies.
>
> If a sculptor had stolen a model head from the works of a Sonneberg doll factory, and tried to sell it to a competing company, he was taken to court and imprisoned for two months; the owner of the competing company was imprisoned for two months and paid a fine of 500 Mark.

The Gebrüder Heubach mold number 7602 is a credit to the Heubach factory sculptor. The pensive expression is quite haunting, and a 10-inch 7602 Heubach boy doll still tied in his original box has every reason to be pensive. This original doll, dressed in a red and blue felt military uniform, was given to a little boy in Saalfeld, Germany by his father just before World War I. His sister received a girl doll at the same time. The father left home to fight in World War I shortly after giving the dolls to his children. The father was killed in one of the first skirmishes of the War. The little boy was so sad that he never took the doll out of the box. The little boy grew up, and was killed fighting in World War II. His sister kept the doll in her attic until she was forced to move into a nursing home. Only then did she sadly part with the doll. Dolls have such stories to tell. They are silent witnesses to so much past history.

Porcelain products are made in current porcelain factories much the same way they were made over a hundred years ago, but the porcelain mixture is no longer pressed into molds as it was earlier, but poured into the

Right: A 3-inch Heubach bisque shoulder head marked "5920." The doll head, with an original mohair wig and bonnet, has an open/closed mouth with upper and lower teeth, and a metal, iridescent fly attached to the nose.

Below: This 10-inch Heubach bisque socket head doll, circa 1912, is marked: "(Heubach in a square) 0//7971//Germany" on a composition baby body. The doll has intaglio eyes with white highlights, single-stroke eyebrows, an open/closed mouth with a molded tongue, and cheek dimples. *Jane Walker Collection.*

Below: An expressive 13-1/2-inch Heubach character doll with a crooked smile marked "5 (Heubach in a square) 8191." The doll has side-glancing intaglio eyes, an open/closed mouth with upper and lower teeth, and a realistic molded tongue. The doll head, circa 1912, is on a composition toddler body.

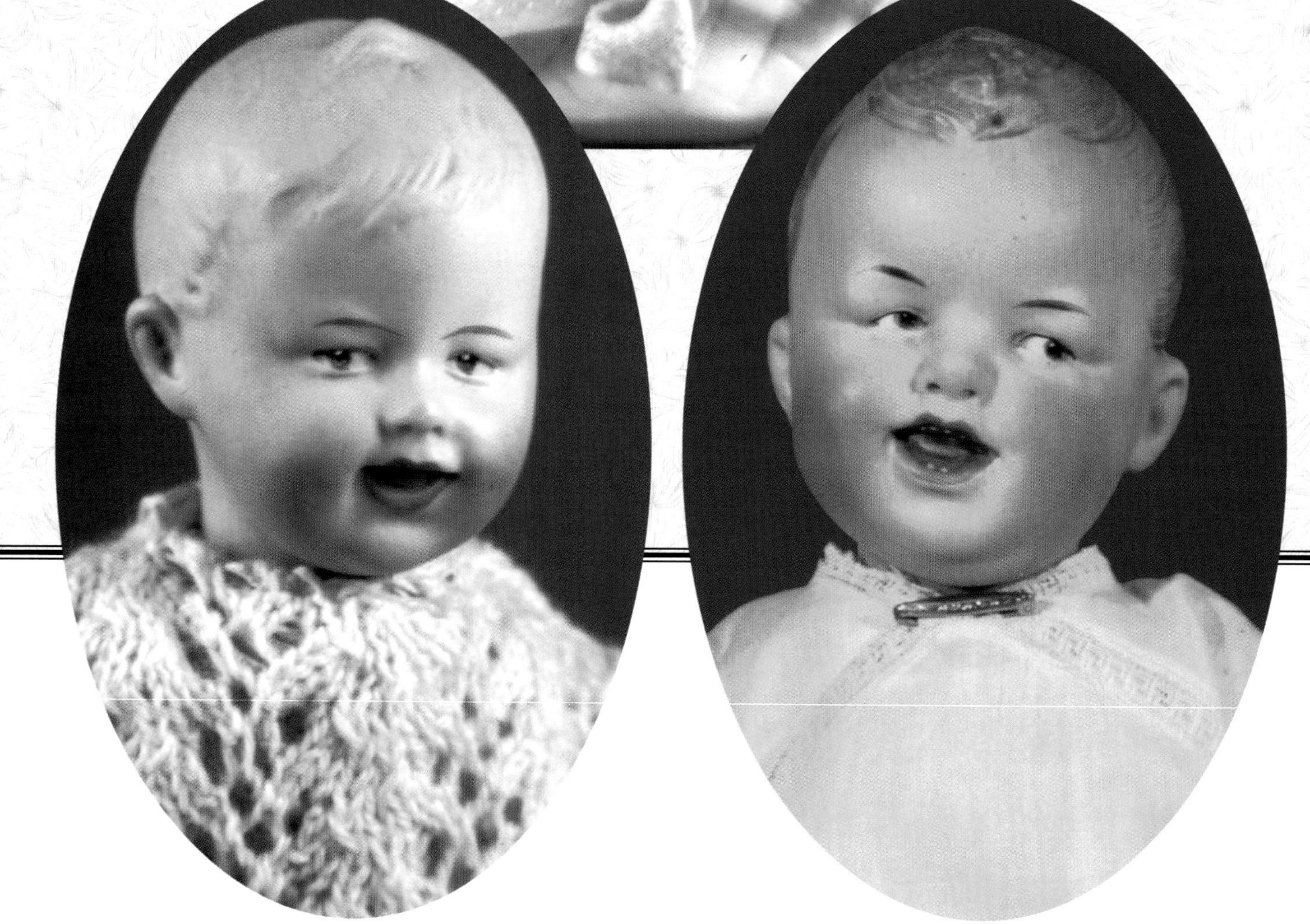

Left: A seldom seen 12-inch Heubach bisque shoulder head character doll, circa 1912, with intaglio eyes, an open/closed mouth with six teeth, and a molded hairstyle featuring coiled braids over each ear. The doll is marked: "0//78 (Heubach in a square) 52 //Germany." The doll's body is kid with bisque arms to the elbow. A hole in the bisque arm connects the arm to the body permitting the arm to bend.

A pair of 3-inch Heubach eggs featuring black and white baby faces and hands. The babies appear to "hatch" from the molded cracks in the surface of each egg.

molds using porcelain slip. In about 1870, a method was developed to add water to porcelain dough to make slip, which could be poured into a mold. The plaster mold absorbs the liquid from the porcelain slip, leaving the porcelain shell. When the molds are taken off, the unfired pieces are a grayish-green color, hence the name greenware. Greenware is still rather soft because the porcelain is not completely dry at this stage, and since it is yet to be fired in the kiln, the feldspar has not melded the ingredients together. Therefore, it must be handled with care. During this stage of production, the eye sockets and mouths are cut out. Sew holes as well as the ear holes are also created with a sharp tool. The porcelain pieces are allowed to dry completely and then fired in a kiln. The next step is called finishing. Workers clean up each piece, removing marks and blemishes as well as sharpening features. The sanding process is very important to the overall quality of each porcelain piece.

Painting each piece is the next step. On bisque and Parian-type doll heads, the last step is the kiln firing that sets the painted colors. On china doll heads, two more steps are necessary. China heads are glazed with a clear coating and then kiln fired a third time.

The Gebrüder Heubach porcelain factory is now the Lichte Porcelain GmbH, still producing porcelain after 178 years. The Heubach factory has gone through a number of changes in the last fifty years. After World War II, the factory was expropriated, and three years later it was nationalized and named VEB Porzellanwerk Lichte (VEB Porcelainwork Lichte), from 1954 to 1972. In 1972, the factory became the VEB Zierporzellanwerk Lichte (from 1972 to 1990). The German word "zier" means "ornamental." In 1994, the factory became the Lichte Porcelain Factory. During the many years of production, the Gebrüder Heubach porcelain factory has made a number of porcelain products in addition to dolls. The factory specialized in luxury items like figures, vases, chandeliers, candleholders and writing utensils. They also made religious items, tableware (including bowls and plates with paintings), and porcelain portraits made from photographs.

Right: A Gebrüder Heubach 6-inch animal-face doll with a catlike bisque socket head. The realistic modeling features green painted eyes and a large smiling mouth. The doll head, marked "KM//13/0," is mounted on a five-piece composition body. The doll is dressed in an original chemise.

Below: A Heubach "Dolly Dimple." The 12-1/2-inch character doll, circa 1912, is marked: "7307//7// (Heubach rising sun trademark) //DEP." The bisque socket head includes blue sleep eyes, multi-stroke eyebrows, an open/closed mouth with two upper teeth, and cheek dimples. The doll has a jointed composition body. *Jane Walker Collection.*

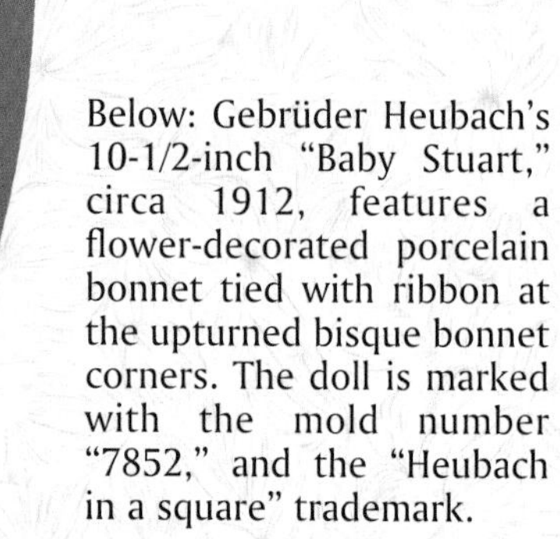

Below: Gebrüder Heubach's 10-1/2-inch "Baby Stuart," circa 1912, features a flower-decorated porcelain bonnet tied with ribbon at the upturned bisque bonnet corners. The doll is marked with the mold number "7852," and the "Heubach in a square" trademark.

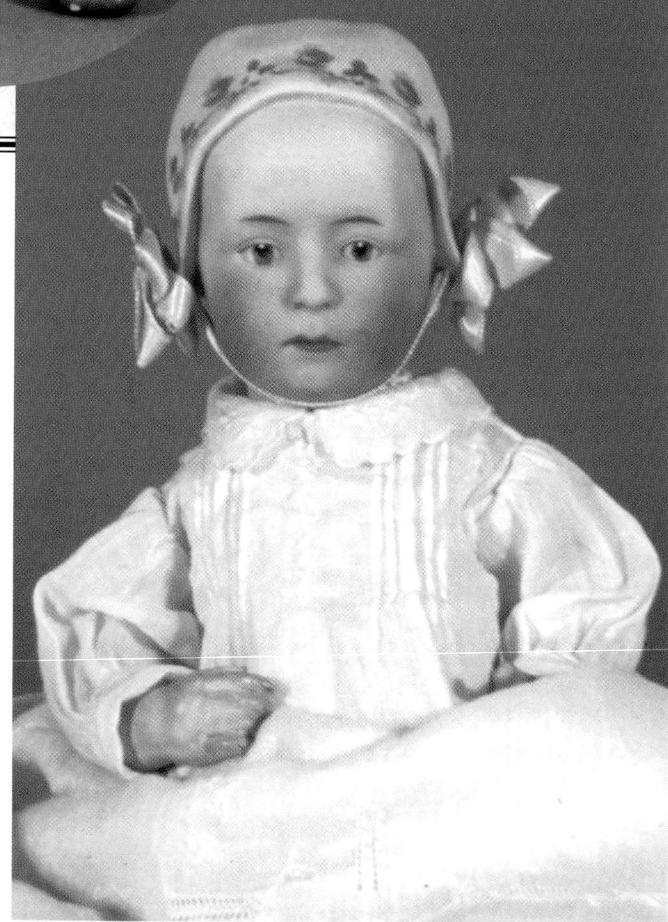

Chapter Thirteen

The Armand Marseille and Ernst Heubach Porcelain Factories

The Armand Marseille Villa, circa 1900, is partially hidden today by the overgrown trees and shrubs that were once part of a 10-acre horticultural haven in Köppelsdorf. The beautiful mansion is now in need of repair. It is hard to picture the days when Marseille walked across the street from his home to his porcelain factory.

Armand Marseille's early life is not well documented. The son of a famous architect at the Imperial Court of the Czar, Marseille was born in St. Petersburg, Russia in 1856. An article by Genevieve Angione in *Spinning Wheel's Complete Book of Dolls* provides additional information on Marseille. Angione quotes a Marseille employee who worked in a mold room at the Köppelsdorf porcelain factory.

The Armand Marseille villa in Köppelsdorf.

A 19-inch Armand Marseille bisque socket head doll marked: "971//A. 6. M. //DRGM 267" made from 1913 on. The doll head, with sleep eyes, multi-stroke eyebrows, and an open mouth with two upper teeth, is on a composition toddler body. *Jane Walker Collection.*

According to the employee, Marseille was a successful butcher before becoming a doll maker. The employee quoted in this article also stated that "His given name and that of his son and grandson was 'Herman.' The name 'Armand' was used only as a business identification." Unfortunately, the employee did not provide any information about his last name. Marseille was a Huguenot descendant, which could account for his "French-sounding" last name.

A 25th Anniversary Booklet produced by the Armand Marseille Company contains important historical information. In 1884, Armand Marseille bought the Mathias Lambert doll and toy factory in Sonneberg. Also in 1884, Marseille married the daughter of a Sonneberg couple named Sieder, and the following year, the Marseilles had a son. Armand bought the Köppelsdorf porcelain factory of Liebermann & Wegescher the same year (1885). After an 1887 lightning strike, Marseille was forced to rebuild his Köppelsdorf porcelain factory. By 1910, the porcelain factory employed 800 workers in the factory and in home trade together. The Anniversary Booklet also contains the statement: "The Armand Marseille factory was the absolutely largest union in the entire German toy industry."

The Marseille porcelain factory made doll heads for Louis Amberg & Sons, W. A. Cissna & Co., Max Handwerck, Maar & Son, Foulds & Freure, Cuno & Otto Dressel, C.M. Bergmann, Otto Gans, Wagner & Zetsche, A. Wislizenus, Butler Brothers, George Borgfeldt & Co., Louis Wolf & Co., E.U. Steiner, Koenig & Wernicke,

Left: This Marseille Googly character doll features a Mohawk hairstyle and a watermelon mouth. The 7-inch bisque socket head, marked: "320//A11/0M//Germany," is on a five-piece composition body with painted shoes and socks. The doll has intaglio side-glancing eyes with white highlights and single-stroke eyebrows. *Jane Walker Collection.*

Right: This original 9-inch Armand Marseille bisque socket head Indian doll, circa 1890's on, is marked: "Germany//7/0." The doll has stationary brown eyes, single-stroke scowling eyebrows, and a five-piece brown composition body.

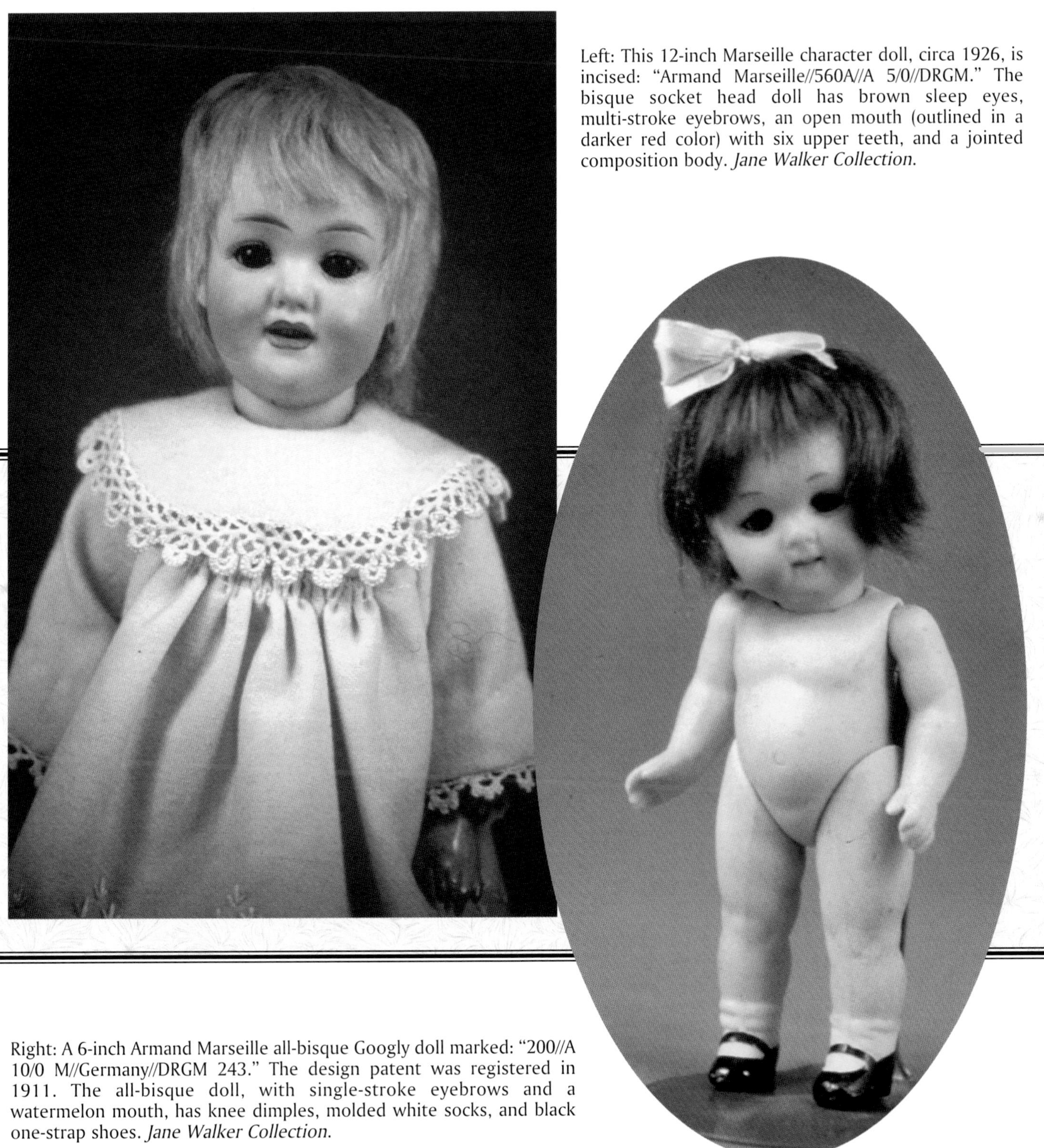

Left: This 12-inch Marseille character doll, circa 1926, is incised: "Armand Marseille//560A//A 5/0//DRGM." The bisque socket head doll has brown sleep eyes, multi-stroke eyebrows, an open mouth (outlined in a darker red color) with six upper teeth, and a jointed composition body. *Jane Walker Collection.*

Right: A 6-inch Armand Marseille all-bisque Googly doll marked: "200//A 10/0 M//Germany//DRGM 243." The design patent was registered in 1911. The all-bisque doll, with single-stroke eyebrows and a watermelon mouth, has knee dimples, molded white socks, and black one-strap shoes. *Jane Walker Collection.*

Gebrüder Echardt, B. Illfelder & Co., Hitz, Jacobs & Co., Arranbee Doll Company, Sears, Roebuck & Co., Montgomery Ward, Wanamakers, F.A.O. Schwarz, and many others.

American importers often called on Armand Marseille. The four largest New York importers sold Armand Marseille dolls. They are as follows: Louis Wolf, founded in 1870; Butler Brothers, founded in 1877; Louis Amberg, founded in 1878 and George Borgfeldt, founded in 1882. George Borgfeldt left the New York importers, Strasburger, Pfeiffer & Co. to found his own importing company.

Armand Marseille also produced doll heads using specific designs for a number of other American importers like Arranbee and Foulds & Freure. American department and toy store representatives were also well

A pair of Marseille bisque head babies. The 8-inch doll on the left, issued in 1914 and 1926, is a "New Born Babe" made for Louis Amberg and Sons. It has a flange neck, a cloth body, and composition hands. The 9-inch doll on the right is a "Dream Baby." Marseille made the #341, closed-mouth babies for the Arranbee New York Doll Company from 1925 on. The "Dream Baby" has a bent-limb composition baby body. In 1926, each of the dolls were dressed, wrapped in a blanket, and tied in a basket. They sold for less than a dollar (wholesale price).

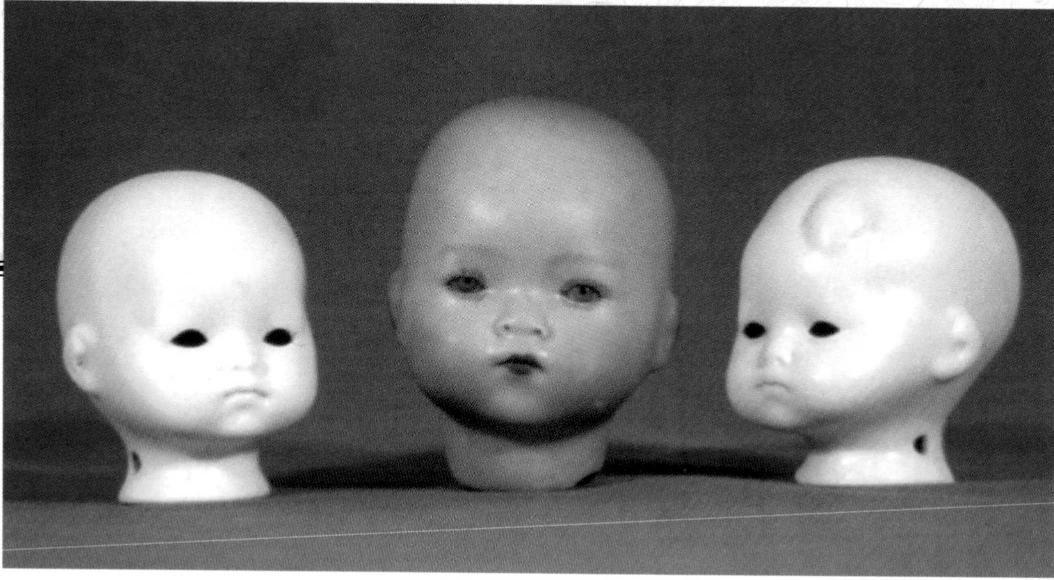

Three "Dream Baby" bisque dome-shaped heads. The 2-1/2-inch painted bisque socket head, marked "AM// Germany//341/4/0K," has blue sleep eyes and a closed mouth. The two unpainted examples, also marked "AM 341," have flange necks and measure 2 inches each. A firing bubble can be seen on the forehead of the doll on the right.

A pair of 11-1/2-inch Armand Marseille bisque socket head dolls marked: "251//G.B.//Germany//A.O. M. //D. R. M. R. 248//1." The 1912 era character heads, with single-stroke eyebrows and open/closed mouths featuring molded tongues, are on composition baby bodies. The dolls were made for the George Borgfeldt Company.

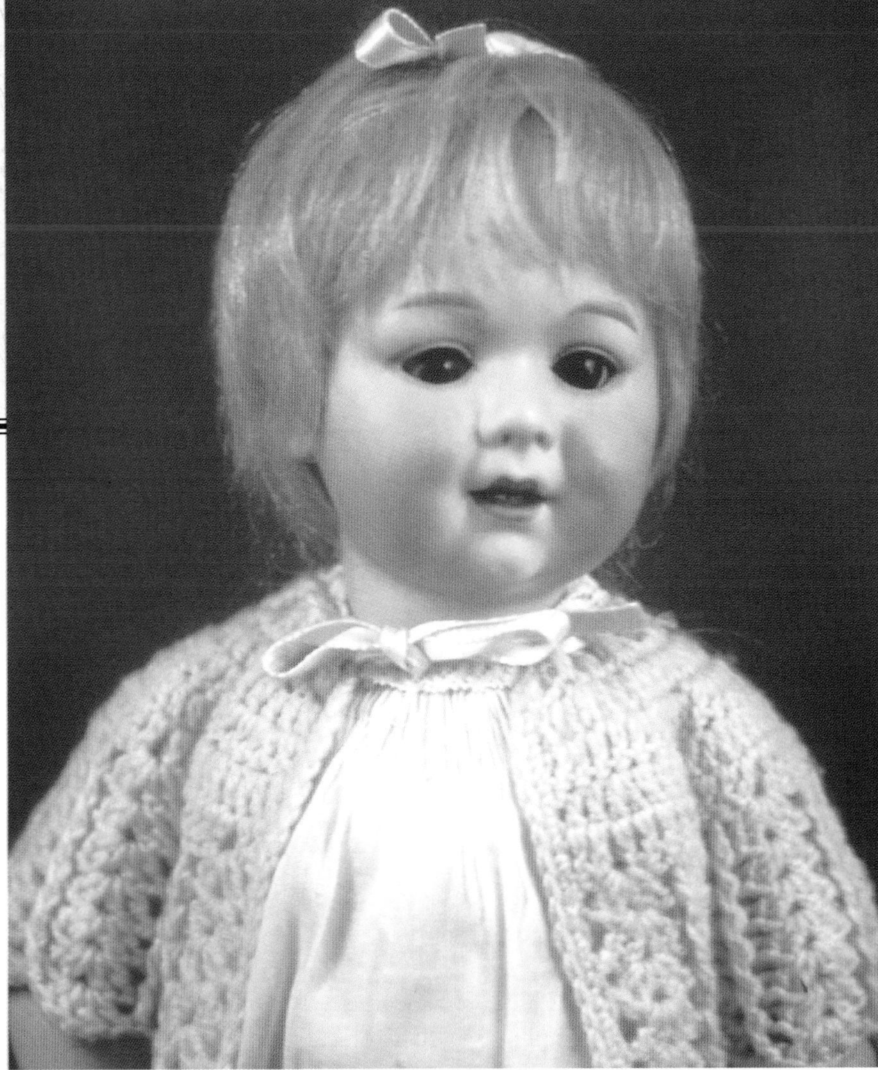

A 13-inch Armand Marseille character baby on a composition toddler body. It is marked: "Made in Germany//G327B//-DRGM-259//A.2/0 M." The doll, circa 1913, was made for the George Borgfeldt Company. It has brown sleep eyes, multi-stroke eyebrows, and an open mouth with two lower teeth. *Jane Walker Collection.*

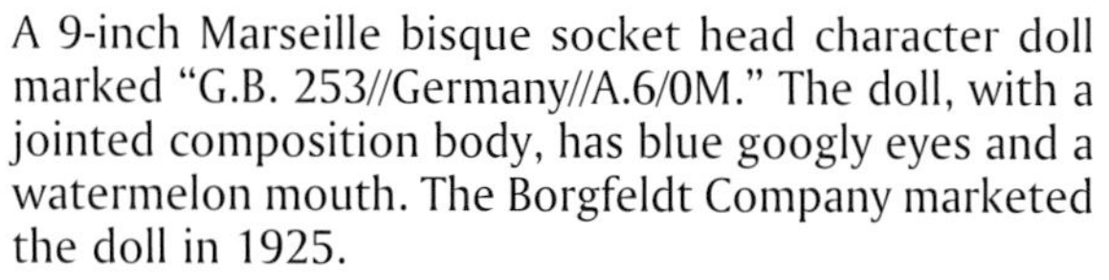

A 9-inch Marseille bisque socket head character doll marked "G.B. 253//Germany//A.6/0M." The doll, with a jointed composition body, has blue googly eyes and a watermelon mouth. The Borgfeldt Company marketed the doll in 1925.

A 12-inch Armand Marseille #253G.B. bisque head doll with large side-glancing googly eyes, a watermelon mouth, and a jointed composition baby body.

A 7-inch bisque socket head Marseille #253 Googly doll with side-glancing blue eyes, a watermelon mouth, and single-stroke eyebrows. The doll has a five- piece composition body that includes painted shoes and socks. The character doll, circa 1925 and in original clothing, was made for the Borgfeldt Company.

The "Nobbi Kid" bisque head is marked: "A.253 M. //Nobbi Kid//U.S. Pat. off. // Germany//10/0."

known in Sonneberg and Köppelsdorf. During the 1870's, American department stores began to add doll and toy departments. The well-known R.H. Macy department store in New York established a doll and toy department in 1875. Marshall Field added a doll and toy department in 1889. During this same time, the John Wanamaker and Woodward & Lothrop stores also sold dolls and toys.

According to the Coleman's research, before World War I, Gimbel Brothers, a New York and Philadelphia department store, placed an annual order of 2,000 dolls over which six or seven large German doll factories competed. These statements serve to explain the price difference from store to store concerning German dolls. For years, Thuringian doll factories made the same type of "dolly-face" doll. Doll factory owners tried to sell their dolls in many different markets, and bidding for an order was common. As each doll factory tried to out-bid the competition, the price would often go down depending upon the size of the order and the opportunity for repeat orders from the same buyer. Of course, the main reason Thuringian doll factories were able to offer their dolls at such low prices was the low wages paid to the home and factory workers in towns like Sonneberg and Waltershausen.

The most famous American retail toy store is F.A.O. Schwarz. It is still considered a child's paradise. It holds the title of the "first American toy store." A Schwarz catalog still carries the following statement: "F.A.O. Schwarz, Children's World, The World's Most Unique Toy Stores Since 1862." F.A.O. Schwarz sold Thuringian dolls

This 11-1/2-inch original Armand Marseille bisque socket head character doll, circa 1914, has a five-piece toddler composition body. It is marked: "Germany//323//A. 3/0 M." The doll has side-glancing eyes, single-stroke eyebrows, a closed mouth, and an original mohair wig.

The Armand Marseille porcelain and doll factory was one of the few Thuringian factories that made complete dolls. Women worked at home or in the factory sewing cloth doll bodies, doll clothes, and accessories. *Ana and Peter Kalinke Collection.*

This pair of unmarked bisque head dolls, measuring 5 and 5-3/4-inches, is similar to many dolls' house dolls featured on Marseille sample sheets. For many years, the A. M. factory sold large quantities of dolls' house dolls to the New York based F.A.O. Schwarz toy store. A 1913 Schwarz catalog advertisement read, "Dolls' house dolls for use in dolls' houses. We have a large variety of small dressed dolls, such as gentlemen and ladies in different costumes. Maids, nurses, waiters, butlers, cooks, etc. The dolls measure five to seven inches, and range in price from 50¢ to $1.50."

Below: A 14-inch original A.M. doll with stationary brown eyes, single-stroke eyebrows, and an open mouth with upper teeth. It is marked: "1894//AM 2/0 DEP//Made in Germany." The doll matches a promotional doll featured on the back of a 1908 edition of the *Brown Book of Boston*. The doll, circa 1894 on, was awarded to each person that sold 15 packages of Smell-Sweet perfume tablets.

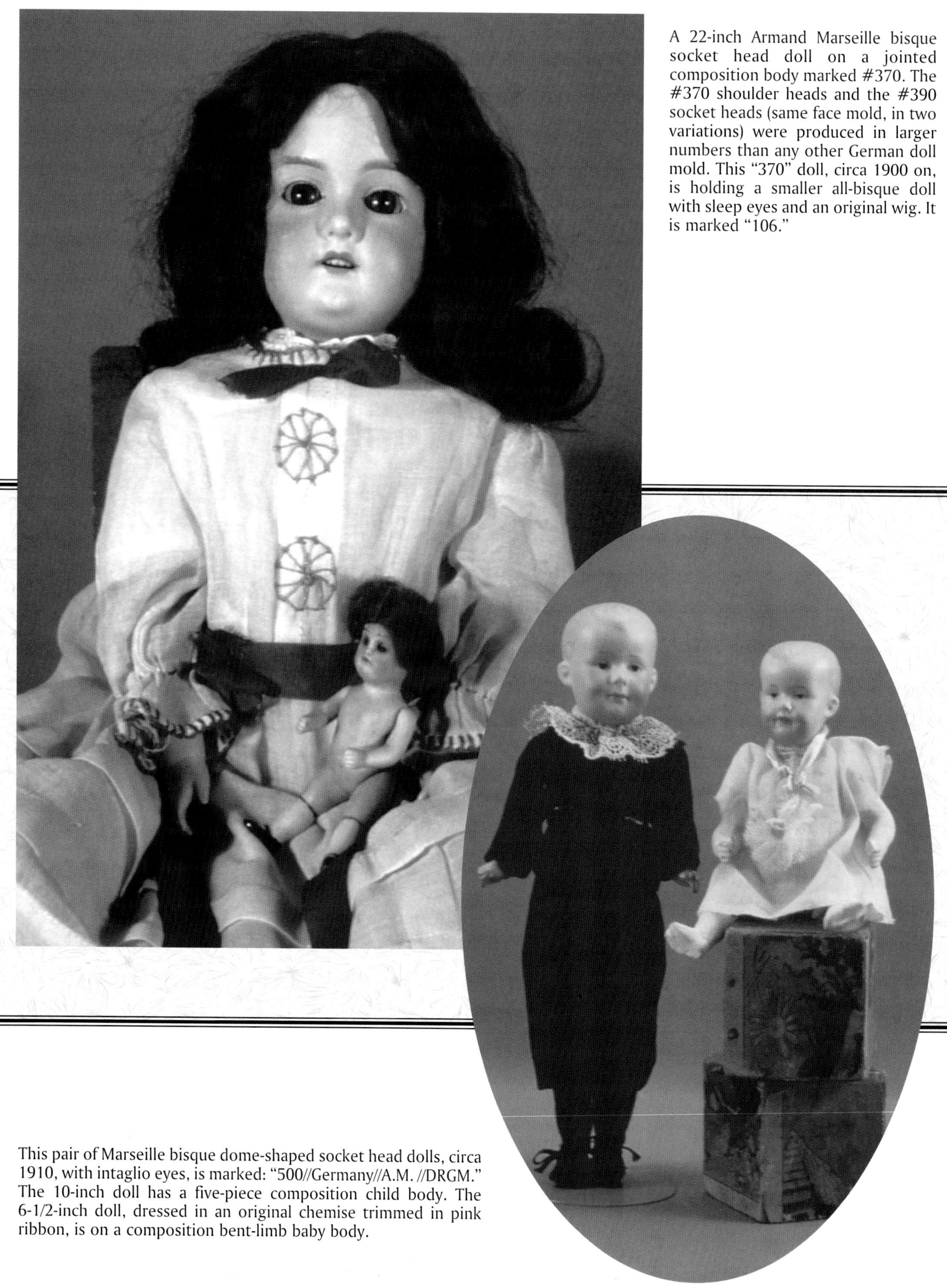

A 22-inch Armand Marseille bisque socket head doll on a jointed composition body marked #370. The #370 shoulder heads and the #390 socket heads (same face mold, in two variations) were produced in larger numbers than any other German doll mold. This "370" doll, circa 1900 on, is holding a smaller all-bisque doll with sleep eyes and an original wig. It is marked "106."

This pair of Marseille bisque dome-shaped socket head dolls, circa 1910, with intaglio eyes, is marked: "500//Germany//A.M. //DRGM." The 10-inch doll has a five-piece composition child body. The 6-1/2-inch doll, dressed in an original chemise trimmed in pink ribbon, is on a composition bent-limb baby body.

Right: A 10-inch #500 A.M. doll on an original Neustadt five-piece composition body. The unpainted socks are indicated on the lower legs with deeply scored multiple lines. The molded shoes feature high heels.

and toys beginning in the 1860's. A Sonneberger by the name of Ernst Thauer was associated with the Schwarz store for many years. Ernst Thauer was born in Sonneberg in 1903. He started working for the toy store in the 1920's. In 1955, as vice-president, he was responsible for all toy purchases, and in 1970, Thauer became president of the company.

A number of A.M. dolls were sold as promotional dolls. A good example of a promotional doll is the A.M. doll that accompanied the 1908 edition of *The Brown Book of Boston*. The A.M. doll is pictured on the back of *The Brown Book*. The ad states:

> Girls. You can obtain one of these pretty dollies absolutely free without any charge to you. It will be your last chance, for we cannot obtain any more like them, and the thousands of girls who have received them are all delighted and wonder how we can afford to give such a handsome doll for so little service.
>
> The doll is nearly a foot and a half tall, has long curly hair and moving bisque head, lovely white teeth, sleeping eyes; hat, shoes, stockings, underwear, etc.; completely dressed from hat to shoes. It is jointed at the knees, body and elbows, and you can move the limbs and head in any direction. It is one of the most beautiful dolls ever given as a premium. Remember we give this beautiful sleeping doll if you will sell for us 15 packages of Smell-Sweet Perfume Tablets, at 10¢ per package. Remember we trust you. Send your full name and correct address and we will send you 15 packages by return mail, at our expense; when sold, send us a money order for $1.50 and we will send the doll to you free of cost, and, if it is not as represented, we will make you a present of the $1.50. Will any other firm do this? Write today. Address your letter this way: Smell-Sweet Perfume Co. 100 and 102 Broad Street, Boston, Mass.

Right: This 14-inch A.M. doll, circa 1910, is marked: "500//Germany//A2M//DRGM." The bisque head features molded hair, blue intaglio eyes, a closed mouth, single-stroke eyebrows, and cheek and chin dimples. The doll has a jointed composition body. *Jane Walker Collection.*

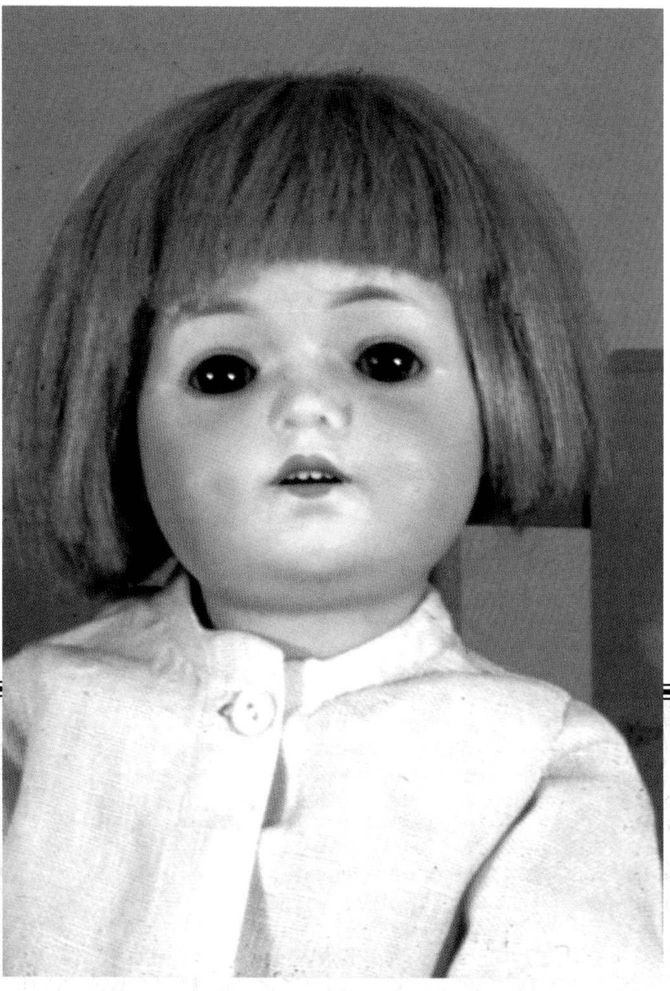

An 18-inch Ernst Heubach character doll marked: "(Heubach trademark horseshoe)//256//2." The dimpled bisque socket head doll has brown sleep eyes, multi-stroke eyebrows, an open mouth with upper teeth, and a jointed composition body. The doll, circa 1920, was made for E. Maar & Son, a doll factory located in Mönchröden near Coburg.

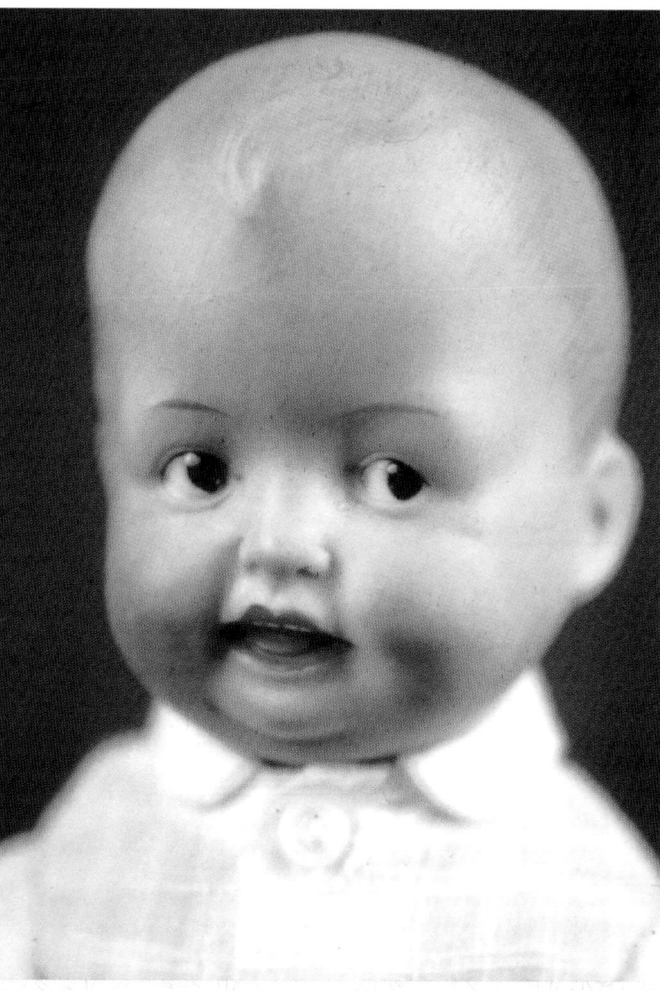

An Ernst Heubach character doll incised: "260-14/0//E.H.Germany//DRGM." The 11-inch doll, circa 1914, has molded hair, side-glancing intaglio eyes, single-stroke eyebrows, and an open mouth with four square upper teeth. It has a kid body with bisque lower arms. *Jane Walker Collection.*

A group of Ernst Heubach bisque socket head character dolls, circa 1920, on five-piece composition baby bodies. The heads are marked: "Heubach Köppelsdorf//300-4/0//Germany." The dolls, ranging in size from 7-1/2 to 13 inches, each have multi-stroke eyebrows, sleep eyes, cheek dimples, and open mouths with two upper teeth.

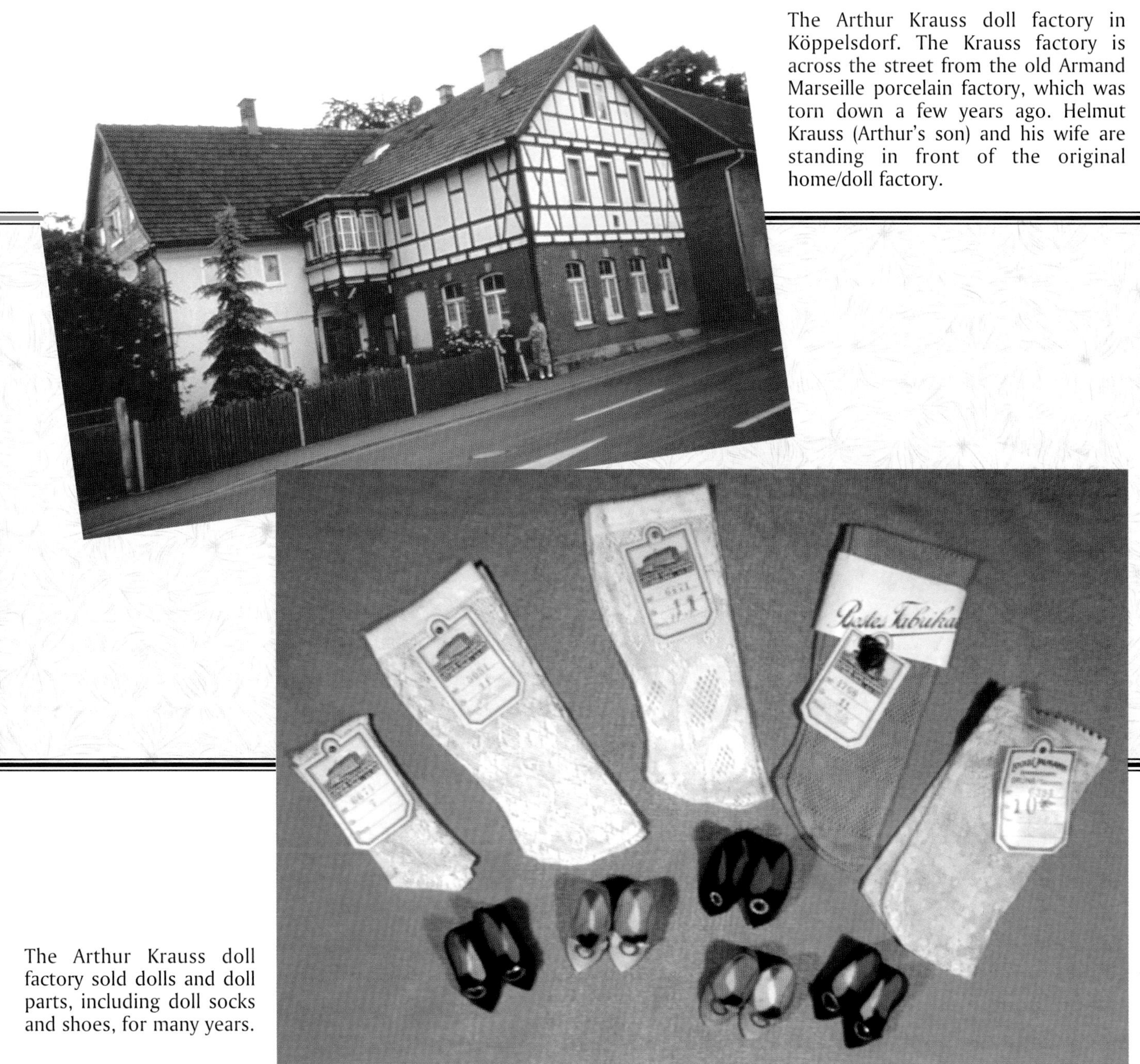

The Arthur Krauss doll factory in Köppelsdorf. The Krauss factory is across the street from the old Armand Marseille porcelain factory, which was torn down a few years ago. Helmut Krauss (Arthur's son) and his wife are standing in front of the original home/doll factory.

The Arthur Krauss doll factory sold dolls and doll parts, including doll socks and shoes, for many years.

The Arthur Krauss doll factory and exporter of dolls was founded in Köppelsdorf in 1919. The old doll factory is still part of the Krauss home. A visit to the original Krauss home/factory helps a doll researcher understand the work carried out in a typical Thuringian doll factory. The doll factory is located directly across the street from the former Armand Marseille porcelain factory. Krauss only had to walk a few steps to pick up doll heads at the A.M. factory. A study of three original ledger books provides information concerning the dolls made by the Krauss doll factory.

Two Krauss ledger books are dated 1925 and 1928, and the third book is dated 1930 through December 31, 1942. The beautiful handwritten entries describe the daily transactions of the Krauss doll factory. One entry in the ledger book tells how Arthur Krauss picked up an order of doll heads at the Marseille factory on December 15, 1934. The heads were used on dolls made for Martin Eichhorn doll factory. Krauss also used Ernst Heubach heads on his finished dolls, according to entries in the 1925 ledger book.

It is only through the study of these three ledger books that cover 17 years of Krauss doll making, that one is able to truly understand doll making in the Sonneberg area. The bookkeeper's handwriting is so clear and precise that it is hard to believe the first book was begun 75 years ago. One book is an accounting book for petty cash. Expenses were listed for the following:

The "Handarbeit" (work made by hand); Linens; Postage; P.O. Box; To the Boss himself; Freight letters; Telephone; Salary and Materials. Accounts payable were Welsch & Co.; Goebel Brothers; To the Bank; To Ernst Ulrich and Danzig (Gdansk, Poland).

An original Arthur Krauss catalog described the "specialties" as: Dressed and undressed dolls; doll house dolls; woolen animals; dressed babies in undershirts; building block sets; babies with clockwork eyes; celluloid and porcelain dolls with moving arms and heads; fabric and leather bodies. Doll parts included: heads made from porcelain, celluloid and papier-mâché; as well as arms, legs, bodies, hands, hairdos, shoes, stockings, underwear, dresses and hats. Items listed for doll hospitals included: rubber cords in all sizes, head spirals, hooks and eyes, celluloid material and make-up, paint, lacquer, eye paint, wooden cranks, loose non-movable eyes, constructions for sleep eyes and eyelashes. Krauss also listed the name of his Sonneberg bank, his Leipzig Fair address and telephone number, as well as his Sonneberg telephone number (648) on one company letterhead. Unfortunately, so much of the original paper relating to German doll making has been destroyed. The archives in museums like the Sonneberg and Waltershausen doll museums will soon be our only sources of original information relating to the old Thuringian doll and porcelain factories.

Left: This original 10-inch Ernst Heubach bisque head character doll, circa 1920, has pierced nostrils. Thuringian doll factories introduced doll lines yearly, which included new, patented features, in order to sell more dolls. The doll head with blue sleep eyes, multi-stroke eyebrows, an open mouth with four upper teeth, and a chin dimple is marked: "Heubach Köppelsdorf//320-12/0//Germany."

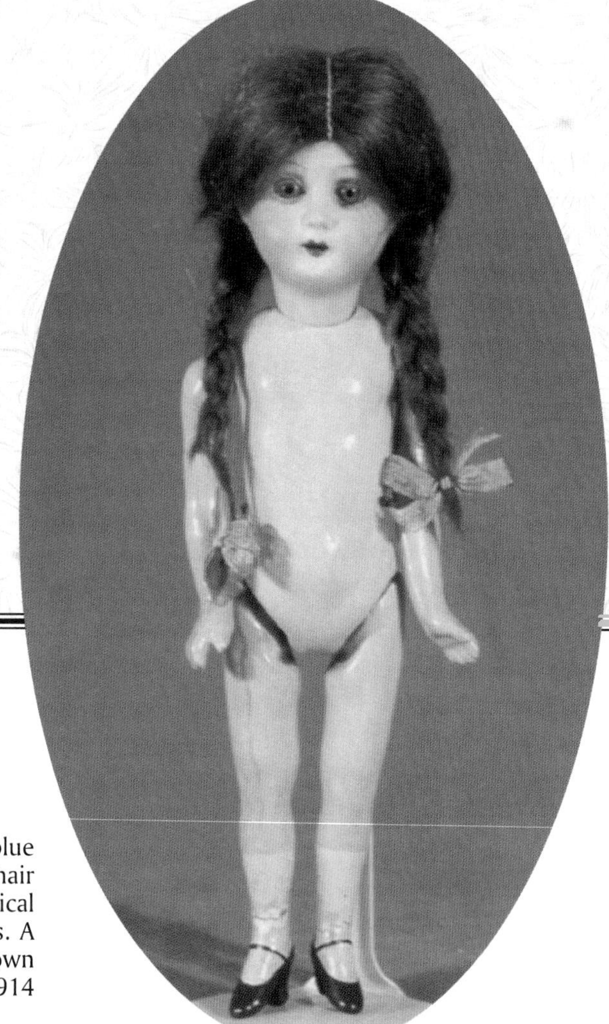

This 8-inch Ernst Heubach "dolly-face" doll has single-stroke eyebrows, blue sleep eyes, an open mouth with four upper teeth, and an original mohair wig. It is marked: "Heubach Köppelsdorf//250-16/0//Germany." Identical bisque heads were often used on a variety of composition body types. A teenage five-piece composition body has white painted socks and brown high-heeled one-strap shoes. The #250 mold number was made from 1914 on.

Chapter Fourteen

The Martin Eichhorn Doll Factory

The Martin Eichhorn doll factory is typical of the hundreds of smaller doll factories that made doll parts and assembled dolls on the majority of streets in Sonneberg. We know so little about doll factories like the Martin Eichhorn factory. The Eichhorn name does not appear, as far as we know, on the back of a doll's head, a doll body, or even a cardboard box. However, the Eichhorn factory assembled dolls in Sonneberg for almost 50 years, and therefore, was a part of the overall picture of German doll making. The "bit players" are just as important as the "major players," as far as the study of Thuringian dolls.

Very little information concerning doll making came out of East Germany for so many years following World War II. Authors Maggie Rogers and Judith Hawkins provide graphic descriptions of the Sonneberg area in the decades following 1945 in their book, *The Glass Christmas Tree Ornament, Old & New.* The authors of the book state, "Central Europe emerged from the war totally devastated. The Potsdam Agreement following the surrender of Germany in 1945 neatly split the Thuringian area in half. Lauscha, Steinheid and Sonneberg fell into the Eastern Democratic Republic, controlled by the Russians; Coburg (annexed to Bavaria in 1923) and Neustadt became a part of the Western Federal Republic, governed by the three Western Allies (United States, France and England)."

The town of Neustadt is 1.65 miles from Sonneberg. Authors Rogers and Hawkins accurately describe the barriers that existed between the two towns in the following way:

> A visitor to Neustadt today (1977) can look from a second story window and see both Sonneberg and Lauscha in the distance, hamlets nestled in the green Thuringian hills. Seemingly only a 'stone's throw' away, formidable obstacles stand between East and West Germany.

The Martin Eichhorn doll factory in Sonneberg.

At the border (Sonneberg) is a complex barrier that deters even the strong-hearted. A strip of grass, heavily impregnated with land mines, lies behind the first fence at the edge of the Western zone. A tall wall of wooden posts demarks the next obstacle of guard dogs leashed onto long lines, but capable of moving about freely to patrol the grounds.

Yet another high fence and minefield looms behind; in the background is a large out-post structure with soldiers keeping watch from the tower. Any person approaching the border is automatically photographed with a telephoto lens, and should any untoward activity occur at the first barrier, it will bring forth a large armored tank whose gun turret will fasten on the offender almost immediately.

The line that separated East Germany from West Germany twisted and turned in many directions. The area below Sonneberg, including Oberlind and Neuhaus, was in East Germany while the towns of Oeslaw, Creidlitz, Kronach and Gundelsdorf were in West Germany. The entire "Northern Doll Making Circle," including the towns of Ilmenau, Gräfenhain, Ohrdruf, Waltershausen and Gotha, was in East Germany.

November 12, 1989 was a memorable day in Sonneberg because the former East German border was opened. Then on July 1, 1990, the interior minister of

A Thuringian border guard tower.

The view from the border tower of the strip of cleared ground that once separated former East Germany from West Germany.

A group of original 3-inch all-bisque dolls with jointed arms and dressed in original regional clothing. The attention to detail is apparent even on dolls that once sold for pennies.

West Germany and the German Democratic Republic official signed a contract to abolish "checkpoints" at the old "Soviet Zone of Occupation." Finally, on September 28, 1991, Sonnebergers were overjoyed when an old steam engine pulled the "Jubilee Train" over the newly reconnected tracks to Coburg.

The last decade has been a decade of major change in Sonneberg. This picturesque valley town has "come alive" again. The restoration, remodeling and repainting of the majority of buildings in Sonneberg is a joy to behold. However, Sonneberg is still a work in progress as a few old buildings are torn down and new, modern buildings are built.

Fortunately for doll collectors all over the world, Hanns Schoenau described and pictured a number of the old doll factories, as well as the owner's homes, in his book *Spurensuche in Sonneberg* (*Looking for Traces in Sonneberg*). Schoenau has been the official doll historian of Sonneberg for many years. The Schoenau family's doll factory was known as the Arthur Schoenau doll factory in Sonneberg since 1884. In 1901, Sonneberg residents Arthur Schoenau and Carl Hoffmeister founded the Schoenau & Hoffmeister porcelain factory in Burggrub. Because of Hanns Schoenau, doll historians and collectors can walk the streets of Sonneberg today and learn about German doll making in a very graphic way. The Martin Eichhorn doll factory is described and pictured in Schoenau's book. It is located at Number 29 Juttastrasse. When one stands in front of the beautifully restored Eichhorn doll factory, it is easy to imagine the days when this factory was an integral part of Sonneberg doll making.

The stories Angelika Tessmer included in her book, titled *Sonneberger Geschichten, Von Puppen, Giffeln and Kuckuckspeifen* (*Sonneberg Stories of Dolls, Slate Pencils and Cuckoo Whistles, From the Workaday World of Our Parents*), are told as remembered by the children and grandchildren of original Sonneberg area home workers. This oral history book paints a graphic picture of the "real" story of German doll making. Through these oral histories, one can learn important details about the home workers and the doll factories for which they made dolls and doll parts.

One Sonneberg resident described the process of making "cardboard lids" that closed doll heads before the wigs were added. The large sheets of cardboard were softened in water and then "sprinkled" with talcum powder, which made the cardboard "elastic" and able to be shaped. This particular story included the following details relating to papier-mâché production in the 1930's:

> In a large press, my grandparents fastened the upper and lower molds, which had the shapes of the arms, leg, head and body halves. On the mold's upper portion was an iron punch. So, in one workshop the halves could be shaped and cut out. The sections were then sorted and dried before my grandfather fit the two halves together with the fastening machine.
>
> So that the seams were not later visible, the joining places had to be glued over with paper strips. For certain dolls, my grandparents even made a paste of chalk and glue, which they smeared on and smoothed out these seams and cracks. Once again, the pieces had to dry out before being worked further. In the

Left: This 12-1/2inch Theodor Hornlein original bisque head character doll, circa 1910, features painted intaglio eyes, an open/closed mouth with painted teeth, and dimples. The Hornlein doll has a jointed composition body similar to bodies made by hundreds of Sonneberg home workers. An identical doll was purchased at a F.A.O. Schwarz toy store in 1915. The doll head is marked: "DEP//T.H.//Germany." *Mary Beard Collection.*

Above: An original 1890's stereoptic card picturing dolls being dressed in Sonneberg. The name on the company sign that is hanging on the wall is J. Franz & Co. The card caption reads, "Women dressing dolls in Sonneberg. Dolls' clothes are so small that many dresses are made by hand. That is what these women pictured are doing."

An original "Druckstimme" (squeeze voice) doll. The unmarked clown from the 1920's has a white bisque face featuring clown face painting, a blue molded cap with a wool pom-pom, and mushroom-like ears. The wooden body has turned wooden limbs. When the bellows mechanism is pressed, the cymbals come together. The Gottlieb Zinner and Söhne doll factory in Schalkau sold the doll originally. The Zinner doll factory was considered the best in the world in mechanical dolls and toys, which were often mistaken for French products. Clown dolls were often used as mechanical toys.

Left: This 7-inch dolls' house doll in original clothing is dressed to represent a German officer. An identical doll was sold at a New York toy store in 1892. The doll has a bisque shoulder head, a closed mouth, a cloth body with bisque arms and molded, painted hair. The original felt uniform is trimmed in intricate, embossed metallic paper. A lead sword and coat of arms hang from the doll's waist. The original price of the doll was 48¢.

A group of dressed dolls attached to original pieces of decorated cardboard. Children often made wigs and clothing for small, inexpensive dolls. The 4-1/2 inch doll, dressed in a red felt coat, is wearing a blue checked cotton dress trimmed in lace, which matches the dresses on the 3-inch dolls. The smallest scraps of material were utilized for dresses on all-bisque dolls.

> next step, they received color and sheen by a bath in skin-colored lacquer.
>
> So that the pieces did not now stick together, they had to be carefully placed on planks with pegs. That was most often my job. My uncle brought the planks into the drying room, on whose ceiling there were many hooks. Sorting of the halves and packing of the finished pieces for delivery was typical work the children did after school.

Fortunately, the Sonneberg oral history book provides an insight into the role the Martin Eichhorn doll factory played in Sonneberg doll making as well. A granddaughter of a Neufang voice maker states, "Every Saturday we made deliveries in a large back basket ("Schanzen") to the Martin Eichhorn, Leven, Kalbitz and Federvogt Companies." Martin Eichhorn must have used a large number of voice boxes in the dolls he assembled to warrant a delivery every Saturday.

From the *German Doll Encyclopedia*, as well as from the Arthur Krauss doll factory ledgers, we learn even more about the Martin Eichhorn doll factory. Eichhorn is listed as an exporter from 1889 to the 1930's. According to the Ciesliks, "His first order for 1000 stiff jointed dolls (in 1889) was placed by Fred Kolb, agent for George Borgfeldt of New York. Eichhorn's wife designed and sewed the doll outfits for the doll factory." The Sonneberg oral history book provides facts about the doll accessories made for assembly factories such as the Eichhorn doll factory. One such story is told by the daughter of a shoemaker who describes the process as follows:

> My father pounded the shoe soles out with a stamping iron and a large wooden hammer. The upper shoe parts were finished by the women and us children from paper and oilcloth. During WWI, we even turned to wallpaper scraps from the painter because the material became so scarce. My mother sewed the upper parts on the sewing machine and glued them over wooden lasts to the soles.

The home workers' jobs were very specialized. The tress makers made hair strands and the braid makers made braids for the wig makers. One child's story is especially poignant:

> As the youngest of seven daughters, I was born in Neufang in 1914. Two of my sisters already died in childhood. I cannot remember my father at all; he fell in 1916 in WWI. Our six-person family lived in our own house in only two rooms, a living room/kitchen in which the home industry was done, and a bedroom for everyone. Of necessity, the other rooms were rented out. My mother worked at home as a braid maker for the Breitung doll factory in Sonneberg. Already at age five, I began to learn tress making from my older sisters. My mother was against it, that I would start to help at such an early age. Secretly I practiced when my mother and older sisters were in the woods gathering the winter supply of wood to burn. As I demonstrated my ability, my mother was greatly impressed by my zeal, and from them on, I was allowed to help.

The study of German doll making is complicated because a few porcelain factories made complete dolls, with the help of home workers. But as a rule, porcelain factories sold doll heads, rather than complete dolls, and the hundreds of small doll factories in Sonneberg bought doll heads from a number of porcelain factories located in every part of Thuringia. Because the majority of smaller factories did not mark their dolls, we often assume that the porcelain factory mark on the back of the head must be the "maker" of the doll. This assumption is often incorrect. A more accurate way to identify a doll is to combine the names of the porcelain and the doll factories. For example, the 1896 bisque head doll, "Uncle Sam," is a product of the Simon & Halbig porcelain factory and the Dressel doll factory. "Uncle Sam" should be identified as a Simon & Halbig/Dressel doll.

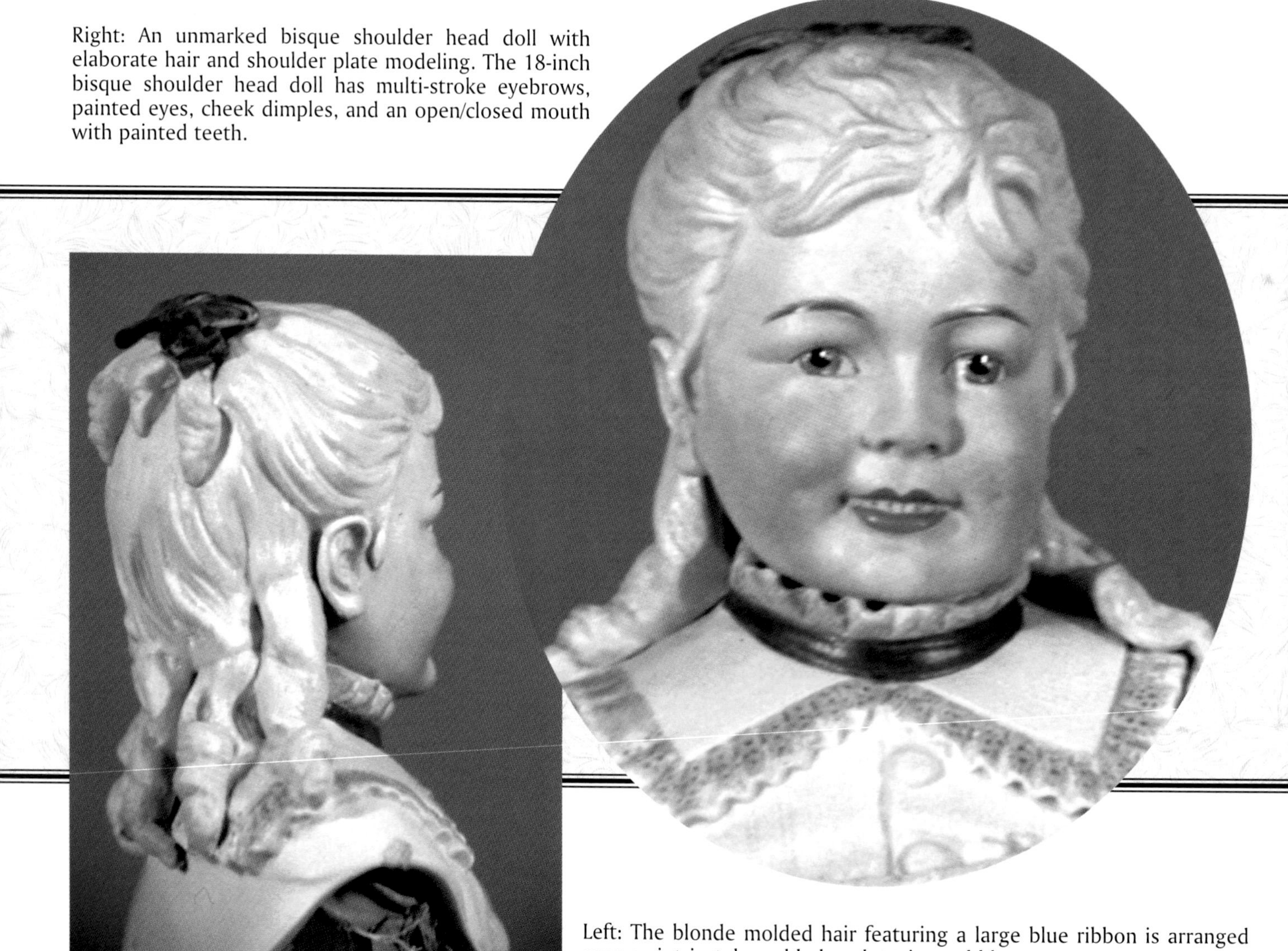

Right: An unmarked bisque shoulder head doll with elaborate hair and shoulder plate modeling. The 18-inch bisque shoulder head doll has multi-stroke eyebrows, painted eyes, cheek dimples, and an open/closed mouth with painted teeth.

Left: The blonde molded hair featuring a large blue ribbon is arranged over an intricately molded eyelet-trimmed blouse.

Chapter Fifteen

Doll Making in Waltershausen

Waltershausen is the center or "hub" of the Northern Doll Making Circle. Sonneberg and Waltershausen are similar in many ways including early town history as well as the history of doll making. Waltershausen, with approximately 17,000 residents today, is about half the size of Sonneberg. Waltershausen is located on the northwest border of the Thuringian Forest. The first documentary evidence of the town is from 1209, but the name "Waltershausen" dates back to the 7th century. A settler named "Walther" built a house at the foot of Burgberg (Castle Mountain).

By the 1200's, about 2000 people lived in Waltershausen, and it had "city" and "market" rights. A city wall with gates and towers enclosed the market area. Farming was the first activity in Waltershausen, but as mentioned in the beginning of this book, the industrious Germans began carving articles from wood during the long harsh winters Soon, the reigning duke conferred beer brewing privileges to several townspeople. By the 19th Century, Waltershausen had become a "booming industrial city" according to the tourist information office.

A typical street scene in Waltershausen.

Right: Clock towers mark the passage of time in the town of about 17,000 residents.

The town is known worldwide for the production of "Cervelatwurst" (salami sausage). Other industries include alabaster finishing, hose and belt "weaving," as well as pipe and clay manufacturing. Today, vehicles, rubber, and jewelry are manufactured in Waltershausen. The town developed slowly over the course of 775 years, and suffered greatly due to a number of devastating fires. A few historical buildings provide a link to the past. The Town Hall, built in 1441, is the oldest half-timbered town hall in Thuringia.

The Castle (Schloss) Tenneberg is of special interest to doll collectors because it serves as a doll museum, exhibiting wonderful examples of dolls, mainly from the Northern Circle of doll making. This castle dominated the Burgberg (Castle Mountain). Both "Schloss" and "Burg" loosely translate to the word "castle." The castle is named after the spruces, called Tannen, that covered the mountain in early years. This imposing Waltershausen castle was built in 518 AD by a Thuringian king, named Baldrich, who lived there for a time. The castle was never conquered according to local history. Later, the castle became the property of various dukes of Thuringia. Duke Balthasar had the walls of the first structure torn down and then had a new castle built in 1391. Through the years, it served as a country court, a hunting castle, and as the home of a widowed duchess. It was remodeled from 1714 until 1729, and the local heritage museum has been using the space since 1929.

By studying the commercial register listings in the *German Doll Encyclopedia* for of the period from 1800 to 1939, we learn that there were once 47 doll factories in Waltershausen. Some were listed for only one year while others were much more important to the history of German doll making. There were no porcelain factories listed in Waltershausen, only doll factories. Fortunately for doll collectors, the Ciesliks provided a walking tour of

Above: The Tenneberg Castle dominates Burgberg hill. The castle was mentioned in town records as early as 1176. The building has been used as a local heritage museum since 1929. Today, doll collectors delight in viewing the fine doll collection on permanent display in the historic old building.

The old Klaustor gate located in the center of town.

Right: An original photograph of a Thuringian doll factory. A large papier-mâché press once used to make dolls and doll parts is located in the left corner. *Ana and Peter Kalinke Collection.*

Eighteen old doll factories have been identified in Waltershausen. The Koenig & Wernicke doll factory, founded in 1912, was once filled with workers assembling dolls.

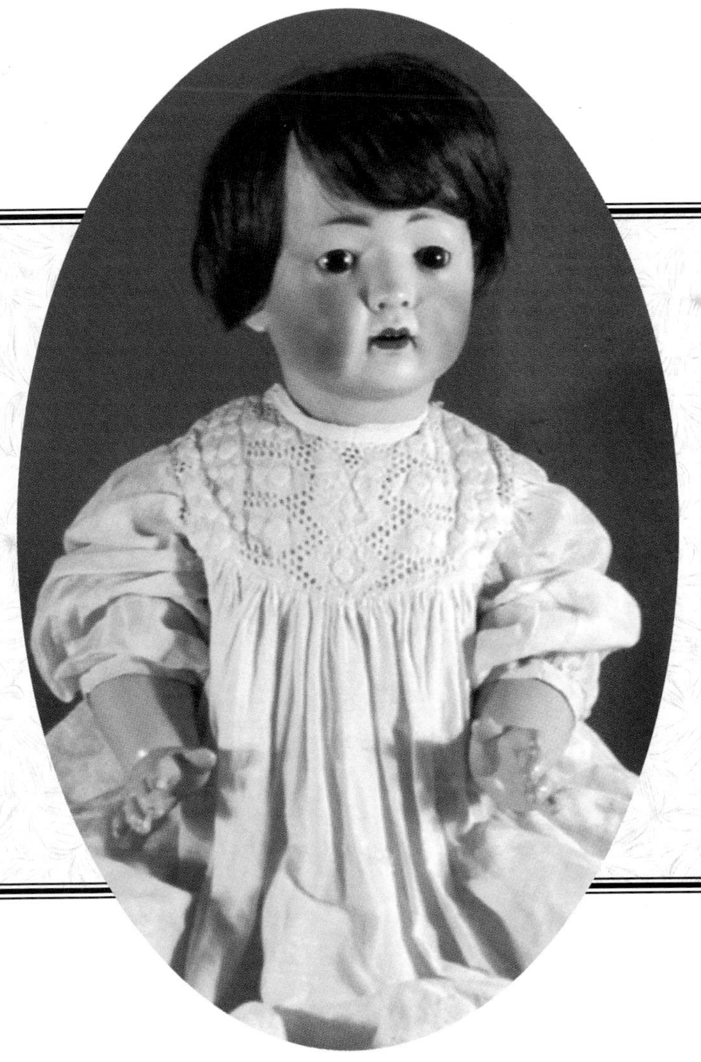

The name of the doll factory is slightly visible today. Every year, more traces of Thuringian doll making disappear from the scene.

This 24-inch bisque socket head character doll, circa 1915, is marked: "K. & W. //13." The head, with sleep eyes and painted lower eyelashes (only), features multi-stroke eyebrows and an open mouth with two upper teeth. The large bent-limb baby body is unmarked. The Baehr & Proeschild, Hertel, Schwab & Co., and the Armand Marseille porcelain factories made Koenig Wernicke bisque heads.

Waltershausen in the February issue of their 1996 *Puppenmagazin*. The 18 doll factories still standing in Waltershausen were pictured and described. The Waltershausen walking tour was also included in the 1999 Cieslik book *German Doll Studies*, which features articles from past issues of their *Puppenmagazin* translated into English. The Ciesliks credit Thomas Reinecke, curator of the Schloss Tenneberg Museum, for his help in locating the old doll factories. One such factory featured was the second home of the Kämmer & Reinhardt doll factory. It is pictured as the 1907 large brick factory that served as the second and main assembly factory for so many years. This factory is now protected by the Waltershausen Historical Trust, and hopefully, will not be torn down in the future. The Waltershausen doll factories located and pictured on the Cieslik tour include: C. M. Bergmann, Rudolf Eckold, Otto Gans, Heinrich Handwerck (factory torn down several years ago), Max Handwerck, Adolf Heller, Adolf Hulss, Bruno Schmidt, Gustav Thiele, Koenig & Wernicke, Schneegass & Söhne, Max Rudolph, Gustav Gessert, Hugo Wiegand, Seyfahrt & Reinhardt, Adolf Wislizenus, Kämmer & Reinhardt and J.D. Kestner, Jr.

"Around 1900, approximately 1,000 to 1,500 people worked in the doll industry of Waltershausen," according to the Ciesliks. "Together with the home-workers the number of people employed by the doll industry during the mid-twenties is estimated to have been between 3,000 to 4,000." This number does not compare with the 35,000 residents from Sonneberg making dolls and toys in 1896 as recorded by a German government survey.

The Adolf Wislizenus doll factory in Waltershausen. Gottlob Schafft founded the doll factory in 1851. In 1870, Wislizenus was either Schafft's partner or owner of the factory. Wislizenus is listed as the sole owner in 1878. The A.W. doll factory was the second doll factory in Waltershausen, founded 35 years after the J.D. Kestner, Jr. doll factory.

Left: The expressive character head, circa 1910, has molded hair painted with comb marks and single-stroke eyebrows. The open/closed mouth includes a molded tongue and two molded upper teeth.

An 11-1/2 inch bisque Adolf Wislizenus socket head doll incised: "110—4// Germany." Many A.W. bodies are unique because of the realistic modeling of fat wrinkles evident on the lower arms and upper legs of the jointed composition body.

Right: The Adolf Wislizenus doll factory made dolls using bisque heads from many porcelain factories including Baehr & Proeschild, Simon & Halbig, and Ernst Heubach (from 1910 on). A Simon & Halbig/Adolf Wislizenus bisque socket head doll is marked: "13//A.W." The 9-inch original doll resembles the group of 1896 dolls in the Dressel "Portrait Series." The doll has a wooden body and lower limbs. The George Washington portrait doll is sitting on a papier-mâché horse that is mounted on a wooden pull toy.

Chapter Sixteen

The Kestner Doll and Porcelain Factory

Johann Daniel Kestner, Jr. was to Waltershausen what the Dressels, Fleischmanns, Lindners, and Müllers were to Sonneberg. Kestner was the only doll maker in Waltershausen from 1816 until 1851. In 1851, Gottlob Schafft founded a doll factory in Waltershausen. In 1870, Adolf Wislizenus became Schafft's partner, and in 1878, he became the sole owner of the factory. There is no question that during his years of doll making, Kestner left a permanent legacy that was unequaled by any other doll maker in the Northern Circle.

Johann Daniel Kestner, Jr. was the son of an innkeeper. He was born September 4, 1787, and by the age of 16, he was selling items to Napoleon's troops. When the troops had withdrawn, he started making wooden shirt buttons and black slates out of papier-mâché. The manufacture of the buttons required the use of a lathe to make the small, thin wooden button rings. Therefore, Kestner decided that it would be more economical if he used the lathe for other wooden items. According to an entry in the *German Doll Encyclopedia*, Kestner began to make jointed wooden dolls in 1816.

"J.D. Kestner, Waltershausen, in addition to dolls' heads and bodies of papier-mâché, also supplies bodies in white leather to match the doll's heads, also looped buttons for white shirts, chemises and ladies clothing," according to a German advertisement from 1823. Kestner didn't receive government approval to produce papier-mâché dolls in Waltershausen until 1822, seventeen years after the Müllers introduced papier-mâché in Sonneberg.

Kestner built a very large doll factory in Waltershausen in 1824. It had a classic design and featured his trademark crown on the side of the building. In the following years, he sold dolls,

The Kestner doll factory, built in 1824, is still standing in Waltershausen today. The Kestner trademark "crown of superiority" is slightly visible on one wall of the large home/factory.

nutcrackers, wooden animals, sheep farms, stables, animal shaped toys with voice boxes, Jack-in-the-boxes, harlequin dolls, slates and slate pencils. In 1830, Kestner's sales totaled over $15,000. By the 1850's, his annual sales had risen to over $150,000. He paid his workers about a dollar a week in 1859 for working 12 hours a day.

From *Reise ins Spielzeugland* (*A Journey in Toyland*) we learn more details about the life of J. D. Kestner, Jr. Author Marion Christiana Müller states, "In 1815, he traded alcohol and tobacco, sausages, 43 different toy figures like cows, zebras, horses and camels; and by 1820, he had added glue, yarn, batiste, rubber and gypsum to his inventory."

German author, Christiane Gräfnitz, provides doll-related facts about Kestner in her book, *German Papier-Mâché Dolls, 1760-1860.* Gräfnitz states, "The first written document describing Kestner's independent trading activities is dated December 6, 1815, not long after his first marriage (to Sabrina Friederike Buschmann)." According to Gräfnitz, Kestner's original and only account book indicates that in 1815, he offered "ladies doll heads in 13 sizes and boys' doll heads in several sizes." These papier-mâché heads, attributed to Kestner, are part of an important study of papier-mâché dolls conducted by Gräfnitz. Many Kestner early sample pages are described and pictured in the author's papier-mâché book, along with actual Kestner dolls from the same years. Doll researchers like Christiane Gräfnitz have added important pieces to the German doll-making puzzle. Gräfnitz has identified early papier-mâché dolls from Sonneberg and Watershausen in her well-researched book. The Gräfnitz book helps collectors identify Kestner, Müller and Voit papier-mâché dolls in their collections.

In 1830, Kestner's main income came from the sale of shirt buttons, which included a button inventory of 15 different designs. By 1830, he was quite wealthy and famous in Waltershausen. One interesting numerical

Right: A papier-mâché shoulder head doll with painted eyes and an elaborately styled wig, circa 1830. Maker unknown (possibly J.D. Kestner, Jr.). The 17-inch doll, with a leather body and wooden limbs, is wearing a blue silk dress and a red necklace. *Christiane Gräfnitz Collection.*

Left: An 1840/50 doll with a papier-mâché head by J.D. Kestner, Junior. The 16-inch boy has a gusseted cloth body with leather arms. The unusual molded papier-mâché hat, with molded tassel, is pictured on Kestner's original sample sheets. *Christiane Gräfnitz Collection.*

Left: This 11-inch Kestner character boy, circa 1909, is marked "177." The doll is probably the first of the Kestner character child series. The bisque socket head features deeply molded blonde hair, well-defined eye sockets, blue intaglio eyes, multi-stroke eyebrows, and an open/closed mouth with a molded tongue. The bisque head is mounted on a Kestner fully jointed composition body. *Jane Walker Collection.*

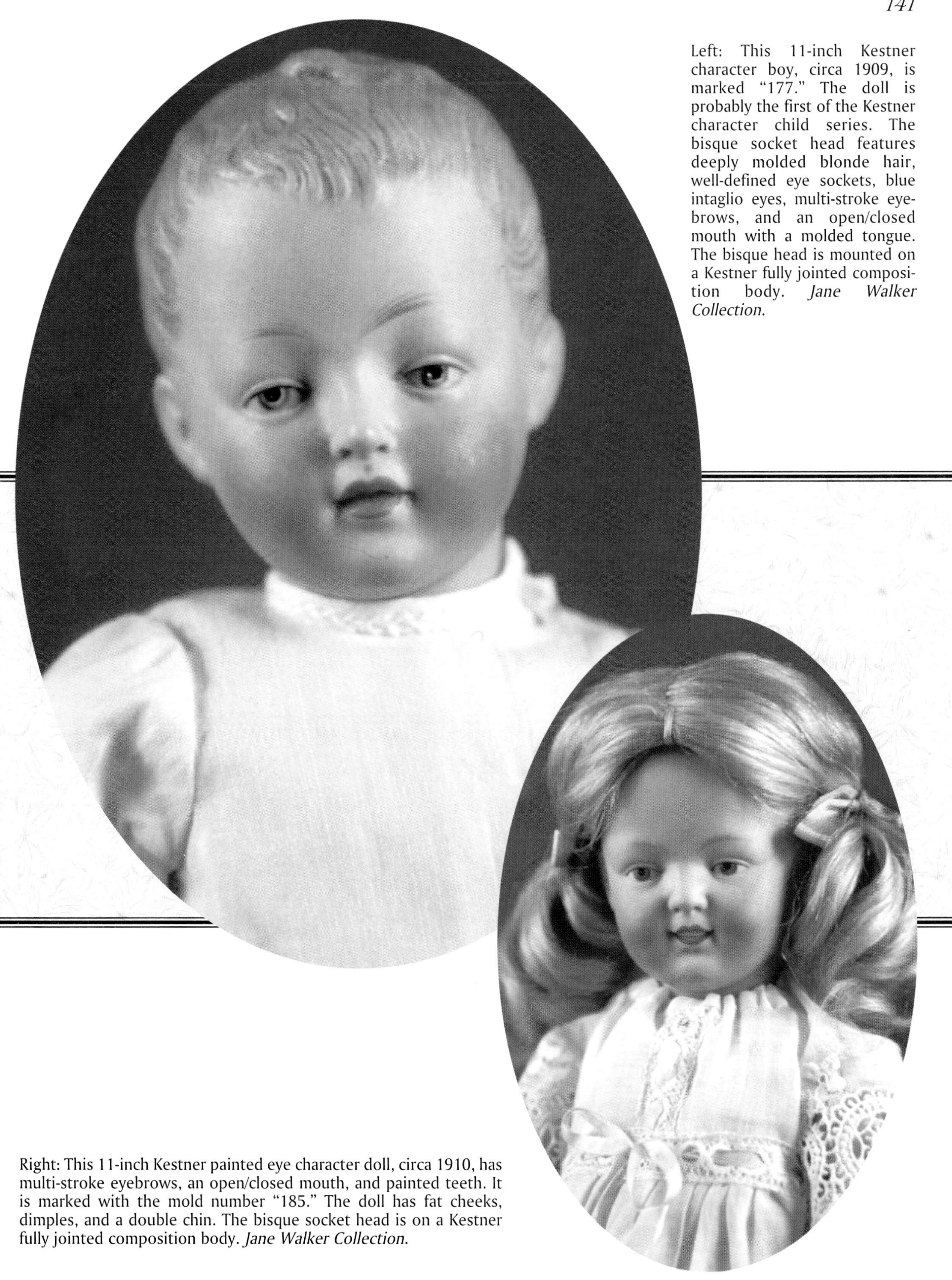

Right: This 11-inch Kestner painted eye character doll, circa 1910, has multi-stroke eyebrows, an open/closed mouth, and painted teeth. It is marked with the mold number "185." The doll has fat cheeks, dimples, and a double chin. The bisque socket head is on a Kestner fully jointed composition body. *Jane Walker Collection.*

figure is found in *Reise ins Spielzeugland*. According to the author, Kestner employed 1,264 persons in 1846 of which 423 of these were children younger than 14. Children were always a very important part of the Thuringian doll making work force in Waltershausen as well as in Sonneberg. Children began to work by the age of three or four. Reports of very young children sitting under a sewing machine for ten hours a day cutting thread are not uncommon. As a child's level of skill increased, he or she would be assigned more difficult duties relating to doll making such as hand sewing, knitting, painting, sanding, matching and setting doll eyes and packing finished products in cardboard boxes.

Home workers did not have much disposable income for clothing or food. Clothing was passed down from older to younger children. Children often owned only one set of clothing. Children shared shoes, and went barefoot inside the house and in the summer. Potatoes were a staple at almost every meal. They were even eaten raw. Meat was a special treat for most home workers in Thuringia. Families often rented small plots of ground outside the borders of doll making towns in order to grow potatoes and other vegetables. Children were expected to take care of the gardens as well as their younger siblings in addition to their doll-related assignments.

Delivery of dolls and doll parts was often the work of

Right: A 14-inch unmarked Kestner child doll with brown sleep eyes, very dark eyebrows and an open mouth with four teeth. The bisque head is mounted on a kid body with bisque lower arms. *Jane Walker Collection.*

Left: A 14-inch "Hilda" Kestner character doll advertised by the George Borgfeldt Company in *Playthings* magazine in January of 1916. The baby doll is marked: "Germany//245//JDK 11//1914//c//Hilda." The bisque socket head is on a Kestner composition bent-limb baby body. The doll has blue sleep eyes, multi-stroke eyebrows, and an open/closed mouth.

Right: A 17-inch Kestner character bisque socket head doll marked: "Made in Germany//JDK//260." The doll, circa 1916, with sleep eyes, hair eyelashes, and multi-stroke eyebrows, has an open mouth with upper teeth and an original brown mohair wig. The bisque head is mounted on a fully jointed composition body.

Left: This 15-inch Kestner character doll, circa 1916, is marked: "Madein//Germany// JDK//260//37-40." The bisque socket head doll has blue sleep eyes, multi-stroke eyebrows, an open mouth with four upper teeth, and a jointed composition body.

a child because the parents needed to work as many hours as possible in order to support the family. The orders had to be delivered on time regardless of the weather. One child described walking three miles each way twice a week to deliver wooden doll limbs. She said that her delivery basket was so tall and heavy that she easily lost her balance while carrying it. She adds in her oral history account that she was small and thin and had little counterweight to balance the "Schanzen" (delivery basket).

J. D. Kestner, Jr. was instrumental in establishing the first railroad line into Waltershausen in 1849. Railroads improved delivery time of doll-related articles in a major way. Kestner's 1824 factory is still standing today in Waltershausen, and it covers almost an entire block. The trademark Kestner "crown" is still slightly visible on the building. Only a small amount of gold paint, which outlines the crown, still glitters in the sunlight today. The crown "symbol of superiority" was registered in the United States on December 24, 1895. While standing in front of this important doll factory, it is easy to picture workers inside this old building, assembling, dressing, and then packing dolls for a shipment to an American department store.

Kestner dolls are treasured today by a large number of doll collectors. However, according to a quote by author Müller in *Reise ins Spielzeugland*, Kestner dolls were not always considered the best. Müller states:

> In the beginning, Kestner traveled to the Leipzig Fair pushing a cart. The Waltershausen townspeople called him "Mr. Nothing." From the beginning,

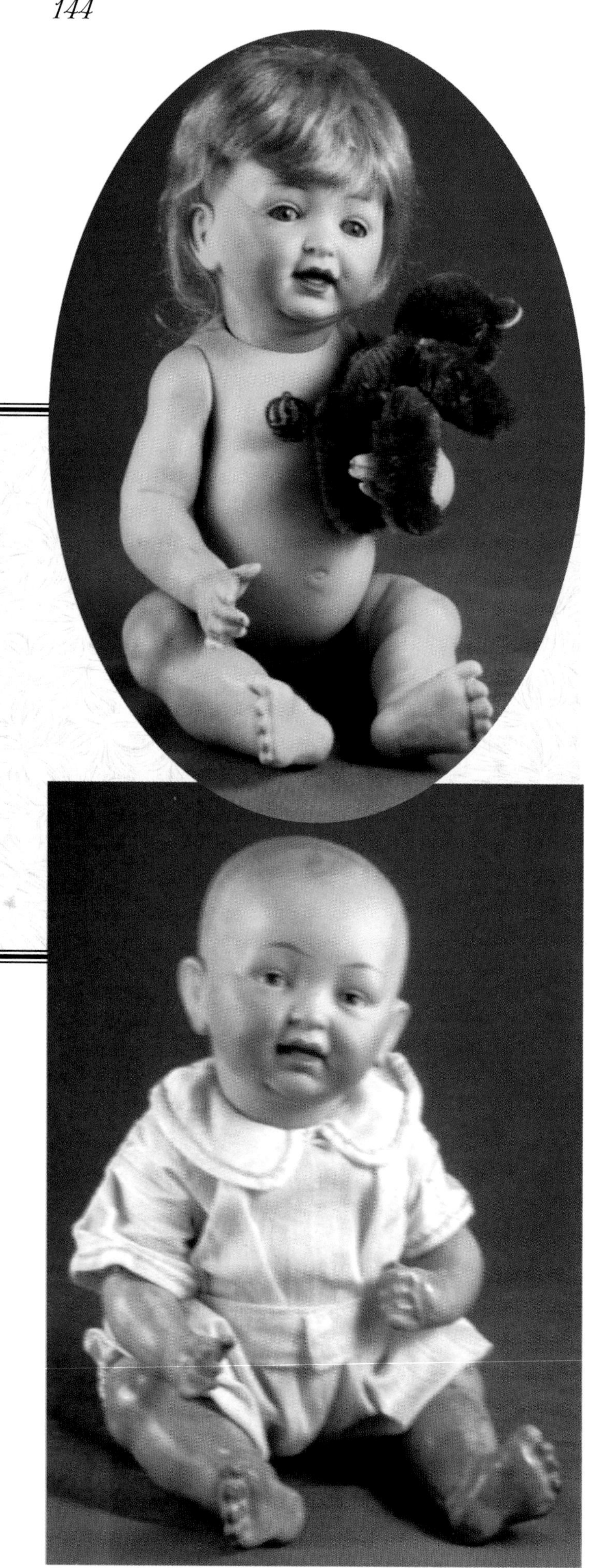

An 11-1/2-inch Kestner doll, circa 1912, incised: "made in//C. 7//Germany//211//J.D.K." "Sammy" has a bisque socket head, brown sleep eyes, multi-stroke eyebrows, an open/closed mouth with molded tongue, kid-lined joints, and an all-bisque body, arms and legs. A Kestner "crown" paper label is attached to the doll's chest. *Jane Walker Collection.*

Kestner dolls were made in his factory, but contrary to the Sonneberg dolls, they were not very attractive. Kestner modelers were called "Fratzenmacher," makers of freak faces. Other than that, they were not much different from the Sonneberg dolls. Their bodies were made of leather, heads made from papier-mâché, the limbs were filled with sawdust and they only wore a simple dress.

Material costs were little, and the hourly wage was only 4 or 5 Pfennige (similar to the value of pennies in U.S. currency). But Kestner was not happy with the prices the dolls brought on the market. Goods were measured by weight, and his expenses for transportation and customs were high. Kestner decided to improve quality instead of making money in quantity. Then his exports more than doubled. Kestner was one of the few doll makers to make entire dolls, heads and bodies.

The Armand Marseille and Schoenau & Hoffmeister doll and porcelain factories were two other companies that made complete dolls.

According to author Christianne Gräfnitz, "In 1836, Kestner has dolls' porcelain heads and limbs made in a factory, probably by the Müller Company in Ohrdruf." Author Gräfnitz also adds that some of the porcelain heads resembled the bonnet head papier-mâché doll heads in Kestner's original sample book. J. D. Kestner, Jr. died on December 11, 1858. Two years later, in 1860, the Kestner doll factory bought the Steudinger, Müller & Co. porcelain factory in Ohrdruf. After Johann's death, his first and second wives ran the business along with the company secretary, H. Oesten, and Eduard Reitz. Kestner's son preceded him in death, and therefore, his grandson, Adolf, managed the doll factory from 1872 until his death in 1918. The Kestner porcelain factory was still making china doll heads in 1928. The doll and porcelain factories closed in 1938.

The Kestner doll factory made character babies from 1912 on. A 10-inch Kestner bisque socket head doll, marked with the size number "7," has painted brown eyes, single-stroke eyebrows, and an open/closed mouth with molded tongue. The doll head is mounted on a composition baby body. *Jane Walker Collection.*

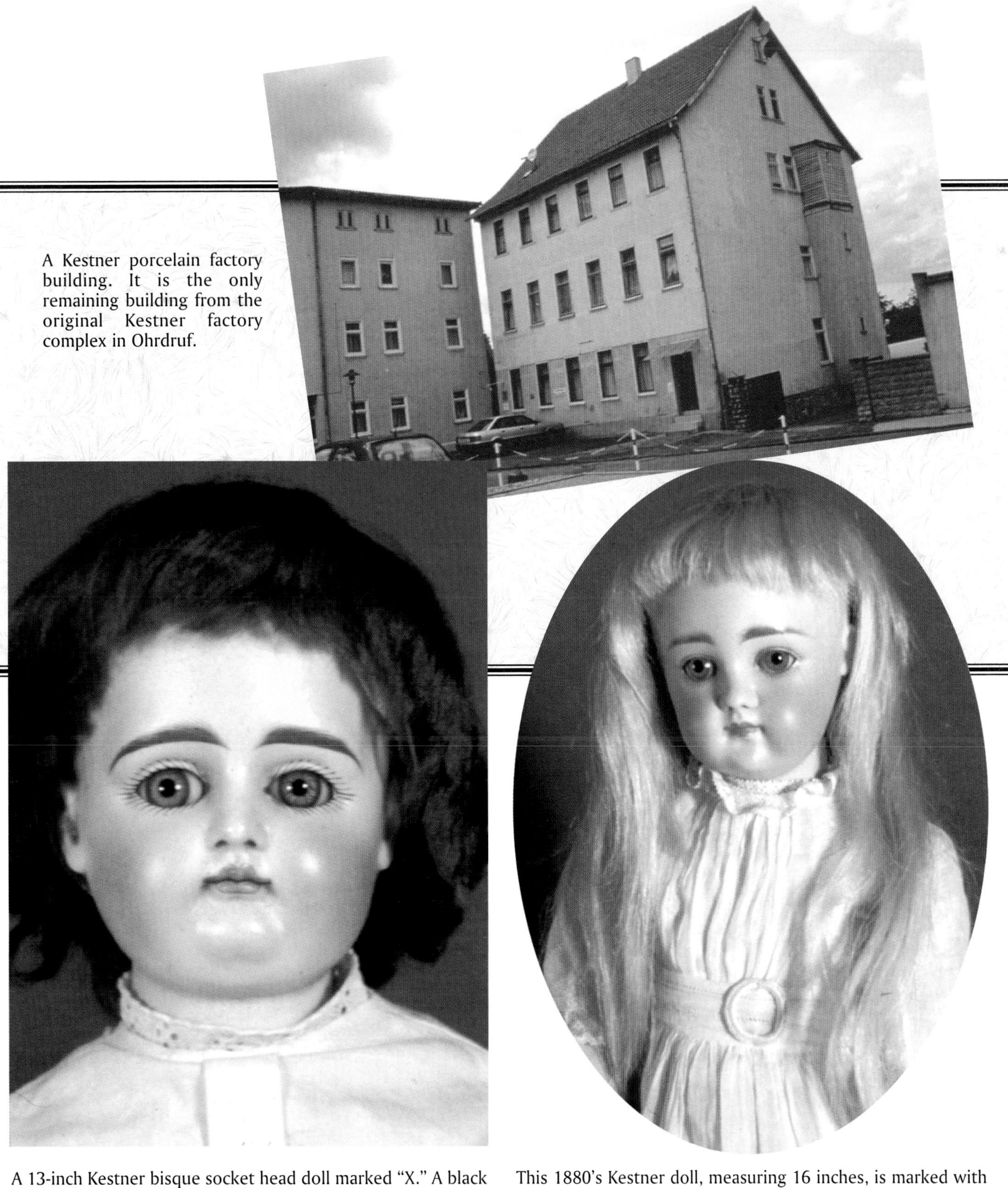

A Kestner porcelain factory building. It is the only remaining building from the original Kestner factory complex in Ohrdruf.

A 13-inch Kestner bisque socket head doll marked "X." A black "X" is also painted on the lip of the cut-off crown. The head, circa 1885 on, has beautifully painted facial features that include multi-stroke eyebrows painted in the French style, a closed pouty mouth with typical Kestner upturned corners, and finely painted eyelashes. The bisque head is mounted on an early ball-jointed composition body with straight wrists and cupped hands.

This 1880's Kestner doll, measuring 16 inches, is marked with the German-style size number "7." The bisque head includes a closed mouth, multi-stroke eyebrows, blue sleep eyes, and an original plaster pate. The head is mounted on a fully jointed composition body with straight wrists and cupped hands. The doll is dressed in original clothing.

Left: An original 13-inch Kestner shoulder head doll marked "D" on the shoulder plate and crown. The original plaster pate is also incised "D 4." The Kestner "alphabet heads" were made for at least twenty years. The well-made kid body has gussets at the knees and bisque lower arms. The doll has blue stationary eyes, multi-stroke eyebrows, an open mouth with four upper teeth, and an original mohair wig.

This 14-inch Kestner closed-mouth bisque doll, circa late 1800's, is marked only with the size number "4." The doll has multi-stroke eyebrows, stationary brown eyes, and a cloth body with bisque lower arms. *Jane Walker Collection.*

Three Kestner bisque socket head dolls marked: "Made in Germany//143." The #143 mold design was registered in 1897, and made for a number of years. The three dolls with blue sleep eyes and open mouths with two teeth measure 7, 9 and 12 inches. The heads are on jointed composition bodies. *Jane Walker Collection.*

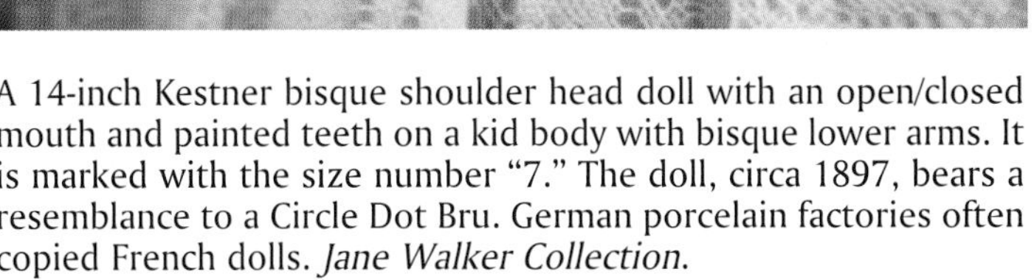

A 14-inch Kestner bisque shoulder head doll with an open/closed mouth and painted teeth on a kid body with bisque lower arms. It is marked with the size number "7." The doll, circa 1897, bears a resemblance to a Circle Dot Bru. German porcelain factories often copied French dolls. *Jane Walker Collection.*

This 8-inch all-bisque "Bru" Kestner doll, patented in 1897, is marked: "132//2/0." The doll has blue stationary eyes, multi-stroke eyebrows, and an open/closed mouth with a molded tongue. The typical Kestner high-heeled painted boots have five black cross straps.

An original all bisque 1880's Kestner doll measuring 6-1/2 inches. The stationary dark eyes and the finely painted eyebrows and mouth illustrate Kestner porcelain factory quality, which is evident on even the smallest dolls.

Kestner bisque head dolls were sold in a number of American stores and catalogs through the years. It is interesting to compare a 1910 Sears, Roebuck & Co. advertisement with a 1911 Montgomery Ward advertisement that describe a "bisque head, kid bodied Kestner doll." The Sears ad reads:

> Kestner, the manufacturer of this doll, is known for the excellence of manufacture, the fine quality features and the general superiority of his dolls. His goods are the standard by which all others are judged. The heads are of absolutely the finest quality bisque with open mouth showing teeth, and moving eyes with natural eyelashes. They are fitted with a long curly wig, parted on one side and tied with a bow of good quality ribbon. They have quality bisque forearms, riveted elbows, shoulder, hip and knee joints, allowing free movement of arms and legs. The doll wears good quality removable colored lace stockings and ribbon tied sandals to match. We buy these dolls direct from Germany and save at least one-third for you. This doll we guarantee to please for many years. Comes in 5 sizes, each carefully packed for shipping. 18 ½ inches - $1.75 and 28 inches-$4.98.

The Montgomery Ward ad is as follows:

> Kestner Kid Body Doll. This doll must be seen to be appreciated. The illustration does not begin to do it justice. It is the handsomest doll we could buy, and sells at a much higher price retail. You will not

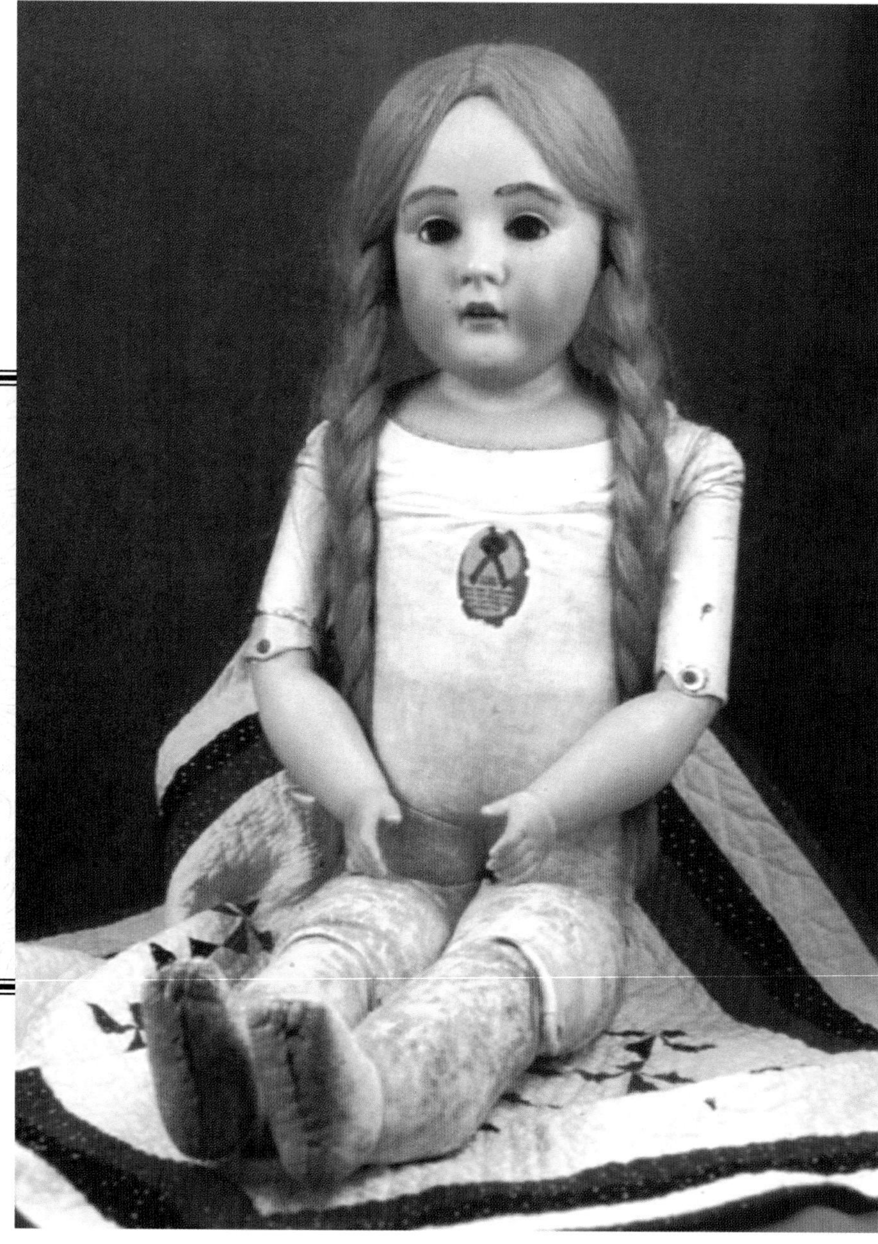

Right: Many doll makers prided themselves on unique facial features and eye movements of their dolls. Kestner often advertised improvements on kid-bodied dolls. A 32-inch Kestner child doll with unusual eyebrows, circa 1910, contains the following description under the Kestner stamped crown and streamers on the kid body: "Real Hair Eyebrows//will not drop out//nor can they be//pulled out." The bisque shoulder head is marked: "Dep. 195.16."

The Kestner paper "crown and streamers trademark" glued on the kid body of the #195 doll. Above the eyebrow description, the label includes the words, "1/2 cork stuffed." *Jane Walker Collection.*

A 20-inch Kestner "Gibson Girl" doll, circa 1910, with a bisque shoulder head marked: "P made in Germany." The doll's upturned chin, slight smile, and high cheekbones accentuate the haughty look that personified Charles Dana Gibson's drawings of the women from that era. The doll, made for the George Borgfeldt Company, has a rivet-jointed kid body. The doll head includes hair eyelashes, painted lower lashes, and blue sleep eyes. *Jane Walker Collection.*

> be disappointed in this doll; it is well worth the price and with care will last indefinitely. These dolls are made with extra fine quality kid, full formed, stout bodies, half arms with ball-jointed shoulders, elbows and wrists, large fine quality bisque head with teeth, moving eyes, eye-lashes and fine sewed wigs, fitted with shoes and stockings. Length 23 inches-$4.25 and 28 inches-$6.60.

A 1906 *Playthings* magazine contains a long article on the Kestner doll factory. From the description provided by the George Borgfeldt New York importing company we learn that Kestner dolls were made much like dolls were made in Sonneberg using many home trade workers. Hundreds of home workers furnished various doll parts, which were assembled in the Kestner factory. The *Playthings* magazine also includes a description of the process used in making Kestner kid bodies. It is as follows:

> In making kid bodies, the sheepskins, while moist, are first tightly stretched on long tables, in order to get their full surface. The skins are then given to experienced cutters, who cut by tin patterns, the bodies, arms and legs, and these are subsequently deftly sewn together on machines. Stuffers then fill the bodies thus sewn together with sawdust, cork or hair.

Kestner made the "Marvel" kid body for the New York importers, Butler Brothers. Kestner made the Bye-Lo Baby heads for George Borgfeldt & Co., a series of baby heads for the Century Doll Company, character heads for Catterfelder Puppenfabrik, and the "Walküre" heads for Kley & Hahn. One of the most popular Kestner dolls was the Kewpie. Designed by Rose O'Neill, the Kewpies took the world by storm. Originally produced by the Kestner porcelain factory, demand outpaced supply. A number of other Thuringian

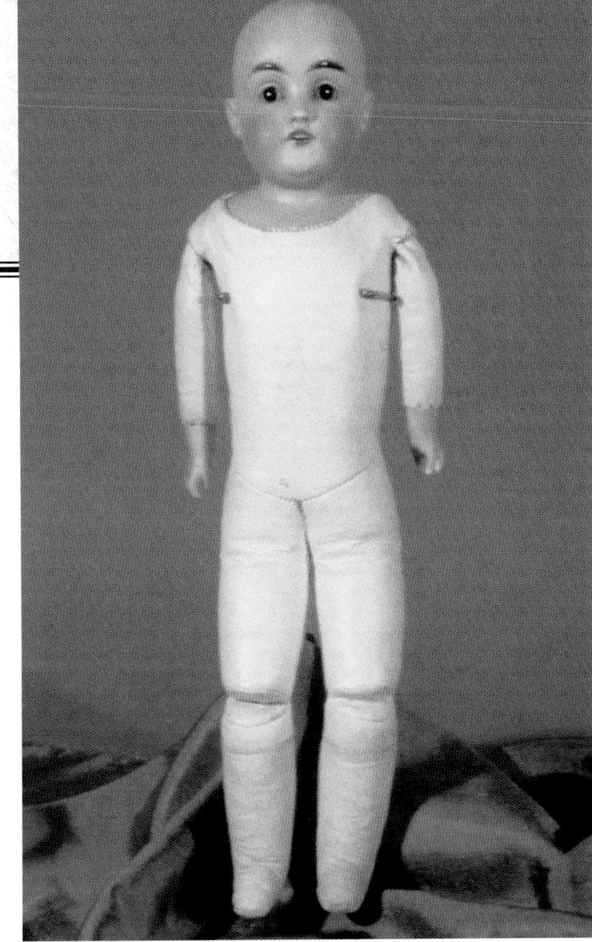

A 15-inch Kestner bisque shoulder head doll marked: "154 dep. 4-1/2." The doll has an original plaster plate, brown sleep eyes, multi-stroke eyebrows, and an open/closed mouth with four molded upper teeth. The Kestner kid body, with cloth lower legs and bisque lower arms, is marked "Marvel" along with the Kestner trademark crown and streamers. The Kestner doll factory made the Marvel kid bodied dolls for Butler Brothers from 1898 until 1913. Montgomery Ward advertised the Kestner #154 mold as late as 1924. Many Thuringian porcelain factories made the same popular doll head molds year after year.

porcelain factories were called upon to help fill the orders, including Gebrüder Voigt, Hermann Voigt, Hertwig, Weiss, Kühnert & Co. and many others.

The Borgfeldt Company owned the exclusive rights to the Kewpies. Apparently, many doll factories tried to copy the Kewpies. A Borgfeldt representative ran the following ad in a German newspaper during the Kewpie craze:

> Kewpie Warning-Signed George Borgfeldt. Warning: Attention: Notice. We have noticed that our patented Kewpie dolls (Patent No. 30,403 of the Berlin Court, product protection mark no. 189,826 of the Reichs National Office) are being copied by an unknown source and we herewith warn of the purchase or sale of those. We will take legal steps against anybody who breaks our legal protection by forbidden manufacturing, purchase and sale.

World War I interrupted Kewpie production. The Colemans indicate that in 1951, all-bisque Kewpies were made in East Germany and imported to America by the Borgfeldt Company who claimed "the quality is about as good as when imported before the War." According to the Colemans, these Kewpies came in three heights, one of which was 6 in., and were stamped "Germany" on the body. This mark, according to the Colemans, rubbed off easily and is difficult to distinguish these 1950's Kewpies from the early ones. Unfortunately, the individual German porcelain factories responsible for Kewpie production did not mark the dolls accordingly. As is true with the Bye-Lo Baby bisque head dolls, the dolls cannot be attributed to a particular maker, only to a group of makers.

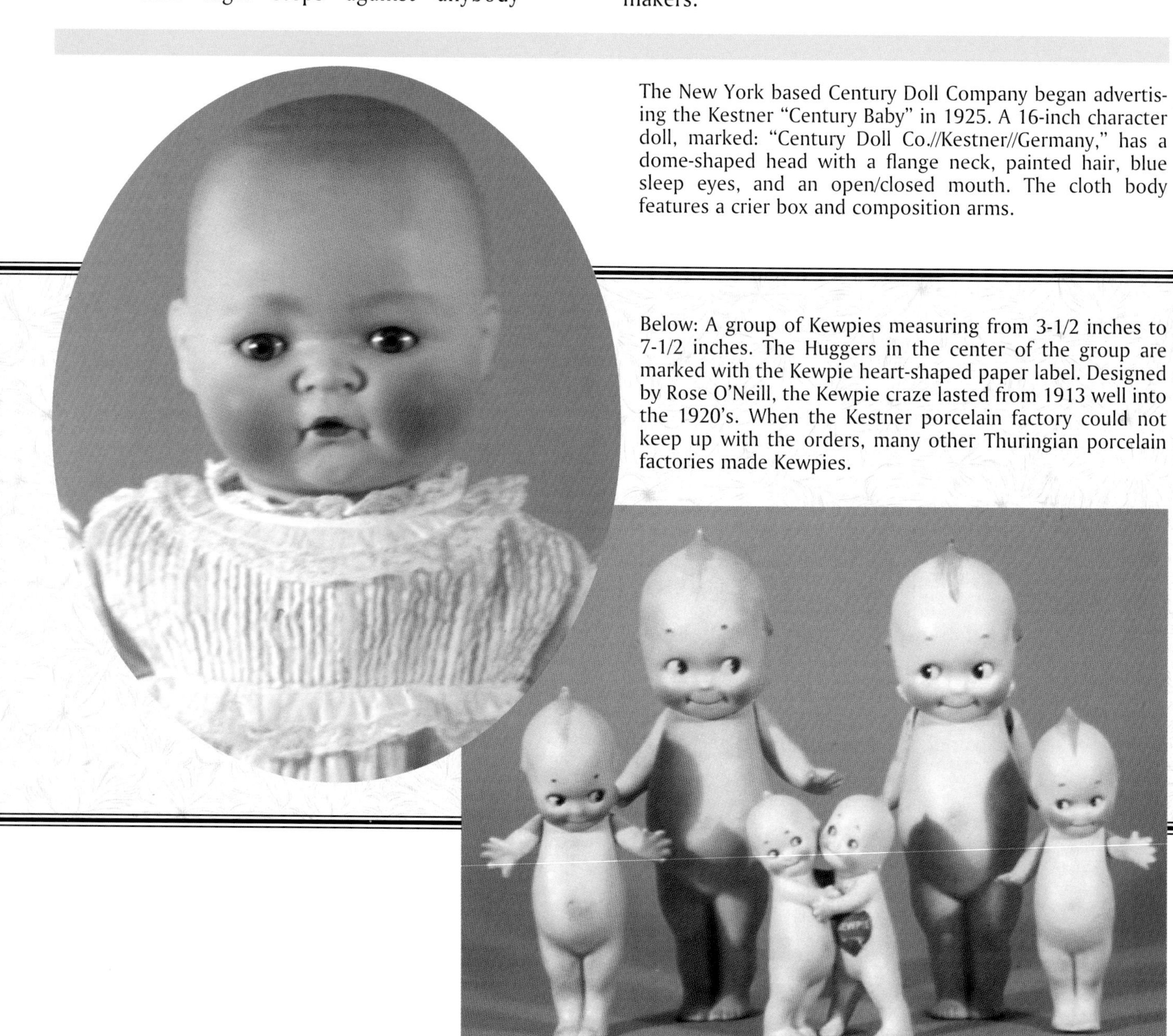

The New York based Century Doll Company began advertising the Kestner "Century Baby" in 1925. A 16-inch character doll, marked: "Century Doll Co.//Kestner//Germany," has a dome-shaped head with a flange neck, painted hair, blue sleep eyes, and an open/closed mouth. The cloth body features a crier box and composition arms.

Below: A group of Kewpies measuring from 3-1/2 inches to 7-1/2 inches. The Huggers in the center of the group are marked with the Kewpie heart-shaped paper label. Designed by Rose O'Neill, the Kewpie craze lasted from 1913 well into the 1920's. When the Kestner porcelain factory could not keep up with the orders, many other Thuringian porcelain factories made Kewpies.

Chapter Seventeen

The Ohrdruf Area Porcelain Factories

Kestner, Kling, Baehr & Proeschild and Hertel, Schwab & Company

Porcelain dolls from Ohrdruf are well known all over the world. The Baehr & Proeschild, Kestner, Kling and Hertel Schwab porcelain factories turned out top quality dolls year after year in the Ohrdruf area. The C.F. Kling porcelain factory was founded in 1834. Doll heads weren't produced until 1870. The Kestner doll factory purchased the Ohrdruf porcelain factory of Steudinger, Müller & Co. in 1860. The Baehr & Proeschild

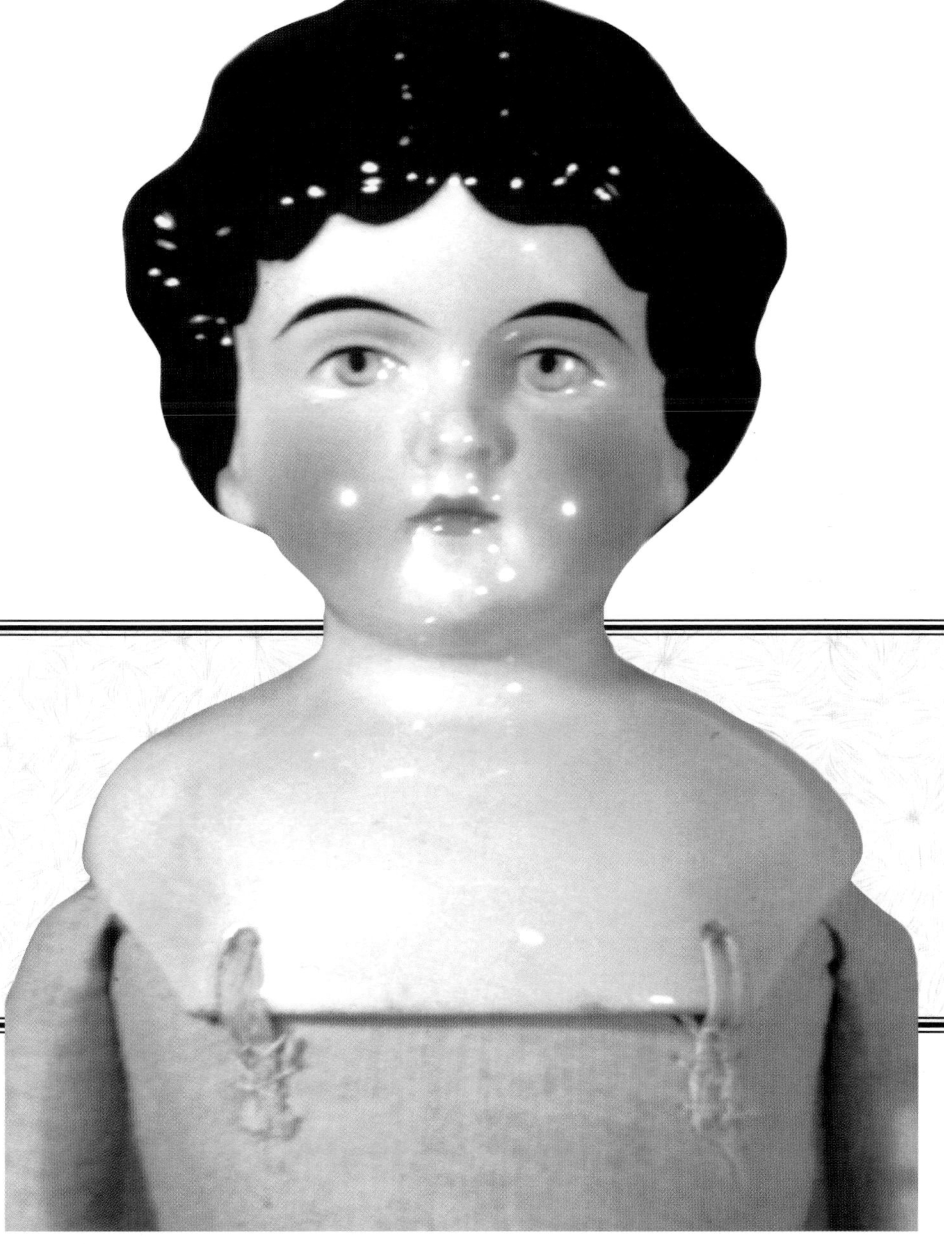

A 20-inch Kling china shoulder head doll, circa 1885, with blue painted eyes, molded black hair, and a cloth body with china lower limbs. The shoulder plate is incised: "Germany//189, and the Kling trademark bell." Kling china dolls often have a childlike look.

The Baehr & Proeschild porcelain factory made a large number of "French trade" dolls. A Baehr & Proeschild doll, circa 1880, has a dome-shaped bisque shoulder head, paperweight eyes, heavy French-type eyebrows, and a closed mouth. The 13-inch doll is wearing original marked Bru shoes with oval metal buckles. The Wagner & Zetsche marked kid body resembles a French "bebe" body including the body shape and bisque lower arms. The shoulder plate features a molded bust in front, and shoulder detail in back.

A Kestner bisque socket head marked: "W//6//Walküre//Germany." The Kestner porcelain factory made the "Walküre" heads (mold design registered in 1903) for the Kley & Hahn doll factory. The 19-inch doll has blue sleep eyes with painted upper and lower lashes, multi-stroke eyebrows, an open mouth with four upper teeth and a fully jointed Kestner composition body.

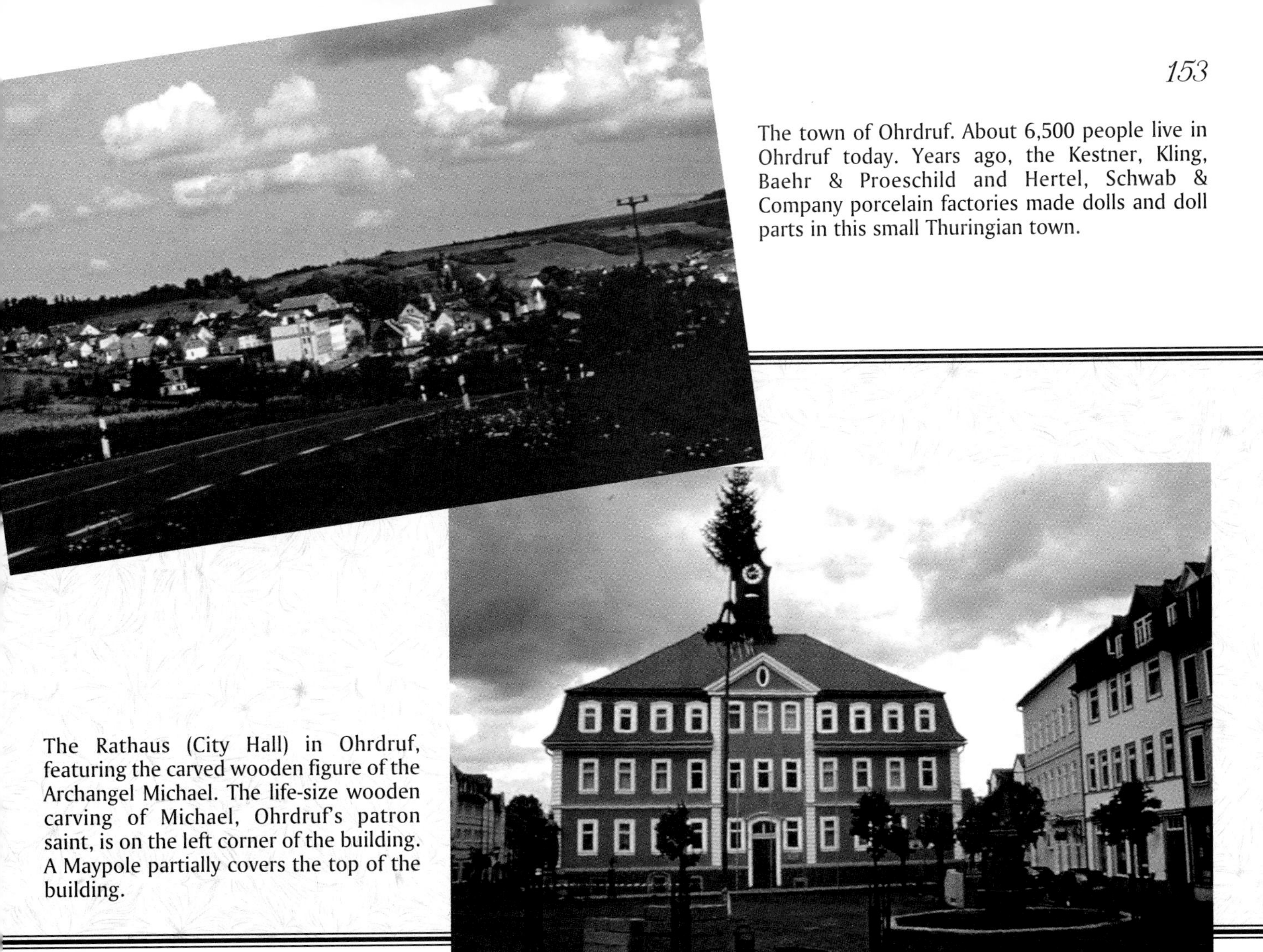

The town of Ohrdruf. About 6,500 people live in Ohrdruf today. Years ago, the Kestner, Kling, Baehr & Proeschild and Hertel, Schwab & Company porcelain factories made dolls and doll parts in this small Thuringian town.

The Rathaus (City Hall) in Ohrdruf, featuring the carved wooden figure of the Archangel Michael. The life-size wooden carving of Michael, Ohrdruf's patron saint, is on the left corner of the building. A Maypole partially covers the top of the building.

porcelain factory was founded in 1871, and according to a document in the Sonneberg Doll and Toy Museum archives, doll heads were listed since the 1870's. The Hertel, Schwab & Co. porcelain factory is located on the outskirts of Ohrdruf in Stützhaus. It was founded in 1910 and was still making doll heads in 1930. Parts of the Kling and Kestner porcelain factories are still standing in Ohrdruf today, and the entire Baehr & Proeschild porcelain factory remains unchanged on the original factory site. The one remaining Kestner porcelain factory building is now an apartment building. It is located next to the main town square in Ohrdruf.

The small town of Ohrdruf dates back to 724–725. Ohrdruf was the primary Church "seat" until the 14th Century, according to German historians. In 1344, the Church "seat" was moved to Gotha because Ohrdruf was unable to protect the Church during the "Wars of the Dukes." It is believed that Ohrdruf received city rights in 1348. Johann Sebastian Bach and his brother Johann Cristoph Bach lived in Ohrdruf from 1695-1700.

Ohrdruf townspeople were industrious, and there were many industries in town besides doll making. There was a lumber mill, a hammer works, a bell foundry, a fabric company, a lead paint factory, and several furniture factories. The charcoal makers provided energy for the kilns in the porcelain factories for many years. In 1865, Carl Eduard Meinung established the first wooden toy factory in Ohrdruf. Meinung is credited with the invention of the rocking horse.

The marked porcelain dolls made by the Kestner factory are well known to doll collectors. Many unmarked Kestner dolls have also been pictured and described in a variety of doll books and magazines, but other Kestner porcelain products are harder to identify. An exception is the beautiful nine-inch figurine pictured in Patricia R. Smith's 1976 book, *Kestner and Simon & Halbig Dolls.* The base of the Kestner figurine is marked with the trademark Kestner crown and streamers found on so many Kestner kid doll bodies. The figurine is the bust of a lady wearing a large, elaborate, molded hat with feathers. The figurine does not appear to have been painted, which may indicate it was a model bust head. We learn more about Kestner porcelain production from the Röntgen book on German porcelain. The author states that the porcelain factory made "dolls, doll heads and parts, figurines, as well as decorative and household porcelain."

The Kling factory buildings are located on both sides of the street. The oldest section of the Kling factory site contained a section of track from a narrow gauge railroad. One of the main buildings was built of brick, and a concrete block section was added at a later date. Across the narrow street from the factory buildings were several other buildings the oldest being quite ornate. The original main doorway was trimmed with large molded winged birds and an ornate crown. Raised medallions over the windows were dated 1808 and 1911. The second office building was newer, and built of red brick. Christian Kling founded the porcelain factory. In 1836, the factory sold "figures and vases at the Leipzig Fair," according to the Ciesliks. The Kling factory was an early producer of porcelain doll heads, in 1870.

Three dated entries from the *German Doll Encyclopedia* provide important historical information about Kling doll production:

> 1886: Advertised children's figures, first-class doll heads and dolls, bathing dolls, figures and vases. 1894: Advertised doll heads, socket and shoulder heads, simple types up to the most hair styled ones, with sleeping eyes and teeth, movable bisque children, bathing dolls, "nanking" dolls, doll arms and legs. 1930: Referred to as porcelain dolls, heads and joints, "nanking" dolls.

Under "Kling remarks," the authors write, "A mystery is the shoulder head series 377 of C.F. Kling, Ohrdruf, who probably had been manufacturing doll heads for Kämmer & Reinhardt before 1902."

Kling dolls after 1880 are often marked with the Kling bell. The early dolls showcase the art of design. Many untinted bisque heads have flowers or other trims accenting their elaborately styled hair. Kling molded blouses often feature ruffles, unusual collars and molded jewelry.

The George Borgfeldt Company donated a number of early Kling dolls to the Museum of the City of New York. One unmarked example is pictured on page 33 in the

Parts of the Kling porcelain factory, founded in 1834, are still standing in Ohrdruf today. Narrow gauge railroad tracks are slightly visible in front of one old factory building.

The oldest Kling building is located across the street from the rest of the factory complex.

A 1-1/2 inch Kling china shoulder head incised: "9/0 K." The black curly "low-brow" hairstyle is from the 1890's. The Kling porcelain factory made doll heads from 1870 on.

An 11-inch Kling bisque shoulder head doll with molded blonde hair, glass sleep eyes, multi-stroke eyebrows, and an open/closed mouth with molded teeth. The doll has a cloth body and composition lower arms and legs

book *The Rose Unfolds* by Rosalie Whyel and Susan Hedrick. The authors state:

> Her head is one of a group imported in the late 19th Century by the U.S. based company of George Borgfeldt. It is illustrated in Colemans' *Encyclopedia of Dolls*, Volume I, page 87, as part of a group donated to the Museum of the City of New York by Fred Kolb, a former president of the Borgfeldt Company. The Colemans have studied Fred Kolb's encoded documentation that came with the doll heads, and feel that this fine example was made by the German firm, Kling.

Five similar Kling dolls are pictured on the same page of the Coleman's Encyclopedia, mentioned above. Marks on the dolls pictured include the following number and letter combinations: 2K3, 5M5,and 5C5.

Kling also made Bye-Lo Babies for the George Borgfeldt Company. The Ciesliks add, under "Kling remarks" in the *German Doll Encyclopedia*, "It is assumed that Borgfeldt was a silent partner in the porcelain factory."

Walking through the gates at the Baehr & Proeschild factory complex is like turning back the century clock. The nearby stream flows into the factory site through a concrete waterway. The factory buildings are quite large and many are built of red brick. One storage building is sided with stacked Baehr & Proeschild discarded molds. The loading docks are intact, and it is easy to imagine the boxes of dolls being loaded first on wagons pulled by horses, and later, on trucks.

The stream behind the factory must have flooded at one time as many doll heads and parts have been washed to the surface of the dumping grounds. One interesting find is a so-called "Belton" shoulder head of an old man. For many years, doll collectors have referred to flat, convex or concave tops of bisque heads, with one, two or three stringing holes as "Belton" heads. The three-inch Baehr & Proeschild bisque head is unique because of a large molded mustache and "bags" molded under the eyes. The molded face has a chin dimple, a large hooked nose, and well-molded ears. The doll head also has an open/closed mouth with molded teeth. The head is turned to the left, so that although the shoulder plate is straight, the head is almost in a profile view. The shoulder plate has three sew holes in back as well as in front. The flattened head contains only one large stringing hole.

The Waltershausen Bruno Schmidt doll factory bought the Baehr & Proeschild porcelain factory in 1918. One beautiful shard from the dumping ground includes the "BS inside the heart" Schmidt trademark. Another little boy with molded combed hair is marked with the Schmidt heart and the mold number 425. According to the Ciesliks, up until the time Bruno Schmidt bought the Baehr & Proeschild porcelain factory, "Schmidt had all his doll heads poured by Baehr & Proeschild after his own models."

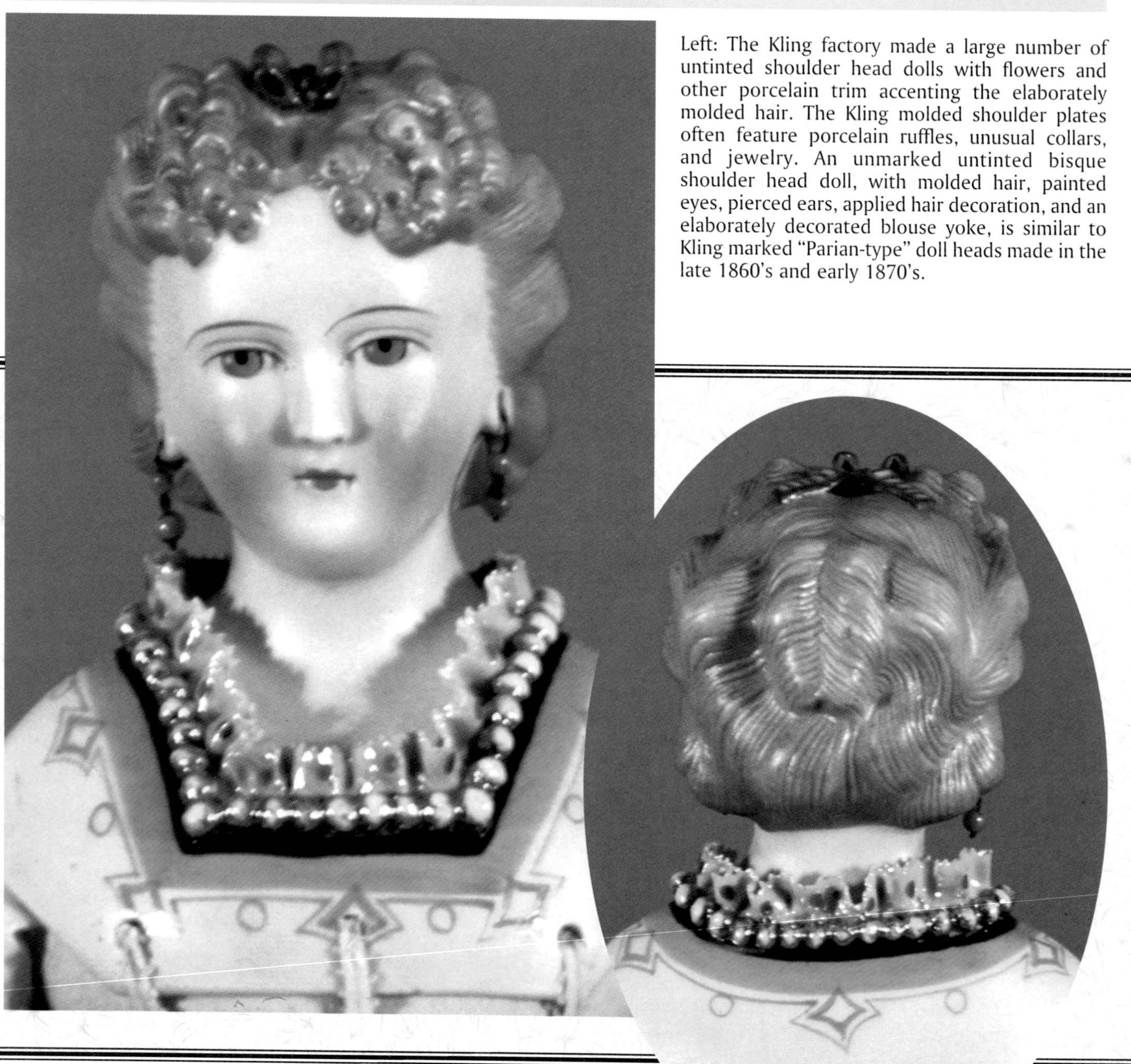

Left: The Kling factory made a large number of untinted shoulder head dolls with flowers and other porcelain trim accenting the elaborately molded hair. The Kling molded shoulder plates often feature porcelain ruffles, unusual collars, and jewelry. An unmarked untinted bisque shoulder head doll, with molded hair, painted eyes, pierced ears, applied hair decoration, and an elaborately decorated blouse yoke, is similar to Kling marked "Parian-type" doll heads made in the late 1860's and early 1870's.

The untinted porcelain shoulder head features well-molded hair and shoulder plate detail.

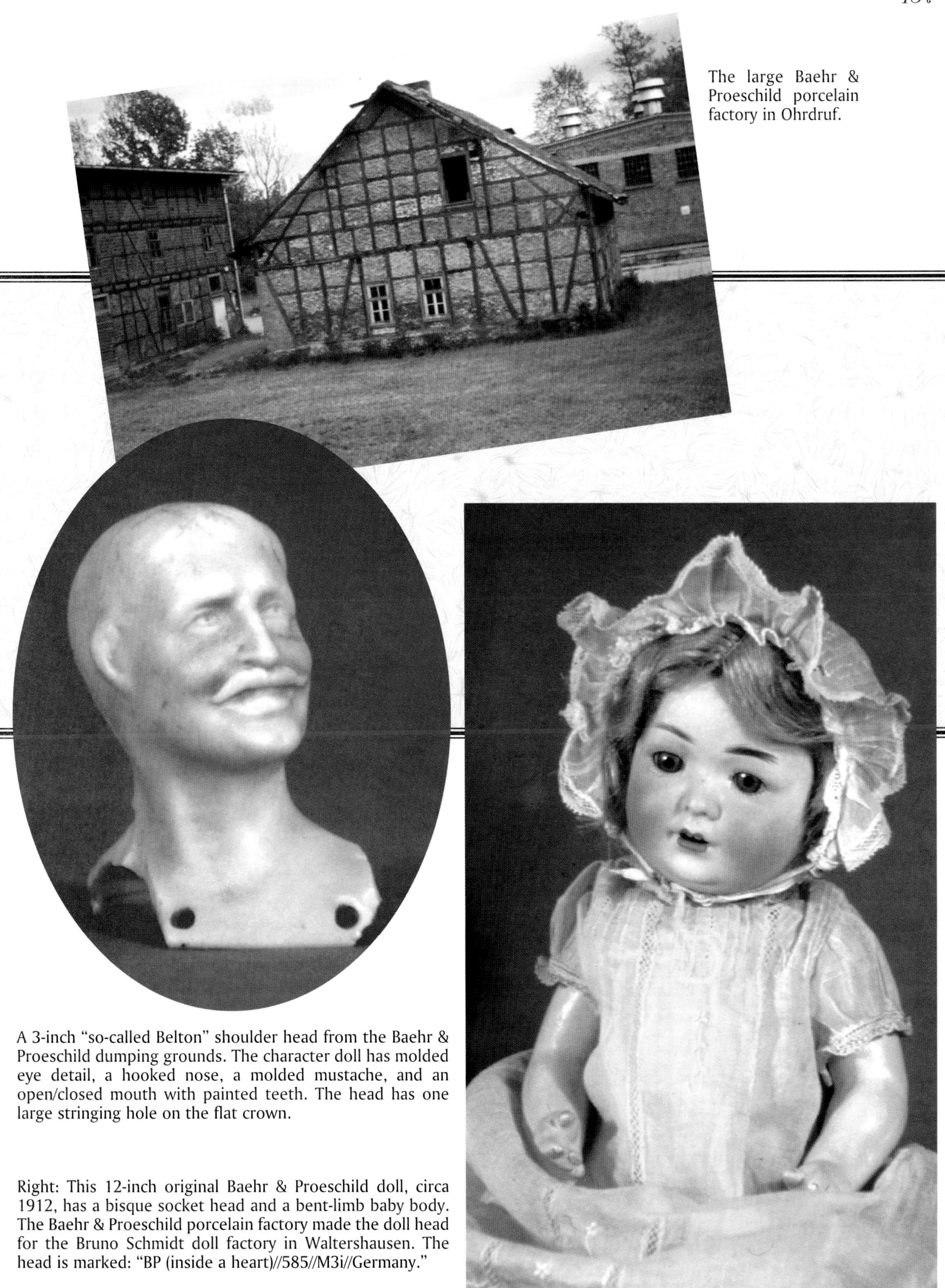

The large Baehr & Proeschild porcelain factory in Ohrdruf.

A 3-inch "so-called Belton" shoulder head from the Baehr & Proeschild dumping grounds. The character doll has molded eye detail, a hooked nose, a molded mustache, and an open/closed mouth with painted teeth. The head has one large stringing hole on the flat crown.

Right: This 12-inch original Baehr & Proeschild doll, circa 1912, has a bisque socket head and a bent-limb baby body. The Baehr & Proeschild porcelain factory made the doll head for the Bruno Schmidt doll factory in Waltershausen. The head is marked: "BP (inside a heart)//585//M3i//Germany."

The Baehr & Proeschild porcelain factory made doll heads for: Adolf Wislizenus; Josef Bergmann; Kley & Hahn; Wiesenthal, Schindel & Kallenberg and Heinrich Stier. A document in the Sonneberg Doll and Toy Museum indicates that in 1871, Heinrich Stier listed heads from Baehr & Proeschild that were wrongly identified as French heads. Even the bodies looked like typical French bodies according to this document.

August Hertel, Heinrich Schwab, Friedrich Müller and Hugo Rosenbusch founded the Hertel, Schwab & Co. porcelain factory. Hugo Rosenbusch was originally a porcelain painter, before he became president of the porcelain factory. The dolls made by the Hertel, Schwab & Co. factory were, for years, credited to the Kestner porcelain factory, especially the 151 and 152 mold numbers. The factory made Bye-Lo babies for Borgfeldt and a number of heads for Kley & Hahn, Koenig & Wernicke, Strobel & Wilken, Wiesenthal, Schindel & Kallenberg and Louis Wolf & Co.

The Kley & Hahn doll factory is also standing today on the outskirts of Ohrdruf. This large doll factory assembled dolls with heads from the Kestner, Hertel, Schwab & Co. and the Baehr & Proeschild porcelain factories. The Hertel, Schwab & Co. porcelain factory

Left: This 10-inch Baehr & Proeschild bisque shoulder head doll, in original clothing, is marked: "73//225." The dome-shaped head has single-stroke eyebrows, blue painted eyes, and an open/closed mouth with two molded upper teeth. The brass cymbals come together when the bellow mechanism is pressed. The turned wooden arms and legs are attached to the voice mechanism with heavy wire. The #225 mold was patented in 1888. Cymbalier dolls sold for under a dollar in French toy stores at the turn of the last century.

Baehr & Proeschild made a number of character dolls during the character doll movement. This 12-inch bisque socket head doll, circa 1914, has multi-stroke eyebrows, sleep eyes, an open mouth, realistically painted hair, and a bent-limb baby body. The doll is marked: "B &P//11//619-3."

This 14-inch Baehr & Proeschild character bisque socket head doll, circa 1915, is marked with the mold number "624." The doll head, with sleep eyes, multi-stroke eyebrows, fat cheeks, and an open mouth with two upper teeth, is mounted on a jointed composition toddler body.

The Baehr & Proeschild porcelain factory made a number of painted eye character dolls. This 12-inch bisque socket head marked: "536//2/0," circa 1912, is on a jointed composition body and was made for the Kley & Hahn doll factory. *Jane Walker Collection.*

An original 1914 picture of the Hertel, Schwab porcelain factory in Stützhaus, a suburb of Ohrdruf. The 103 factory employees are seated and standing in front of the factory.

Right: The Hertel, Schwab & Co. factory made a number of character babies formerly identified as Kestner porcelain products. The Hertel Schwab bisque doll heads, with the #151 and #152 mold numbers, were attributed to Kestner until the 1980's. The wigged dolls are marked with the mold number "151," and the doll with the dome-shaped head is marked "152." The three dolls, measuring from 14 to 16 inches, have bisque socket heads, blue-gray sleep eyes, open/closed mouths with two upper teeth and molded tongues, "fly-away" painted eyebrows, and composition baby bodies.

The large Kley & Hahn doll factory is located on the outskirts of the town of Ohrdruf.

made the 100 mold number series. The Kestner porcelain factory made the 200 mold series doll heads in addition to the "Walküre" doll heads. The Baehr & Proeschild porcelain factory made the 500 mold number series.

Although the Ohrdruf area porcelain factories often worked together to fill large orders, (for instance, the Borgfeldt Bye-Lo Babies and Kewpies) many doll heads were produced for use by doll factories located in Sonneberg. There is no question that the Ohrdruf area porcelain factories created beautiful porcelain products especially in the early years, but there were definitely more porcelain factories making doll heads in the Southern Circle than in the Northern Circle. One can also conclude that many Southern Circle porcelain factories made porcelain heads before the porcelain factories in the Northern Circle by comparing the dates that doll heads were first produced in the 17 porcelain factories in

This 7-1/2 inch Kley & Hahn bisque socket head doll, circa 1912, is marked "549." It has dark sleep eyes, multi-stroke eyebrows, a closed mouth, and a jointed composition body. The Baehr & Proeschild porcelain factory made the "500" series bisque heads for Kley & Hahn. *Mary Beard Collection.*

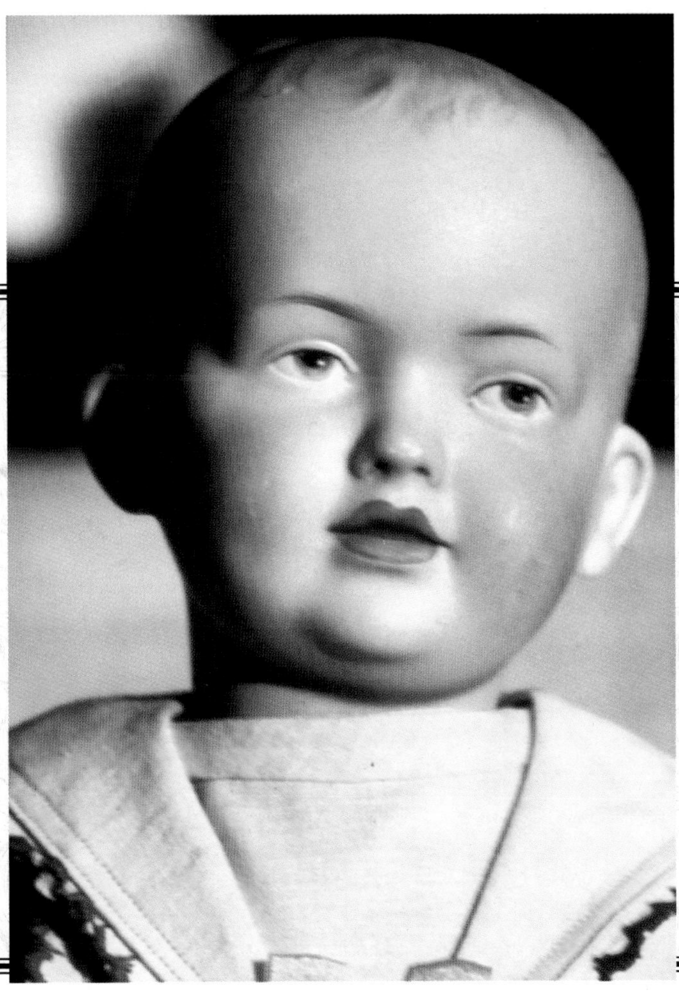

This 18-inch Baehr & Proeschild bisque dome-shaped socket head doll, circa 1912, has molded hair, big molded ears, expressive intaglio eyes, and an open/closed mouth with a molded tongue. It is marked with the mold number "531." The Baehr & Proeschild porcelain factory made the #500 mold number series for the Kley and Hahn doll factory. *Jane Walker Collection.*

the Northern Circle with the 61 porcelain factories in the Southern Circle.

Thuringian porcelain factories manufactured millions of wholesale generic doll heads and doll parts primarily for exporting internationally. The doll heads were attached to bodies and dressed in hundreds of doll factories all over Germany for well over a hundred years. Most of the heads, especially the early group of glazed porcelain heads, were only marked with a size number. Doll factories in both circles ordered from a number of factories. They also changed factories when they were not satisfied with the quality or prices of the heads ordered. Fine quality porcelain dolls were made in a number of porcelain factories located in the Southern as well as the Northern Circles. Therefore, we can no longer conclude that the Southern Circle dolls were later and of poorer quality than the dolls made in the Northern Circle.

Left: This 16-inch Hertel, Schwab & Co. bisque socket head doll, circa 1912, is marked: "K. & H. (inside a banner)//Germany//160-9." The character head has blue sleep eyes, typical Hertel, Schwab "fly-away" eyebrows, an open/closed mouth with a molded tongue and two upper teeth, and large protruding ears. The doll head is on a well-made bent-limb composition baby body.

Below: Seven Bye-Lo babies ranging in size from 4-1/2 to 14 inches. A number of Thuringian porcelain factories made Bye-Lo babies including Hertel, Schwab & Co., C. F. Kling & Co., J. D. Kestner, Jr., and Alt, Beck & Gottschalck. The mold design was copyrighted in 1922. The New York importers, George Borgfeldt & Company, had the exclusive marketing rights to the Bye-Lo babies. Designed by Grace S. Putnam, they were made for the American market. The bisque dome-shaped heads with flange necks are incised: "Copr.by//Grace S. Putnam//Made in Germany." The five larger doll heads are on cloth bodies with celluloid hands. Kestner is credited with making the all-bisque Bye-Los. The all-bisque dolls, with molded and wigged hair, circa 1925 on, are marked (on the back of the body): "G-12//Copr.by//Grace S. Putnam//Germany."

Chapter Eighteen

The Simon & Halbig and Alt, Beck & Gottschalck Porcelain Factories

The beautiful porcelain doll heads we associate with the Simon & Halbig porcelain factory were made in the small town of Gräfenhain with a population about 1,500 residents. First referred to as "Gräfenhagen" in early town records, a more common spelling was "Gräfenhahn" in old writings "Graf" translates to the word "count" and "Hahn" translates to the word "cock." The rooster is prominently featured on the Gräfenhain coat of arms.

The town became the property of Duke Erwin von Gleichen in 1168. In 1230, the Dukes Ernst and Heinrich von Gleichen sold part of the Georgenthal monastery for 60 silver marks and a horse according to the town records. The townspeople were technically free during this time, but they had to do "master services" (Frondienste). In other words, residents living on the Duke's land had to work the land and repay the Duke with goods or money.

Early town records mention the mining of cobalt and slate. As was common in many of the Thuringian early mining towns, townspeople were promised a piece of property where they could build a small house in exchange for their promise to work in the mines. They were required to give a large part of the mined ore to the town monastery or "Käfernburger." After the Reformation, Gräfenhain belonged to the Georgenthal area under a "privileged" Duke who had the right to vote in the election of a king.

In 1416, Gräfenhain had a christening chapel, and in 1593, the first school was mentioned. By about 1690, Gräfenhain merchants transported their goods in covered wagons on trade routes to Holland. Ore mining ended, for the most part, by 1780. The early 1800's were a period of population expansion for this peaceful village on the north side of the Thuringian Forest.

In 1869, Carl Halbig and Wilhelm Simon founded the Simon & Halbig porcelain factory in Gräfenhain. The April, 1999 issue of the *Kreis Gotha* newspaper provides a wealth of information on Carl Halbig and the porcelain factory. Carl Halbig worked as an accountant for the Alt, Beck & Gottschalck porcelain factory in Nauendorf before founding his own porcelain factory. Halbig was 29

The Gräfenhain coat of arms painted on the side of a building in Gräfenhain—a town of about 1,500 residents.

when he left the Nauendorf factory to start his own business. He received financial help from Wilhelm Simon, a successful Hildburghausen merchant as well as doll factory owner. Simon founded his own doll and toy factory in Hildburghausen in 1846.

Carl Halbig bought the "old pastor's house" on Main Street in Gräfenhain in March of 1868. According to the Gotha newspaper, it took Halbig a year to have the pastor's house converted into a porcelain factory. The Simon & Halbig porcelain factory began making doll heads in 1869. To quote the newspaper article, "Dolls dressed in silk outfits were made of 'bisquit' porcelain in the beginning. Later the company specialized in doll heads made in many different patterns."

The small towns of Gräfenhain and Nauendorf share a museum named the "Dorfmuseum." A few Simon and Halbig as well as Alt, Beck & Gottschalck doll-related items are currently on display including a Simon & Halbig large "Badepuppe" (bathing doll). One Simon & Halbig bisque shoulder head is of particular interest. According to the museum brochure, "Carl Halbig was known to be an enthusiast of classical art, and his partner Simon preferred the playful Rococo style." The brochure also reported that "Halbig thought the doll heads, which were mainly manufactured for export, were tacky. He longed for a classical profile for a doll head."

Soon, the doll that collectors refer to as the "Little Women" type, mold number 1160, emerged from the hands of a Simon & Halbig sculptor. Halbig exclaimed, "Looks like Nefertiti!" The Dorfmuseum brochure continues, "The word (Nefertiti) made the rounds in the factory, and his (Halbig's) workers, mainly young

The Simon & Halbig porcelain factory in Gräfenhain was originally the "old pastor's house." Halbig spent a year converting the building into a porcelain factory. The factory was located across the street from the Halbig villa. It was torn down several years ago.

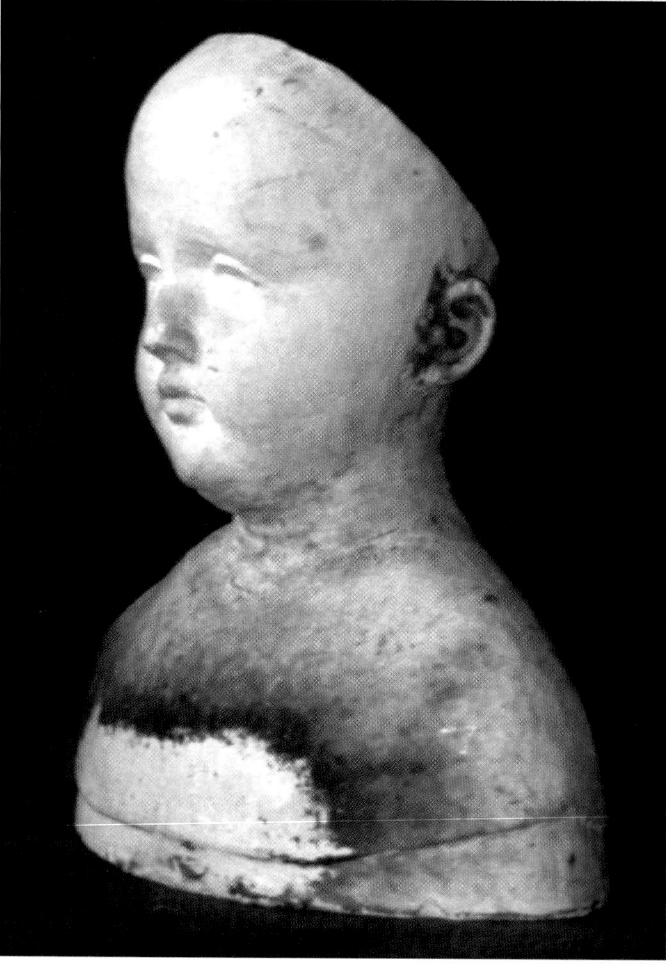

An original hand-carved plaster Simon & Halbig model head. *Roland Schlegel Collection.*

The Simon & Halbig porcelain factory was founded in 1869. Doll heads were made the same year. This 9-inch S & H bisque shoulder head doll, circa 1870, has molded, painted blonde hair and a black molded hair band. The doll head includes a black line painted around the blue iris of each eye, a white highlight eye dot, and multi-stroke eyebrows. A dark red painted line separates the upper and lower lips. The swivel head is attached to a kid-lined shoulder plate. The Simon & Halbig cloth body includes camel colored high-heeled bisque boots that are trimmed in black.

Below: Three Simon & Halbig bisque shoulder heads, circa 1894, are wearing original mohair wigs. The doll heads range in size from 2-1/2 to 3 inches. The two larger doll heads are marked with the number "1" in the middle of the front shoulder plate and: "S & H//1160-1" on the back shoulder plate. The smaller doll head has the number "0" on the front shoulder plate, and no marking in back. All three doll heads have stationary glass eyes. Two of the doll heads have single-stroke eyebrows, and the third has multi-stroke eyebrows.

porcelain painters between 14 and 18, asked the Secret Council (Halbig) the question, what 'Nefertiti' means?"

Halbig returned to the porcelain factory the next day with an encyclopedia under his arm, so that he could explain the word "Nefertiti" to his workers. A few days later, one of the workers added a "Nefertiti-styled" headdress to the shoulder head. Now the doll head actually resembled the early 14th Century BC Egyptian queen. It rested on Carl Halbig's desk for a short time, and then he gave the shoulder head back to "the lady porcelain painter who kept it safe," according to the museum brochure. Today, this historical 1160-shoulder head is on display at the Dorfmuseum, complete with Egyptian headdress. Descendants of the "lady" porcelain painter donated the doll head to the museum. The 1999 *Kreis Gotha* newspaper provides further interesting information about Halbig's life as well as his S&H dolls. The author states, "The girl toys with the product mark of the 'sitting Chinese' were loved mainly in Great Britain and Overseas (America). This must be the reason that most of the products are nowadays found in North America." The "sitting Chinese mark" refers to the company trademark found on Simon & Halbig boxes and labels.

Little information is known about Halbig's personal life during his first marriage. The author of the newspaper article mentions that he and the widow Gottschalk had two daughters and a son named Arno. After the death of his first wife in 1887, he remarried. His second wife was Minna Seyferth Halbig. They had a daughter named Elisabeth, nicknamed Lisa. For many years, the growing Halbig family lived unpretentiously in the neighboring rooms of the factory or in the tower, a little fortress-like building on the Gräfenhain meadow.

The tower was a summer home in 1893, and the Halbigs moved into the villa next to the tower in 1900.

The Carl Halbig villa is located across a wide meadow on a wooded hillside in Gräfenhain.

The Carl Halbig family moved into the villa in 1900. Halbig's daughter, Elisabeth, lived in the villa until her death in 1980. *Original artwork by Mary Krombholz.*

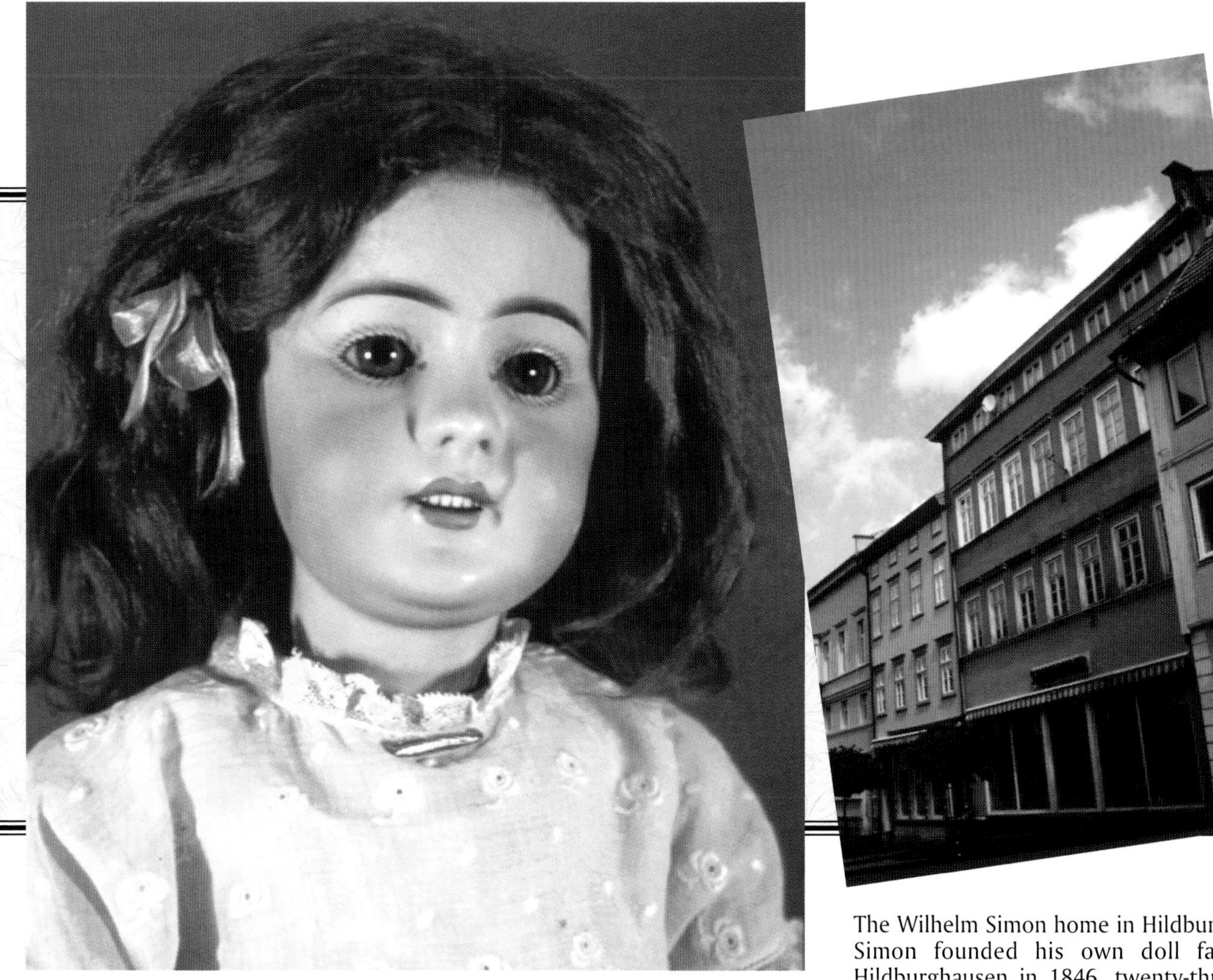

A 21-inch Simon & Halbig bisque socket head doll on a jointed composition body. Although the doll head is categorized as a "dolly-face," it has a "character look." The doll head is marked in one line along the head rim: (in script) "S.7 H., 769 DEP." The doll, circa 1888, has a closed mouth, multi-stroke eyebrows, stationary eyes, and a high forehead.

The Wilhelm Simon home in Hildburghausen. Simon founded his own doll factory in Hildburghausen in 1846, twenty-three years before the Simon & Halbig porcelain factory was founded.

Halbig was 61 when he moved into the mansion, which still dominates the Gräfenhain hillside. He died in the villa at the age of 86, on June 23, 1926. Halbig's daughter Elisabeth lived in the villa until her death in 1980.

Carl Halbig was well loved in his hometown. He was generous to the townspeople in a number of ways. He funded the installation of gaslights in Gräfenhain. In 1887, he built a funeral hall at the cemetery. In 1891, he opened a children's home for the children of his employees. The home later became the town "Kindergarten." Halbig also established housekeeping and cooking schools for girls.

Carl Halbig became sole owner of the Simon & Halbig porcelain factory in 1894, when Wilhelm Simon died. Wilhelm Simon was a very successful businessman before he became Halbig's partner in 1869. Simon lived in the Southern Circle, 18.6 miles from Sonneberg while Halbig lived in the Northern Circle. Wilhelm Simon's house is still standing just one street from the main town square in Hildburghausen. Wilhelm Simon is buried in the Simon family cemetery located outside the town of Hildburghausen.

In 1886, Simon's doll factory was written up in the *Chronicles of Hildburghausen*. The *Chronicle* quote read,

> The world-known toy factory of Wilhelm Simon who owns a business . . . exports to all European states, to North and South America, Java and East India. In 1900 the company advertised: "Fine toys, music toys, dolls and porcelain services for children.

Wilhelm's son became the sole owner of the factory in 1894; and the Wilhelm Simon doll and toy factory continued as a separate company until 1927. The Simon & Halbig porcelain factory was extremely successful until

Below: This Simon & Halbig 18-inch character doll, circa 1912, is marked: "151//S&H//3." The bisque socket head includes an original mohair wig, blue intaglio eyes, single-stroke eyebrows, and an open/closed mouth with painted teeth.

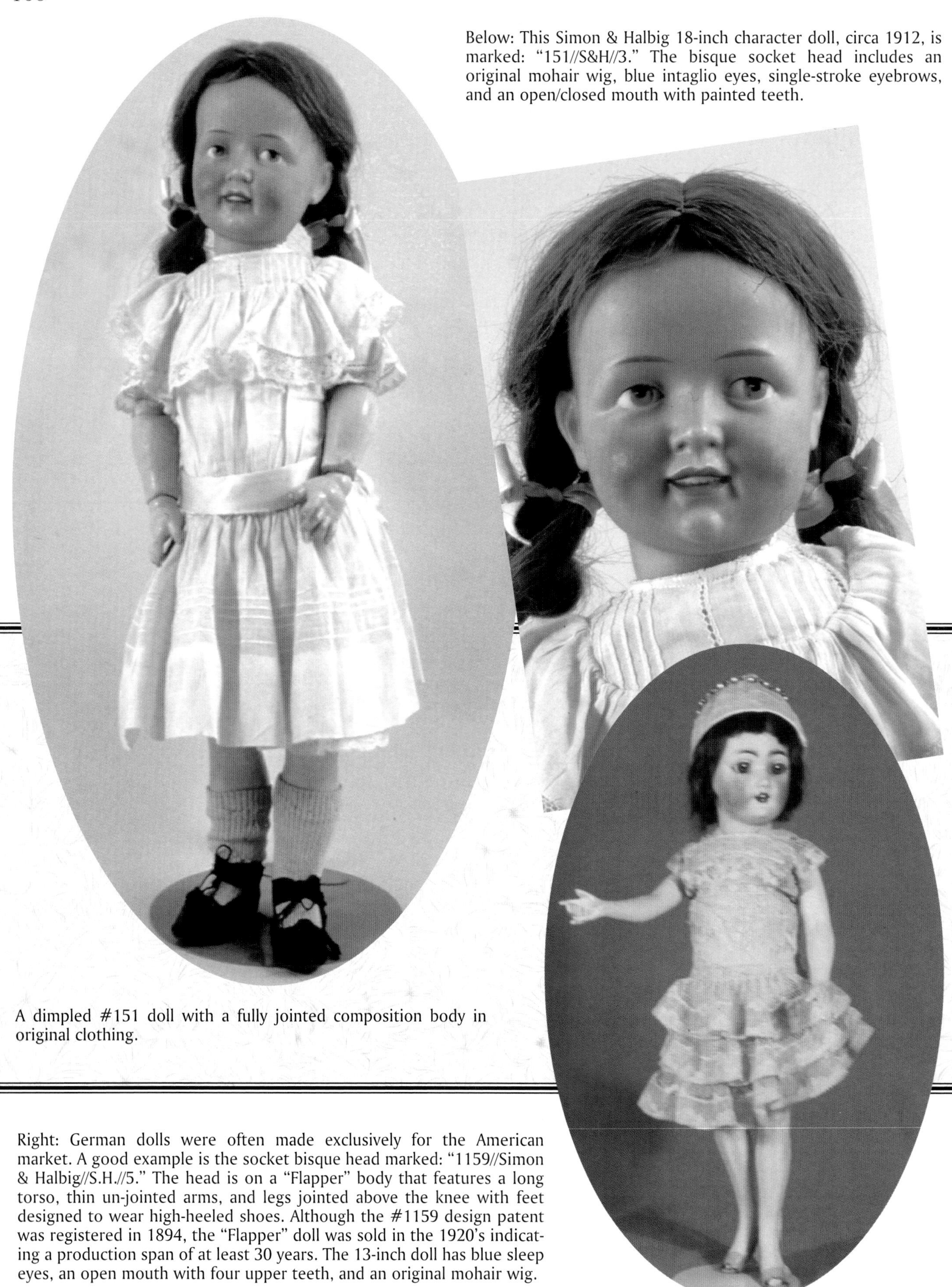

A dimpled #151 doll with a fully jointed composition body in original clothing.

Right: German dolls were often made exclusively for the American market. A good example is the socket bisque head marked: "1159//Simon & Halbig//S.H.//5." The head is on a "Flapper" body that features a long torso, thin un-jointed arms, and legs jointed above the knee with feet designed to wear high-heeled shoes. Although the #1159 design patent was registered in 1894, the "Flapper" doll was sold in the 1920's indicating a production span of at least 30 years. The 13-inch doll has blue sleep eyes, an open mouth with four upper teeth, and an original mohair wig.

Left: An original "DEP" doll in a marked Jumeau box. The Simon & Halbig bisque socket head is marked with only three letters: "DEP." The "DEP" heads were made for the Fleischmann & Bloedel doll factory. Fleischmann was the first director of S.F.B.J. (the amalgamation of a group of French doll factories) in 1899. The doll has sleep eyes, multi-stroke eyebrows, an open mouth with four upper teeth, and pierced ears.

The head is marked "DEP" and stamped in red "Tete Jumeau."

A 16-inch Simon & Halbig "DEP" with an original mohair wig and earrings. It is undressed to show the French composition body.

1914 when American importers stopped buying German dolls. By 1918, Carl Halbig was forced to sell the largest part of the business to the Bing Company in Nuremberg. In 1919, Carl Halbig, his son Arno, and Leo Benarie (from the Bing Company) were listed as owners of the Simon & Halbig porcelain factory. Arno Halbig died in 1923, and Elisabeth's husband, Ernst Rosenstock, took Arno's place.

According to the *German Doll Encyclopedia*, Simon & Halbig manufactured doll heads for the following doll companies: C.M. Bergmann (Eleanore & Columbia); Carl Bergner (double and multi-face dolls); Cuno & Otto Dressel (Jutta and the Portrait Series-1896); Edison phonograph dolls (Nos. 719 & 917); R. Eeckhoff (Holland); Fleischmann & Bloedel (heads marked DEP for the French market); Hamburger & Co. (Imperial and Santa); Heinrich Handwerck; Adolf Hulss; Emile Jumeau (number series 200); Kämmer & Reinhardt (from 1902 on all heads); Louis Linder & Söhne; Roullet & Decamps (Ondine); Franz Schmidt; S.F.B.J., Paris (from 1900 to 1914); Carl Trautmann; Welsch & Co.; Hugo Wiegand; Wiesenthal, Schindel & Kallenberg; and Adolf Wislizenus (Old Glory).

There is no question that Simon & Halbig's porcelain heads were attached to a variety of doll bodies. As doll collectors, we generally place much more value on a doll's head than the body, but during the years of Thuringian doll making, doll heads were not always the most expensive part of a doll, especially considering the price of papier-mâché heads. From the earliest days of doll making, doll bodies played a very important part in the sale of a doll. From the early wooden jointed bodies to the later ball jointed composition bodies, the price of a doll was often determined by the quality of the body. Doll makers strove for a body as close as possible to a human body with cost the main consideration. Kid doll bodies were popular for decades. Kid bodies were more expensive to produce than similarly shaped cloth bodies. Cloth and kid bodies were stuffed with many different materials including sawdust, wood wool (excelsior), ground cork, hair, grass, straw, wool, cotton, and kapok.

Left: This 16-inch Simon & Halbig bisque socket head character doll, circa 1912, has blue sleep eyes, multi-stroke eyebrows, and an open mouth four upper teeth. It is marked: " Simon & Halbig//600//6-1/2." The doll's expressive bisque head is mounted on a jointed composition body. *Jane Walker Collection.*

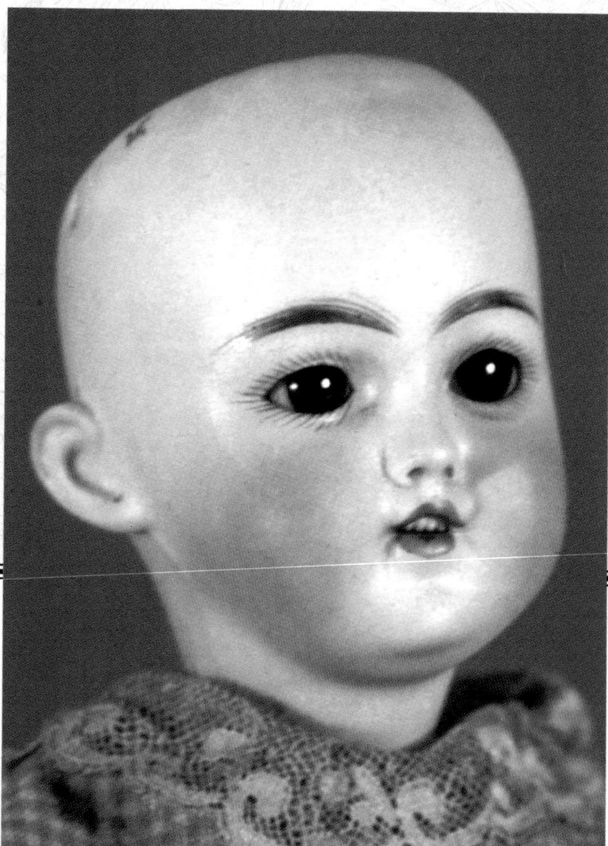

Right: A "Santa" Simon & Halbig bisque socket head doll, circa 1898, made for Hamburger & Co. The head is marked: "S & H 1249-4//DEP//Germany//Santa." The right upper crown is also marked in red with the number "25." The 14-1/2-inch doll has brown sleep eyes, multi-stroke eyebrows, protruding pierced ears, an open mouth with four upper teeth, and the distinctive "Santa" lip shading—a lower lip that features a triangular, darker red shading.

Above: A 14-inch unmarked Simon & Halbig black doll similar to the mold number "1358," circa 1910. The bisque socket head doll has stationary dark brown eyes, original earrings, and an open mouth with six upper teeth. The black composition body is fully jointed. *Jane Walker Collection.*

Above: This Simon & Halbig bisque socket head, circa 1912, is marked: "1295//F.S.&Co. //Made in//Germany//30." The character doll has blue sleep eyes, an open mouth with a movable tongue, and pierced nostrils. The "F.S.&C." head marking indicates that the Simon & Halbig porcelain factory made the bisque head for the Franz Schmidt and Co. doll factory in Georgenthal.

An original cardboard box containing twelve Simon & Halbig bisque heads with flange necks marked with the letter "D." The 2-inch heads, with painted, molded eyebrows, smiling closed mouths, and red painted wrinkles, resemble the "Uncle Sam" bisque heads from the 1896 Dressel Portrait Series.

The Simon & Halbig porcelain factory made doll heads for a number of French and German doll factories. A Roullet & Decamps walking doll is marked: "S. & H. 1039//DEP//5//Germany." The bisque socket head doll has pierced ears, flirty eyes, original silk thread eyelashes, multi-stroke eyebrows, and an open mouth with four upper teeth. The head is mounted on a jointed composition body with straight legs. The key-wind clock mechanism is the Roullet & Decamps patent no. 222661 of June 28, 1892. The #1039 mold design patent was registered in 1891. The doll throws kisses as she walks.

A pair of Simon & Halbig black dolls. The dolls have bisque swivel heads on shoulder plates, black stationary eyes, closed mouths, and original caracul wigs. The dolls' bodies are black kid with black bisque hands. The 12-inch doll is marked "51/3" and the 18-inch doll, circa 1888, is marked "949" on the shoulder plate. The dolls are wearing original clothing.

Porcelain shoulder heads, made from the 1840's on were usually attached to cloth or kid bodies although a few early shoulder heads were attached to wooden jointed bodies. Gussets and innovative jointing at the knees, hips, elbows and shoulders were added to kid and cloth doll bodies by many Thuringian doll factories. A number of unusual doll bodies surfaced during the 1850's, including the Täufling body. In the 1870's, ball-jointed composition bodies ushered in a more realistic body type that increased doll sales in a major way. This type of doll body was made through World War II, and is still being made today as a replacement body for antique dolls. The "Puppen Doktor" in Neustadt makes fine quality composition doll bodies from old molds.

Gräfenhain is located only a few miles from Ohrdruf, as is Nauendorf, the "home" of the Alt, Beck and Gottschalck porcelain factory. Nauendorf is a small village of about 500 residents. It is older than Gräfenhain by a few years. A monastery was built here in 1152. Early town documents indicate that the town was also referred to as "Nuwendorf" in 1360.

As in Gräfenhain, the early residents were free, but had to do "master services." Some of the early occupations listed in town records are carpenters and blacksmiths. The town has had village mayors (called Heimburgen) since 1525. In 1642, Nauendorf was officially declared a village.

Both towns (Gräfenhain and Nauendorf) provided workers for an Ohrdruf factory. The home workers in this area made "Zwirn" buttons. Zwirn is a very tough linen thread. The Dorfmuseum in Nauendorf owns the "Button star" mold used in button manufacturing in 1892. The Museum brochure states, "People made 'Zwirn' buttons at home. Everybody helped, children and grandmothers. They received only 3 Pfennige (similar in value to our pennies, 100 Pfennige equal 1 Mark) for 100 buttons, which was very important for their survival." Nauendorf is located about a mile from Gräfenhain. The towns shared a post office and school at one time. The Alt, Beck & Gottschalck porcelain factory is on the main highway that joins the towns. The Alt home is directly across the street from the factory.

The Alt, Beck & Gottschalck porcelain factory in Nauendorf. The Alt home is across the street from the factory.

This 11-1/2-inch bisque shoulder head Alt, Beck & Gottschalck doll, circa 1880's, has molded blonde hair and painted eyes. The doll, dressed in an original Scottish kilt and accessories, has a cloth body and bisque lower arms and legs.

A pair of closed mouth unmarked Alt, Beck & Gottschalck dolls, circa 1885 on, measures 12 and 23 inches with the typical turned shoulder heads, blue stationary eyes, closed mouths, and eyebrows painted with a flat lower edge. The bisque shoulder heads are mounted on kid bodies with bisque lower arms. *Jane Walker Collection.*

Although the porcelain factory was founded in 1854, doll heads were not mentioned until 1882. Ciesliks' 1882 entry for the factory is: "Large export of doll heads to U.S.A." A porcelain worker's story explains porcelain production in factories like the Alt, Beck & Gottschalck factory. His story is as follows:

> One had to be very careful during the firing. Just by making a little mistake, a weeks worth of work could be ruined. Already the filling of the oven was an art form. The porcelain to be fired was stored in firing capsules made of "Schamotte." In order for each piece not to get baked to another, they would be individually placed on top of a type of porcelain plate, the so-called "Bomse." Those plates were sprinkled with a fine sand of "clay dirt hydrate" that also countered the "baking together" of the "Bomse" and the goods. The filled capsules were closed up and arranged in a circle in the firing chamber. The fine decorative porcelain was placed on the inside of the circle.
>
> In those days, there were no thermometers that could withstand such high temperatures and measure them. Somehow, the firer had to determine when the temperature was high enough, and when the firing was long enough. There were no set times, and the quality and heating power of the coal varied and played a significant role during firing. Once all six fireplaces surrounding the oven were burning, one put on three or four shovels full of coal. Slowly, the firing increased to 5 to 7 shovels full. After 12 hours, the warming up phase was completed, and the temperature of 1,400 degrees Centigrade was reached. Now the "sharp firing" could begin.
>
> The trick to knowing when the "sharp firing" was ready was to put a sample piece and three firing cones on top of a capsule by the window. We could see into the oven because we left a brick loose at eye level, to watch the sample pieces. When the first "Kegel" (cone) broke, the temperature had reached 800 degrees Centigrade. The second Kegel broke at 1,000 degrees Centigrade, and the last Kegel broke at 1,400 degrees Centigrade. Now we had the correct temperature. The oven temperature had to be watched carefully, so that it wouldn't drop or rise too much, or the goods would crack. The "sharp firing" lasted 12 to 14 hours. Slowly the firers started taking down a few bricks out of the wall. The temperature was so great that flames would shoot out of the firing chamber. Once the oven had cooled down enough, the men could walk into the oven wearing special suits. The men took the firing capsules out of the firing chamber. The capsules were emptied, and the goods were checked for cracks and sorted, before they were sent to the painting department.

An unmarked Alt, Beck & Gottschalck "Blue Scarf" untinted bisque shoulder head doll with stationary blue eyes. It is from the 3rd Quarter of the 19th Century. According to doll historians, the molded "blue scarf" is representative of the one Empress Louise of Prussia wore to cover a swollen neck when she descended the stairs at Schönbrunn Palace. She was on her way to meet Napoleon to plead for her people. The "Blue Scarf" image of Louise was also painted on porcelain objects such as vases and plates.

Two Alt, Beck & Gottschalck china shoulder heads measuring 4 and 6 inches. The "Highland Mary" doll heads, circa 1890, have blue painted eyes and black, curly hair with combed bangs. The china shoulder plates are marked with the mold number "1000." A.B.G. glazed porcelain heads often have a distinctive white highlight eye dot painted on each iris.

A 22-inch unmarked Alt, Beck & Gottschalck china shoulder head doll with a cloth body and china lower arms and legs. The original lower legs feature boots with high heels and molded buttons; the black boots match a shard from the factory dumping grounds. The doll head has black curly hair and exposed ears. The well-painted face includes the typical A.B.G. darker line between the closed lips and a painted white highlight dot on each eye.

Robert E. Röntgen's book, *Marks on German, Bohemian and Austrian Porcelain,* contains a short entry of Alt, Beck & Gottschalck porcelain production. It states, "1854-1953, figurines, dolls, doll heads, decorative porcelain and religious articles."

The Alt, Beck & Gottschalck dolls on display at the Dorfmuseum are quite interesting. Many were dug up next to the factory when the building was remodeled. The shards tell the story of Alt, Beck & Gottschalck doll making. One board contains pieces of 12 dolls mostly all-bisque dolls. Two are favorites of American collectors, the Orsini "Didi" and "Mimi." Many examples of Alt, Beck & Gottschalck doll heads are found on Wagner & Zetsche and Fischer, Naumann & Co. bodies.

Left: A 22-inch Alt, Beck & Gottschalck "Bonnie Babe" designed by Georgene Averill. The New York importers, George Borgfeldt and Company began marketing the dolls in 1926. The character dome-shaped bisque head with a flange neck is marked: "Copr. By//Georgene Averill//1005/3652//Germany." The doll has painted hair, brown sleep eyes, an open mouth with two lower teeth, and a molded tongue. The cloth body made by K&K Toy Co. has composition arms and legs and includes a crier box.

A 12-inch Alt, Beck & Gottschalck bisque shoulder head doll, in original clothing, marked "870 No. 3." The mold design was registered in 1895. The dome-shaped head includes stationary blue eyes, multi-stroke eyebrows and a closed mouth, with a darker line between the upper and lower lip. The head is on a marked Wagner & Zetsche kid body.

Left: This Alt, Beck & Gottschalck 15-inch bisque shoulder head doll in original clothing, circa 1880, is marked "698-4." The doll has stationary blue eyes, multi-stroke eyebrows, and a closed mouth. The original one-strap shoes with oval metal buckles are marked "Jumeau." The doll head is on a marked Wagner & Zetsche kid body.

Chapter Nineteen

The Kämmer & Reinhardt Doll Factory

The Kämmer & Reinhardt doll factory was founded in Walterhausen in 1885. Reinhardt was the practical, business-oriented side of the partnership while Kämmer, as a sculptor, was interested in the creative side of doll making. The house that served as the first place of business is still standing. In 1907, the partners moved to the huge brick building that served as the factory until the 1930's. In 1994, the Kämmer & Reinhardt factory building was added to the Waltershausen historical protection list, which means the building will be preserved rather than demolished like the Simon & Halbig, Heinrich Handwerck and the Armand Marseille factories.

As doll collectors, we treasure the entire series of character dolls from the 100 mold number series produced by the Kämmer & Reinhardt doll factory. The tinted, unglazed porcelain heads were made by the Simon & Halbig porcelain factory in Gräfenhain. The story of the character movement is an important part of K & R history.

The Munich Art dolls receive credit for starting the character doll movement in 1908. The beginning of the character movement has been well documented. It all began in 1908, when an exciting event took place at the Hermann Tietz department store in Munich. Max Schreiber was the director of the toy department in the Munich branch of the Tietz store. He thought that the declining doll sales at the store were due to the similarity of current dolls. In an effort to revive the Tietz doll sales, Schreiber acted upon a friend's suggestion to

The Kämmer & Reinhardt doll factory in Waltershausen. The large brick building served as the doll factory from 1907 until the 1930's.

A Simon & Halbig bisque head character for K & R incised: "K (Star) R//Simon & Halbig//117/53." The 21-inch original doll, circa 1911, has blue sleep eyes, multi-stroke eyebrows, a closed mouth, a human hair wig, and a ball-jointed composition body.

Three S & H/K&R dolls marked: "K (Star) R//Simon & Halbig//126//26." The doll heads, circa 1914, are on three different types of composition bodies. From the left: a baby body, a toddler body, and a standard child body. The dolls have the same face mold, but they look very different. The 10-inch doll with the baby body has a very dark complexion; the 15-inch doll in the middle has flirty eyes; and the 23-inch doll on the right has a separate wobble tongue.

Three Simon & Halbig/ Kämmer & Reinhardt baby dolls marked with the mold numbers "121" and "122." The (character) dolls, circa 1912, have bisque socket heads, blue sleep eyes, multi-stroke eyebrows, and open mouths with two upper teeth. The doll heads are on composition baby bodies. The doll on the right, marked with the #122, has a separate wobble tongue.

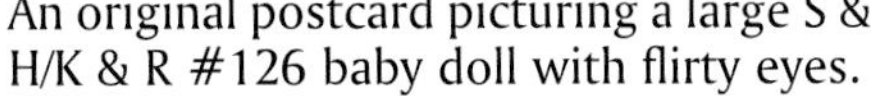

An original postcard picturing a large S & H/K & R #126 baby doll with flirty eyes.

Right: This S & H/K&R bisque socket head character doll, circa 1914, is marked: "K (Star) R//Simon & Halbig//126-62." The 26-inch doll has blue sleep eyes, multi-stroke eyebrows, an open mouth with two upper teeth, and a wobble tongue.

locate artists not connected to doll making, and hold a doll design contest. The only requirement was that the dolls must resemble "street children." The dolls caused a sensation because they represented a completely new doll type.

Public approval was immediately apparent, especially for the dolls designed by Marion Kaulitz. They were described as "full of individuality and character, and yet childish, so true hearted and bright, so charmingly pert and rakish." They were also referred to as dolls with "animated expressions."

According to the Colemans' research, Marie Marc-Schnür, Paul Vogelsanger, and Josef Wackerle designed the composition heads. Marion Kaulitz hand-painted the faces. Lilian Frobenius, Alice Hageman, and others dressed the dolls. In the Library of the Musee des Arts Decoratifs, Paris, there is a large scrapbook containing pictures of Munich Art Dolls. One page, dated 1908, shows dolls designed by Paul Vogelsanger, Marie Marc-Schnür, and Josef Wackerle. According to a museum curator, Joseph Wackerle designed dolls for the Cuno & Otto Dressel doll factory. A few of the Wakerle/Dressel dolls are currently on display in the Sonneberg Doll and Toy Museum. The Cincinnati-based Arnoldt's Doll Company, as well as Gimbel Brothers department stores in New York and Philadelphia, served as two distributors of the Munich Art dolls.

In 1909, Kämmer & Reinhardt showed their character dolls at a small exhibit in the Berlin Tietz store. The event was for invited guests only. In 1910, Alfred Golschiner,

Left: A 14-inch Munich Art doll dressed in original regional clothing, circa 1908, with a bald composition head, blue painted eyes, and closed mouth. The Dressel doll factory made the fully jointed composition body.

A 19-inch #101 Kämmer & Reinhardt character doll, circa 1909, identified as "Marie" when dressed as a girl and as "Peter" when dressed as a boy. The Simon & Halbig bisque socket head is marked: "K (Star) R//101-34." The doll has blue painted eyes with deeply molded upper eyelids outlined in black, single-stroke eyebrows, a closed mouth, and a fully jointed composition body. *Jane Walker Collection.*

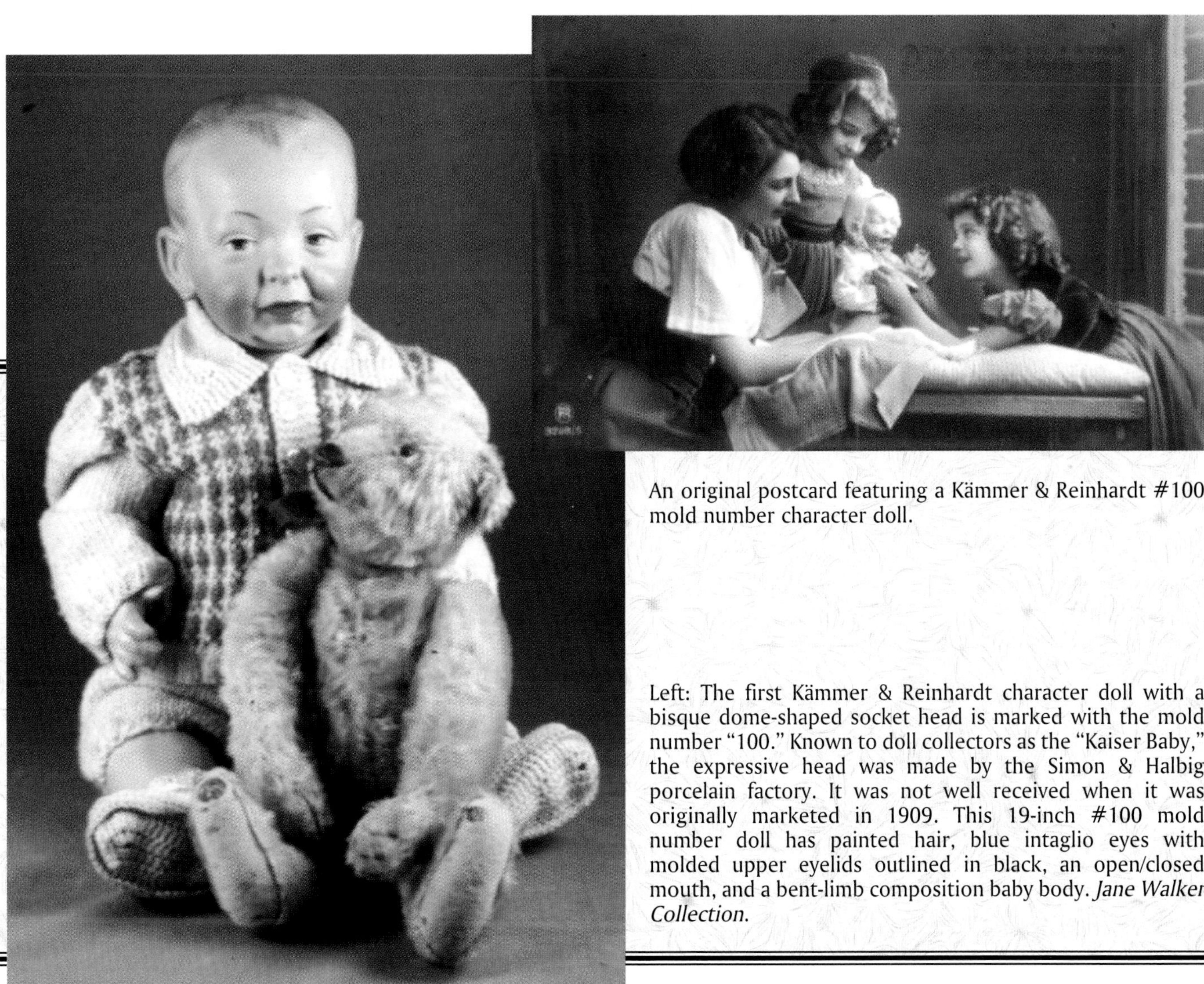

An original postcard featuring a Kämmer & Reinhardt #100 mold number character doll.

Left: The first Kämmer & Reinhardt character doll with a bisque dome-shaped socket head is marked with the mold number "100." Known to doll collectors as the "Kaiser Baby," the expressive head was made by the Simon & Halbig porcelain factory. It was not well received when it was originally marketed in 1909. This 19-inch #100 mold number doll has painted hair, blue intaglio eyes with molded upper eyelids outlined in black, an open/closed mouth, and a bent-limb composition baby body. *Jane Walker Collection.*

manager of the Berlin Tietz toy purchasing department, "filled a whole floor of the store" with the new character dolls. Kämmer & Reinhardt held its first public display of character dolls at the Berlin Tietz exhibition.

The name of the sculptor of the first K&R character baby, mold number 100, has been something of a mystery, but this mystery was solved by the Ciesliks and was revealed in their *Puppenmagazin* in 1987. The Ciesliks spent 10 years searching for the name of the sculptor. They finally found an article from the *Thüringer Allgemeine Zeitung*, dated April 24, 1928, which stated, "The first dolls of this type were created based on the head of a baby modeled from nature by Professor Lewin-Funcke." The Ciesliks state, "Professor Lewin-Funcke was afraid he would tarnish his reputation as a famous sculptor and teacher in Berlin if it became known that he modeled the doll heads." The Ciesliks visited the sculptor's family and found out that the Professor also sculpted the bust for the K&R mold numbers 102 and 107 (Karl) in 1898. The "Karl" prototype still belongs to a family member.

Karl Krauer sculpted the 114 mold number doll head for Kämmer & Reinhardt. "Hans and Gretchen" were introduced at the Leipzig Easter Fair in 1910. Franz Reinhardt's nephew was the model for these captivating doll heads. The attention to detail is apparent in the original clothing designed for many of the dolls that make up the 100 mold number character series.

One original "Gretchen" doll has never been undressed, and therefore, tells the viewer much about Thuringian doll dressing. Her coiled, braided hair remains as it was originally styled. "Gretchen" is dressed in a regional costume featuring braid-trimmed coordinating layers of cotton clothing. The doll is dressed in a white, lace-trimmed underclothing that is covered by a petticoat made of striped blue and lavender cotton material.

A crisply pleated, maroon cotton skirt makes up the next layer of "Gretchen's" ensemble. The skirt is tied with a narrow floral ribbon. Over the pleated skirt, the doll is wearing an apron of maroon-flowered cotton material tied with a ribbon made of another floral-patterned material. She is wearing a pale blue cotton scarf with fringes over her white cotton blouse with contrasting cuffs. A lace bib peaks out from under her blouse.

Her vest is made of several colors of cotton, and is laced with braided cord. The brass hooks attached to the vest hold the cord in place. "Gretchen" is wearing a gold chain necklace. Two small gold coins decorated with a cross and other symbols are attached to the chain with small rings. Between the coins, a small green quartz heart is attached to the chain necklace. Her perky triangular black hat is lined with gauze and trimmed with a large black ribbon bow with streamers that are finished in gold metallic fringe. "Gretchen" is wearing white cotton socks that are tied at the knee with original bows of red silk ribbon. Her black patent shoes are trimmed with silver buckles.

Ernst Kämmer died on a vacation trip in 1901. Heinrich Handwerck died on May 17, 1902 and Reinhardt bought the Handwerck's Waltershausen doll factory shortly thereafter. Handwerck was only 44 years old when he died. The Handwerck doll factory, with Gottlieb Nüssle as its director, remained a separate entity from the Kämmer & Reinhardt doll factory. Simon & Halbig manufactured doll heads for Heinrich Handwerck before his death. By buying the Handwerck factory, Reinhardt was able to have his doll heads made by the Simon & Halbig porcelain factory.

The 100 series dolls display every human emotion unlike the standard "dolly-face" doll that depicts the ideal, but imagined child. Monetarily, the Tietz store exhibitions may not have rewarded all of the exhibitors, but the doll displays may be compared to dropping a small pebble in a puddle of water—the circles continue to widen and expand. One small event in 1908 changed doll making forever. The large German words on the top of the Kämmer & Reinhardt doll factory in Waltershausen translate to: "Always ahead-never backward." The company logo is indeed prophetic considering the value collectors place on Kämmer & Reinhardt dolls today.

Left: A Simon & Halbig bisque socket head character doll, marked: "K (Star) R//114//26," made for the Kämmer & Reinhardt doll factory. Named "Gretchen" when dressed as a girl and "Hans" when dressed as a boy, the all-original 10-1/2-inch doll, circa 1909, has a bisque socket head, painted blue eyes, single-stroke eyebrows, a closed pouty mouth, and a jointed composition body.

The Kämmer & Reinhardt doll factory bought the Heinrich Handwerck doll factory in 1902 following the death of Handwerck. Kämmer & Reinhardt composition bodies are ranked among the best as far as overall quality. *Ana and Peter Kalinke Collection.*

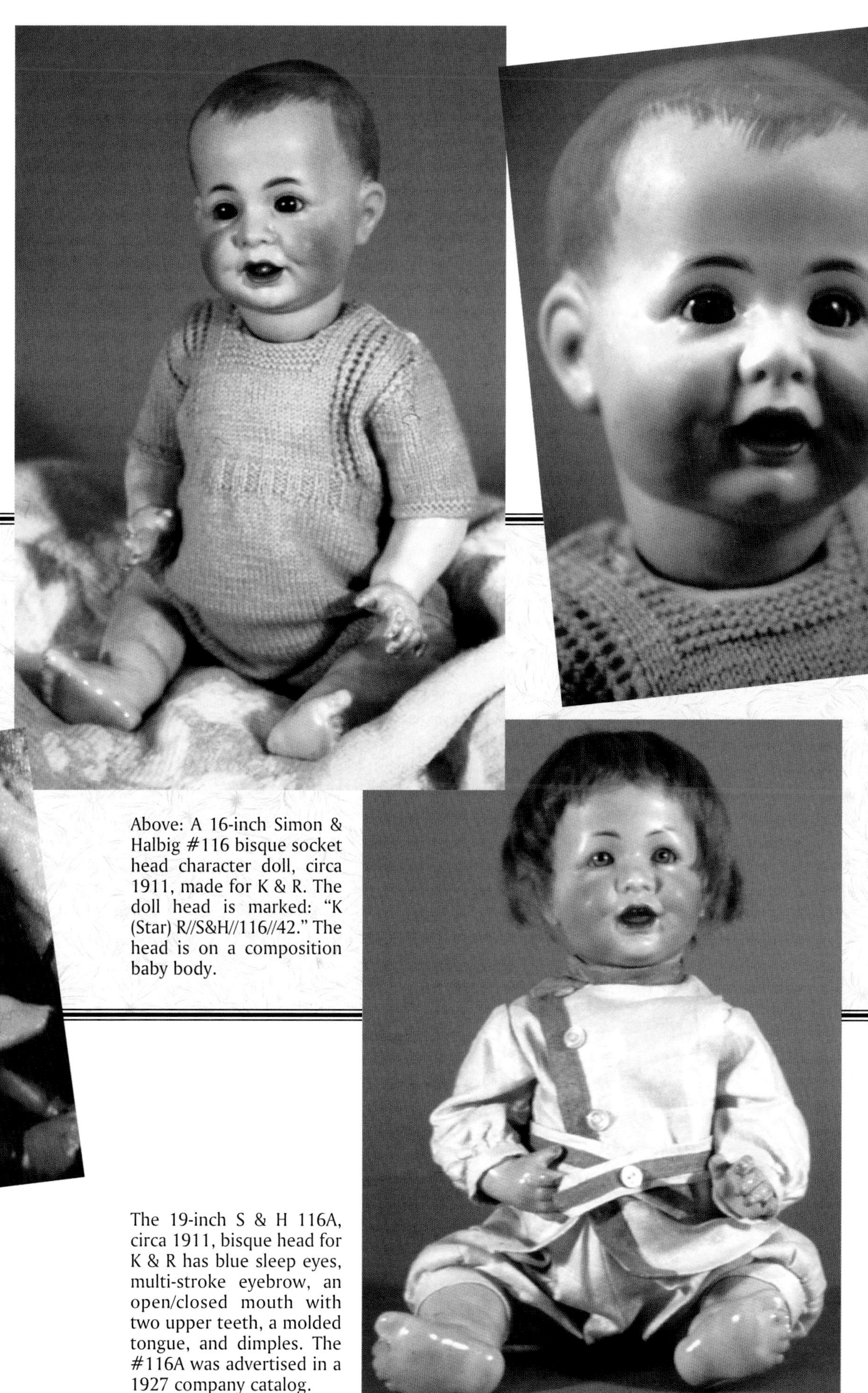

Above: A 16-inch Simon & Halbig #116 bisque socket head character doll, circa 1911, made for K & R. The doll head is marked: "K (Star) R//S&H//116//42." The head is on a composition baby body.

Above: The Kämmer & Reinhardt #116 has painted hair, dark sleep eyes, and an open mouth with a wobble tongue.

The 19-inch S & H 116A, circa 1911, bisque head for K & R has blue sleep eyes, multi-stroke eyebrow, an open/closed mouth with two upper teeth, a molded tongue, and dimples. The #116A was advertised in a 1927 company catalog.

Above: The #116A is on a bent-limb composition baby body; it has an original English angora mohair wig.

Above: A 14-inch Kämmer & Reinhardt cloth character doll from the 1920's. The doll has an expressive painted face and black painted hair. It also has a wired armature body with wooden feet.

A pair of bisque socket head dolls with heads by the Simon & Halbig and Kestner porcelain factories. The 16-inch doll, circa 1914, is marked: "K (Star) R131." The #131 has blue googly eyes, a watermelon mouth, a brown mohair wig, and a jointed composition body. The 14-inch doll, circa 1913, is marked: "JDK 221." The Kestner character doll has brown googly eyes, distinctive eyebrows, a watermelon mouth, and a jointed composition toddler body. *Karen Lintala Collection.*

Chapter Twenty

Doll Making in Thuringia Today

Doll making is alive and well today in Thuringia. The 9th Annual Puppen Festival in Neustadt is a wonderful experience. It is apparent that doll collectors from all over the world admire the German doll artists' newest creations. Antique dolls share the stage with exciting new dolls from many small home workshops as well as larger doll factories in this old doll making area.

Many new workshops open every year in towns like Sonneberg and Lauscha. Although many doll making skills have been lost, many new skills and materials have been introduced. Some workshops are still using old tools and methods according to information from the Sonneberg oral history book. It describes a couple in Zella-Mehlis as "a harness-maker couple" specializing with "old tools and old patterns, in the production of small shoes and purses for antique, artistic and reproduction dolls."

The Lauscha hillsides are also revived with new workshops. Lauscha, located 9.3 miles north of Sonneberg, was once called "the town of doll eyes." Almost every family in town had a part in the production of human or glass doll eyes, glass figurines and Christmas tree glass ornaments. Beautiful glass has been made in Lauscha since 1597. The glassmakers also made glass "pearl" necklaces and art glass. More doll eyes were made here than in any other place in the world.

The annual Neustadt Puppen Festival showcases antique and modern dolls of every size and description.

The Lauscha Trade School taught glass blowing. Students worked hard to attain the title of "Glass Art Master" or "Doll Eye Master."

Today, compressors have replaced the old bellows in achieving the necessary pressure for a gas flame used to make doll eyes. The process for making doll eyes can be summarized as follows:

> First, the white glass tube is blown and shaped. A rod of colored glass the color of the iris is melted onto the white blown eye. The threads of the iris are set onto the eye. The glassblower draws very thin colored threads of glass onto a colorless glass rod to accomplish the "threading" step. Variations in the colors of the threads make the eyes look even more natural. After the threads are set, and applied to the eye, the pupil (black) is added. Following the application of the pupil, the eye is finished with a clear crystal layer of glass.
>
> During the work process, the iris must be heated and re-blown once or twice to create a flat uniform effect. Following this step, the completed eyeball is blown to the size needed to fill the order. And, the finished eye must be heated once more to remove the inner tension.
>
> At this point, the blown glass eye is still attached to the "stem" of the glass tube. The end piece is removed to finish the eye by scoring the "stem" and tapping it with a steel hammer. The eyes must now be paired or matched in size and coloring.

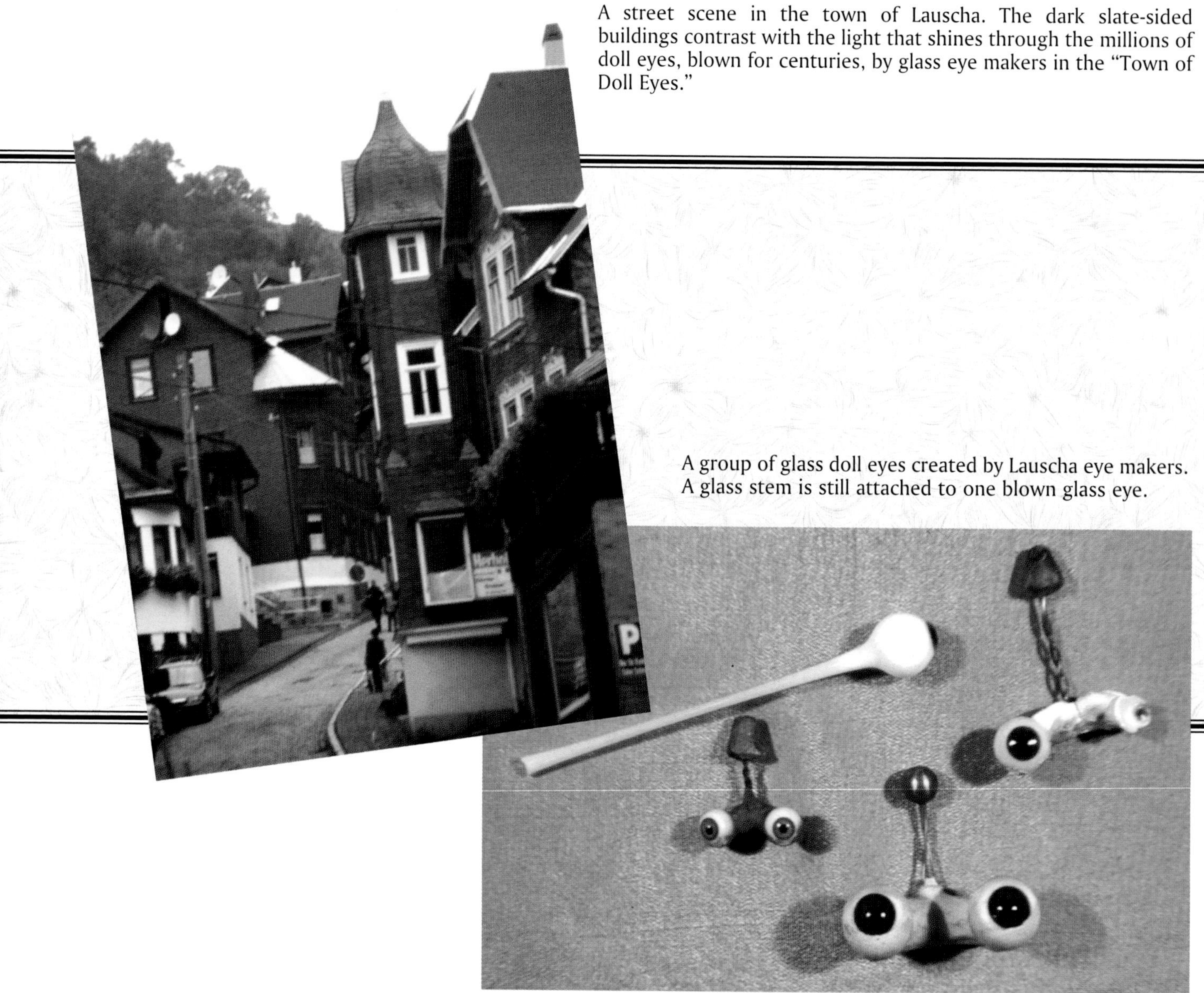

A street scene in the town of Lauscha. The dark slate-sided buildings contrast with the light that shines through the millions of doll eyes, blown for centuries, by glass eye makers in the "Town of Doll Eyes."

A group of glass doll eyes created by Lauscha eye makers. A glass stem is still attached to one blown glass eye.

Three current offerings from talented German doll artists. The 12-inch doll, with a composition head and cloth body, is wearing a paper tag marked: "Sonneberger Puppenstube." The designers are Regina Helmschrot and Bettina Klemm. The doll is named "Stefanie." Two 9-1/2-inch cloth-bodied dolls are marked: "Sonneberger Blütenlese," by Martin. The dolls have composition heads, arms, and legs.

According to the preceding oral history from a Lauscha doll eye maker, from 100 finished eyes, only about 60 or 70 are close enough in size and color to be considered a matched pair.

In 1900, a U.S. dollar was worth the equivalent of 4.20 German Mark. By converting a 1900 Mark into American dollars, we learn that the doll eye makers were paid 86¢ for blowing 100 eyes at the turn of the last century. One family of four glassblowers earned $10.71 a week, and they had expenses (gas, glass tubing) of $3.57. Their total net living wages were $7.14 for one week of work.

More and more signs are evident in Lauscha today advertising glassblower's workshops. The shops are full of beautiful Lauscha glass products. And so, the "Green Heart of Germany" is beating again. Thuringia may not dominate the world doll market again, but it is definitely a key player.

Much has changed from the days when this area was the world's largest doll and toy center. Horses and wagons are no longer used for delivery. Electric lights have replaced the candles and oil lamps. Electric kilns have replaced the old wood and coal fired beehive kilns. But, creativity still abounds in Thuringia. In the Sonneberg and Waltershausen areas, more and more dolls are currently being produced. Doll magazines are full of pictures of the newest Thuringian dolls. We can only hope that, in the future, more and more dolls will continue to be made reflecting the legacy passed down from hundreds of years of fine workmanship.

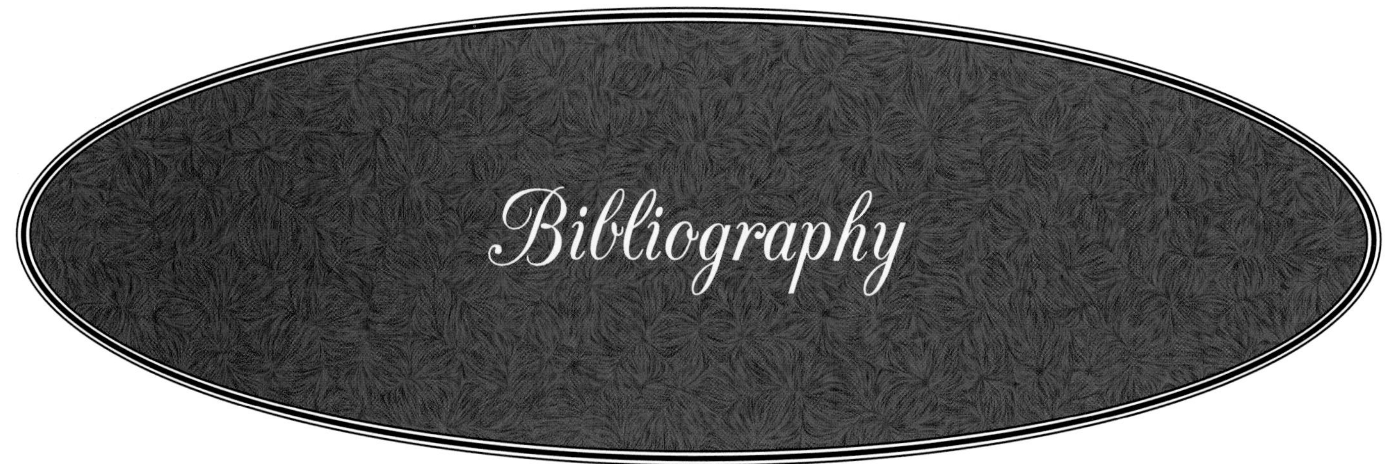

Bibliography

1. Angione, Genevieve. *All-Bisque & Half-Bisque Dolls.* Exton, PA: Schiffer Publishing, Ltd., 1981.
2. Angione, Genevieve. *Armand Marseille Dolls. Spinning Wheel's Complete Book of Dolls.* New York: Galahad Books, 1949-1975.
3. Angione, Genevieve. *Armand Marseille, Prizes and Surprises. Spinning Wheel's Complete Book of Dolls.* New York: Galahad Books, 1949-1975.
4. Angione, Genevieve. *Armand Marseille's Goo-Goos and Pixies. Spinning Wheel's Complete Book of Dolls.* New York: Galahad Books, 1949-1975.
5. Angione, Genevieve. *Simon & Halbig—Master Craftsmen. Spinning Wheel's Complete Book of Dolls.* New York: Galahad Books, 1949-1975.
6. Angione, Genevieve. *The Brothers Heubach. Spinning Wheel's Complete Book of Dolls.* New York: Galahad Books, 1949-1975.
7. Angione, Genevieve. *Competition for Goo-Goos. Spinning Wheel's Complete Book of Dolls.* New York: Galahad Books, 1949-1975.
8. Battie, David. *Sotheby's Concise Encyclopedia of Porcelain.* London: Conrad Octopus Limited, 1990, 1994 and 1995.
9. Borger, Mona. *Chinas, Dolls for Study and Admiration.* San Francisco: Borger Publications, 1983.
10. Bristol, Olivia. *Dolls, A Collector's Guide.* London: De Agostini Editions Ltd., 1997.
11. Bullard, Helen and Callicot, Catherine. *Kestner Dolls, From the 1890's to the 1920's. Spinning Wheel's Complete Book of Dolls.* New York: Galahad Books, 1949-1975.
12. Cieslik, Jürgen and Marianne. *Puppen Sammeln.* Munich: Emil Vollmer, 1980.
13. Cieslik, Jürgen and Marianne. *German Doll Encyclopedia, 1800-1939.* Cumberland, MD.: Hobby House Press, 1985.
14. Cieslik, Jürgen and Marianne. *German Doll Studies.* Annapolis, MD: Gold Horse Publishing, 1999.
15. Crowley, Jean H. *More About Snow Babies. Spinning Wheel's Complete Book of Dolls.* New York: Galahad Books, 1949-1975.
16. Coleman, Dorothy S., Philip Goldsmith (1844-1894). *An American Dollmaker. Spinning Wheel's Complete Book of Dolls.* New York: Galahad Books, 1949-1975.
17. Coleman, Dorothy S., Elizabeth Ann and Evelyn Jane. *The Collector's Encyclopedia of Dolls.* New York: Crown Publications, Inc., 1968.
18. Coleman, Dorothy S., Elizabeth Ann and Evelyn Jane. *The Collector's Book of Dolls' Clothes, Costumes in Miniature, 1700-1929.* New York: Crown Publishers, Inc., 1975.
19. Coleman, Dorothy S., Elizabeth Ann and Evelyn Jane. *The Collector's Encyclopedia of Dolls, Volume Two.* New York: Crown Publishers, Inc., 1986.
20. Desmond, Kay. *Dolls and Dolls' Houses.* London: Charles Letts & Co., 1972.
21. Doll Collectors of America, *Doll Collectors Manual,* 1983. Cumberland, MD: Hobby House Press, 1980
22. Fawcett, Clara Hallard. *Dolls, A New Guide For Collectors.* Boston, MA: Charles T. Branford Co., 1964.
23. Foulke, Jan. *Doll Classics.* Cumberland, MD: Hobby House Press, 1987.
24. Foulke, Jan. *Focusing on Dolls.* Cumberland, MD: Hobby House Press, 1988.
25. Foulke, Jan. *Focusing on Gebruder Heubach Dolls.* Cumberland, MD.: Hobby House Press, 1980.
26. Foulke, Jan. *Kestner, King of Dollmakers.* Cumberland, MD: Hobby House Press, 1982.
27. Foulke, Jan. *Simon & Halbig Dolls, The Artful Aspect.* Cumberland, MD: Hobby House Press, 1984.
28. Gauss, Renate. *Gotthelf Greiner & Christian Fleischmann, Manufakturier und Lohnarbeiter in der Porzellanmanufaktur Limbach.* Grossbreitenbach, Germany: Buchbinderei Weissplug, 1986.

29. Gerken, Jo Elizabeth. *Wonderful Dolls of Wax.* Lincoln, NE: Doll Research Associates, Calico Print Shop, 1964, 1965.
30. Gerken, Jo Elizabeth. *Wonderful Dolls of Papier Mache.* Lincoln, NE: Doll Research Associates, Union College Press, 1970.
31. Goodfellow, Caroline G. *Understanding Dolls.* Woodbridge, Suffolk, England: Antique Collector's Club. Baron Publishing, 1983.
32. Goodfellow, Caroline G. *The Ultimate Doll Book.* New York: Dorling Kindersley, Inc., 1993.
33. Gräfnitz, Cristiane. *German Papier-Mache Dolls,* 1760-1860. Duisburg, Germany: Verlag Puppen & Spielzeug, 1994.
34. Gunzel, Hildegard. *Creating Original Porcelain Dolls, Making, Molding and Painting.* Cumberland, MD: Hobby House Press, 1988 and 1990.
35. Hart, Luella. *Marks Found on German Dolls and Their Identification. Spinning Wheel's Complete Book of Dolls.* New York: Galahad Books, 1949-1975.
36. Hart, Luella. *United States Doll Trademarks, 1913-1950. Spinning Wheel's Complete Book of Dolls.* New York: Galahad Books, 1949-1975.
37. Hillier, Mary. *Dolls and Doll Makers.* New York: G.M. Putnam's Sons, 1968.
38. Hillier, Mary. *History of Wax Dolls.* Cumberland, MD: Hobby House Press, 1985.
39. King, Constance Eileen. *The Collector's History of Dolls.* New York: St. Martin's Press, 1978.
40. King, Constance Eileen. *The Collector's History of Dolls' Houses, Doll's House Dolls and Miniatures.* New York: St. Martin's Press, 1983.
41. Langer, Christa. *Charakterpuppen, (Character Dolls, From Portrait to Model).* Duisburg, Germany: Verlag Puppen & Spielzeug, 1993.
42. Low, Frances H. *Queen Victoria's Dolls.* Newnes, Ltd., 1894.
43. MacDowell, Robert and Karin. *The Collector's Digest of German Character Dolls.* Cumberland, MD: Hobby House Press, 1981.
44. Mathes, Ruth E. and Robert C. *Dolls, Toys and Childhood, The Mathes Collection and Philosophy.* Cumberland, MD: Hobby House Press, 1987.
45. Merrill, Madeline O. *The Art of Dolls, 1700-1940.* Cumberland, MD: Hobby House Press, 1985.
46. Müller, Marion Christiana. *Reise ins Spielzeugland.* Erfurt, Germany: VHT Verlaghaus Thüringen, 1997.
47. Noble, John. *Dolls.* Toronto: The Ryerson Press, 1967.
48. Richter, Lydia. *Heubach Character Dolls and Figurines.* Cumberland, MD: Hobby House Press, 1992.
49. Rogers, Maggie with Hawkins, Judith. *The Glass Christmas Ornament, Old & New.* New York: Timber Press, 1983.
50. Röntgen, Robert E. *Marks on German, Bohemian and Austrian Porcelain, 1710 to the Present.* Atglen, PA: Schiffer Publishing Ltd., 1897.
51. Scherf, Helmut. *Thüringer Porzellan.* Wiesbaden, West Germany: Ebeling, 1980.
52. Shuart, Harry Wilson. *Snow Babies. Spinning Wheel's Complete Book of Dolls.* New York: Galahad Books, 1949-1975.
53. Smith, Patricia. *Kestner and Simon & Halbig Dolls, 1804-1930.* Paducah, KY: Collector Books, 1976.
54. Smith, Patricia. *German Dolls, Featuring Character Children & Babies.* Paducah, KY: Collector Books, 1979.
55. Stanton, Carol Ann. *Heubach's Little Characters, Dolls & Figurines, 1850-1930.* Enfield, Middlesex, England: Living Dolls Publications, 1978.
56. St. George, Eleanor. *Dolls of Three Centuries.* New York: Charles Scribner's Sons, 1951.
57. St. George, Eleanor. *Old Dolls.* New York: M. Barrows and Co., Inc., 1950.
58. Tarnowska, Maree. *Rare Character Dolls.* Cumberland, MD: Hobby House Press, 1987.
59. Tessmer, Angelika. *Sonneberger Geschichten.* Hildburghausen: Verlag Frankenschwelle, 1995.
60. Tessmer, Angelika. *Sonneberger Geschichten, Von Puppen, Griffeln and Kuckuckspfeifen.* Hildburghausen: Verlag Frankenschwelle, 1996.
61. Wendl, Martin and Schäfer, Ernst. *Spass am Sammeln, Altes Thüringer Porzellan.* Rudolstadt, Germany: Greifenverlag, 1984 and 1990.
62. Whyel, Rosalie and Hedrick, Susan. *The Rose Unfolds.* Bellevue, Wash.: Doll Art Inc., 1996.
63. Winkler, John K. *Five and Ten, The Fabulous Life of F.W. Woolworth.* New York: Robert M. McBride & Co., 1940.

About the Author

Mary Gorham Krombholz was born on the Island of Cyprus, in the Mediterranean Sea. Her father was a mining engineer, as well as an archaeologist. He reopened copper mines in Cyprus used by the Romans 1700 years before him. From Cyprus, Mary's family moved to the mountains of Northern Mexico, where they lived for 10 years. Her American grandmothers feared that she would be a tomboy with only her brothers to play with—so they kept Mary well supplied with dolls. Mary still has every one of her childhood dolls, which form the nucleus of her collection. In 1974, Mary found her grandmother's doll in her parents' attic. It was tagged: made in Sonneberg, Germany. Thus, she was off and running. Mary has been researching German dolls for the last 25 years, hoping to find the maker of her grandmother's Belton-type doll. In 1993, she made her first trip to Sonneberg, and plans to return every year for the rest of her life. This May Mary will be making her eighth trip.

In May of 1989, Mary Gorham Krombholz wrote her first column on antique dolls for a weekly newspaper based in Knightstown, Indiana called *Antique Week*. She has written a monthly column, titled "Gems of the Doll World" by Mary Gorham for the last 12 years. Answering the letters from *AW* readers allows Mary to keep up-to-date on her doll research. The newspaper has a circulation of 60,000 readers, and her column now appears in the Central, as well as the Eastern, Editions.

Mary has lectured on Thuringian dolls at the UFDC (United Federation of Doll Clubs) National Conventions in Anaheim, New Orleans, Chicago, Atlanta and Dallas. She is also an accredited UFDC National Antique Doll Judge. She has served as a Contributing Editor of the UFDC magazine, *Doll News*, for the past two years writing 7 articles. In addition, Mary has given highlight tours in German museums for the Lytle Puppentours. Mary states, "I think of myself as a doll archaeologist, because I am currently digging in the dumping grounds of a number of Thuringian porcelain factories. Of course, the dumping grounds only yield objects that are about 100 years old, rather than prehistoric." Mary is currently researching the 100 plus German porcelain factories with the hopes of writing another book.

In collaboration with Cynthia E. Musser

Author, lecturer, authority in the history of dolls and paper dolls, Cynthia Erfurt Musser has been studying and photographing dolls and paper ephemera for many years. Her articles and photographs about dolls and paper dolls have appeared in various collectors' publications including *Doll News*, *Doll Reader*, *Vintage Fashions*, and *Antique Doll World*. She is the author of the books, *Precious Paper Dolls* and *Classic Celebrity Cutouts*, both published by Hobby House Press.

Cynthia holds a Bachelor of Science Degree majoring in Clothing and Textiles from the Ohio State University. Her knowledge of fashion history has proved most valuable in the study and identification of dolls and paper dolls. She views dolls, paper dolls and other related toys as physical evidence of the history of attitudes toward children and of the society in which they lived.

Cynthia frequently lectures about dolls and toys. She has spoken at many United Federation of Doll Clubs national conventions and regional meetings; and at regional and national Paper Doll Conventions as well as on the famous cruise ship, the Queen Elizabeth II. She has been an accredited UFDC judge of antique dolls for over 15 years. Cynthia puts dolls and toys into historical perspective in her lectures. In addition to dolls she also lectures about antique valentines and vintage clothing.

Having collected dolls for most of her life, Cynthia joined the United Federation of Doll Clubs in 1972. She is currently the Editor of *Doll News*, UFDC's magazine. She is also a member of the Doll Collectors of America.